Praise for

SOARING TO GLORY

"All Americans owe Harry Stewart Jr. and his fellow airmen a huge debt for defending our country during World War II. In addition, they have inspired generations of African American youth to follow their dreams."

—**HENRY LOUIS GATES JR.**, Alphonse Fletcher University Professor, Harvard University

"In *Soaring to Glory*, my friend Harry Stewart's extraordinary life is beautifully told by another friend, Philip Handleman. The struggles of the Tuskegee Airmen and our success against enormous odds makes for inspiring reading. I strongly recommend this book for anyone who wants to know more about the pioneering flyers who broke barriers and changed the world!"

—**LIEUTENANT COLONEL ALEXANDER JEFFERSON**, USAF (ret.), cofounder, Tuskegee Airmen Inc.

"It is marvelous when a fascinating, well-written book turns out to be socially important as well. *Soaring to Glory* is exactly that, and arrives at a time when its message is badly needed by the nation. This is a book that can be recommended for a wide variety of reasons, the most important of which is the standard it sets for aviation literature."

—**WALTER J. BOYNE**, former director, Smithsonian Institution's National Air and Space Museum and best-selling author

"Starting in the early 1940s, Tuskegee Institute was at the forefront of helping prepare young African-American pilots to fight for freedom in the skies. Harry Stewart is one of those aspiring aviators who came to our campus as a first step in earning their wings, and then went on to become proudly identified as a Tuskegee Airman. His story of serving our country and overcoming obstacles—not to mention the legacy the Tuskegee Airmen leave us with—is an inspiration for us all."

—**LILY D. McNAIR**, president, Tuskegee University

"This book is a masterpiece. It captures the essence of the Tuskegee Airmen's experience from the perspective of one who lived it. The action sequences make me feel I'm back in the cockpit of my P-51C 'Kitten'! If you want to know what it was like fighting German interceptors in European skies while winning equal opportunity at home, be sure to read this book!"

—**COLONEL CHARLES E. McGEE**, USAF (ret.), former president, Tuskegee Airmen Inc.

SOARING TO GLORY

SOARING
TO GLORY

A TUSKEGEE AIRMAN'S
FIRSTHAND ACCOUNT
OF WORLD WAR II

PHILIP HANDLEMAN WITH
LT. COL. HARRY T. STEWART JR.

REGNERY
HISTORY
Washington, D.C.

Copyright © 2019 by Philip Handleman

All rights reserved. No part of this publication may be reproduced or transmitted in any form or by any means electronic or mechanical, including photocopy, recording, or any information storage and retrieval system now known or to be invented, without permission in writing from the publisher, except by a reviewer who wishes to quote brief passages in connection with a review written for inclusion in a magazine, newspaper, website, or broadcast.

Regnery History™ is a trademark of Salem Communications Holding Corporation
Regnery® is a registered trademark of Salem Communications Holding Corporation

Cataloging-in-Publication data on file with the Library of Congress
First trade paperback published 2021
ISBN 978-1-68451-191-4
Library of Congress Control Number 2020302547

Published in the United States by
Regnery History, an Imprint of
Regnery Publishing
A Division of Salem Media Group
Washington, D.C.
www.RegneryHistory.com

Manufactured in the United States of America

10 9 8 7 6 5 4 3 2 1

Books are available in quantity for promotional or premium use. For information on discounts and terms, please visit our website: www.RegneryHistory.com.

To Delphine and Mary—the loves of our lives—
and to dreamers everywhere
who, refusing to be deterred by the inevitable naysayers,
look to the boundless sky and reach for the impossible

Contents

Prologue

DOGFIGHT

There can be no courage unless you are scared.
—Eddie Rickenbacker

Harry Stewart was five thousand feet over the Luftwaffe base at Wels, Germany.

His flight's element had been reduced to seven planes when the eighth was disabled by mechanical problems. Still, they would be more than a match for the four German fighters they called out below. "Our seven Mustangs cranked over in a mass dive on the enemy aircraft," Harry recalls.

But suddenly the hunters turned into the hunted—as "the sky filled with at least another dozen fighters bearing Luftwaffe insignia."

The German fighters that the American airmen had spotted first were decoys. The Mustangs had been lured into an ambush. The confrontation was certain to end with some of the planes zooming down from the sky in spectacular crashes. Harry began breathing heavily. Everything was happening so fast now.

Barely out of his teens and never before engaged in a dogfight, Harry was almost overwhelmed by the powerful emotions flashing through his mind. There was the anger at having been suckered into a trap. There was the terror of the high-stakes dueling about to transpire. Then the most primordial urge—the instinct for survival—kicked in. The young pilot's feelings of fear and doubt, a sinking feeling in the pit of his stomach, gave way to an unbounded determination, bolstered by his training.

Just days before, Harry had been promoted to first lieutenant, a sign of his superiors' confidence in him. But matters of rank were the farthest thing from his mind as he locked eyes on the two enemy planes beneath him. He advanced toward his prospective quarry as individual skirmishes broke out among the other combatants. As Harry bore down on the tails of the planes in front of him, he saw that they were the long-nosed Focke-Wulf Fw 190D-9s, the finest piston-powered fighters in the Luftwaffe's arsenal!

Indeed, an earlier version of the Fw 190, nicknamed the "butcher-bird," was described in intelligence reports to Allied pilots as "one of Germany's best fighters...." U.S. military authorities had given the pilots only an incomplete description of this new, technologically superior version—though their intelligence manual did include a surprisingly accurate artist's rendering. The brass were clearly concerned about this stunner of German engineering.

The baseline design had been conceived in 1937 by Focke-Wulf's brilliant Kurt Tank as a follow-on to the then world-beating Messerschmitt Bf 109. Tank's original concept incorporated the 1,550-horsepower BMW 139 twin-row radial air-cooled engine, in a departure from the conventional wisdom that favored the newly developed 1,050-horsepower liquid-cooled DB 601A. While the Fw 190 A through C series and the F series had the same general configuration, the D series was a response to the perceived need for a high-altitude fighter.

The D series design returned to the idea of a liquid-cooled engine. Focke-Wulf selected the 1,776-horsepower Junkers Jumo 213A-1

12-cylinder inverted-V inline engine. The engine was combined with a MW 50 methanol-water injection boost system capable of upping the horsepower rating to 2,250 at sea level for short durations. The Jumo's size necessitated the elongated nose as well as a lengthened aft fuselage with increased tail surface area to enhance stability. The resulting airframe became an instant classic, one of the most attractively proportioned and aesthetically agreeable to ever roll out of a factory and grace the sky.

And Harry's element was now facing the ultimate iteration, the D-9 model, known as the "Dora-Nine." By all accounts, it was a match for the Americans' Mustangs.

The armament of the German plane was impressive not only for its firepower but for its ingenious placement. Two MG 131 13-mm machine guns were housed in the upper nose, directly in line with the pilot. Additionally, a pair of MG 151 20-mm cannon were installed in the wing roots, one per side. In the hands of a capable pilot, the Dora-Nine could be incredibly lethal against even the most advanced Allied fighters.

The Mustang's speed brought Harry within firing range. He concentrated on the closer of the two German aircraft, then squeezed off a few short bursts from his fighter's six wing-mounted .50-caliber machine guns.

Smoke and flames suddenly sprouted from the Dora-Nine's fuselage, a ghastly picture that was permanently imprinted in Harry's memory.

As events evolved in a sequence defined in fractions of a second, Harry knew only to stay on the fighter's tail. He contemplated another burst. But the plane in his gunsight had already started to break apart. An eagle's wings had been clipped; the staff officers at Allied intelligence could scratch off one more Luftwaffe fighter, and a damn good one at that!

But there was no time to relax and savor the air-to-air victory. There was another enemy fighter dead ahead. When the second Luftwaffe pilot realized what had happened to his trailing wingman, he yanked his plane hard right in an attempt to shake Harry off his tail. But Harry turned just as tightly, pulling high Gs which stretched the Mustang to the limits of its design envelope and pressed Harry down in his seat.

The high-G maneuvering wrung beads of sweat out of Harry's upper forehead. The sweat came gushing down Harry's face like currents cascading down a waterfall, leaving him drenched. He and his opponent were entwined in a primal struggle, gladiators exerting every ounce of brawn to undo the other contestant; only here the weapons were planes heavily laden with finely engineered barrels pumping out deadly projectiles.

In the minuscule space of another fleeting second, Harry trained his sight on the tail of the bolting fighter. The opportunity to fire looked real, but how could Harry tell for sure in the madness of the fracas, the roughhousing of the planes in the roiled air? He couldn't be sure, but with nothing to lose, he squeezed off another burst. An instant later—in a sight that would also be seared in Harry's memory—the plane started to disassemble "in a cloud of black smoke and orange flame just like the first one."

Harry had scored his second victory of the day. But before he could even breathe a sigh of relief, he heard a squadron mate's urgent call: "Bandit on your tail!" It was Carl Carey, who had scored against two of the Fw 190s himself.

Just then, tracer rounds started to whiz past Harry's cockpit. They were frightfully close. The sinking feeling in the pit of his stomach came back, but as before it was quickly suppressed by the imperative of survival.

This time Harry used his fighter's speed, hoping to outrun his opponent. But the pilot of the Focke-Wulf was tenacious, just like Harry had been moments earlier when he was the pursuer. With the enemy glued to his tail in a sprint at treetop height, Harry reefed his mount over into an extreme right turn, like the one that had served him well moments before—only now it was a desperation maneuver. The German plane followed him, turning and turning in a test of strength and will, the G-forces almost unbearable, but secondary to the lust to come out of this brawl alive.

Men and machines were ratcheted to the limits of their capacity. Something had to give.

Chapter One

"THE GUTS TO FLY THIS THING"

Thou shinest on though clouds hide thee from sight,
And through each break thou sendest down thy light.
—James Weldon Johnson, "Prayer at Sunrise"

On the morning of May 8, 1939, a rickety red-and-cream Lincoln-Page biplane, propitiously yet incongruously nick-named *Old Faithful*, rose from Chicago's Harlem Airport on a mission to change the world. The send-off was hopeful, even joyous. The biplane's two African American pilots, Chauncey Edward Spencer and Dale Lawrence White, brimmed with high expectations, too rapt by the audacity of their project to entertain its probable limits.

Both Chauncey and Dale belonged to a fledgling group of flying enthusiasts who, despite stinging setbacks, held to the notion that aviation was the means to an emancipatory realm. The members of the mostly black National Airmen's Association of America (NAAA) and its precursor, the Challenger Air Pilots Association, saw the sky as a medium inherently devoid of the artificial barriers erected by one class of men to block another. The law of the air, their thinking held, is fair and equitable; it applies uniformly without exception to all people regardless of race, color, creed, gender, ethnicity, ancestry, and national origin—for it is not man's law but nature's law.

The sky as a metaphor for freedom was not a new idea. Mythology, poetry, and liturgy had long celebrated the kingdom where the birds sing as an idyllic oasis, a place of unfettered freedom, where the enslaved could escape oppression and the soul could find fulfillment. Up high enough and you were in heaven, utopia, the Elysium.

For dreamers, the airplane was the symbol of ascension come true, the real-life "sweet chariot" in the melodic Negro spiritual that sustained African American congregations at Sunday services with the promise of "coming for to carry me Home." Chauncey and Dale, riding high on the enthusiasm of their supporters, believed that flight portended great things, not just entry into the previously denied domain of the open air but fruition, wholeness, equality. If only the gateway, the staircase to this near but distant nirvana, could be pried open, all the way open—for everybody.

As described by Chauncey in his 1975 autobiography and as reported by Michael Laris in a 2003 feature in the *Washington Post,* the Spencer-White flight, formally known as the Goodwill Flight, set out to demonstrate that blacks could fly as well as whites, if given a chance. With the government about to roll out the Civilian Pilot Training Program to prevent a pilot shortage in case of war, blacks did not want to be left out. If barriers were going to be shattered, why not the one prohibiting blacks from flying the hottest planes of all—those of the Army Air Corps? Aviation, already well out of its infancy and maturing now into a big and enduring enterprise, ought not to be tainted by the prejudice enforced with unwavering certitude in every other part of daily life for African Americans.

The flight plan, such as it was, called for the biplane to wend its way from Chicago to Washington, D.C. Several stops along the way would serve as warm-ups for a triumphal arrival in the nation's capital. The flight was a unifying event in the black community, a cause to trumpet. Backing came from the black press, starting with a powerful endorsement from the pilots' hometown newspaper, the *Chicago Defender*, whose city editor, Enoch P. Waters Jr., knew the key members of the NAAA and had championed the idea of a flight to Washington at one of their meetings.

Chauncey and Dale were breaking new ground, going where black pilots hadn't gone before. Yes, as chronicled by historian Von Hardesty, there had been other famous long-distance flights by African Americans, like the 1932 transcontinental flight of James Herman Banning and Thomas Cox Allen and the 1934 Caribbean island-hopping flight of Charles Alfred Anderson and Albert Forsythe. But this time the pilots' destination was the seat of government, the center of political power. Moreover, this would not be symbolism alone; if the flight unfolded as contemplated, the pilots would roam the halls of Congress pleading the cause of black aviation to any lawmaker willing to lend an ear.

Because the white press reported nary a word on the Goodwill Flight, the flyers' progress was known only to African Americans who read black newspapers or who heard about it by word of mouth from those who did. News of each waypoint reached and each leg completed infused blacks who were paying attention with feelings of pride, hope, and inspiration. As the biplane plodded ahead ever so determinedly, its followers were moved to prayer for the two Chicago pilots, frontiersmen on the cusp of a new destiny.

The fact that the flight was underway constituted a near miracle. It almost never happened, for the costs of aircraft rental, fuel, lodging, meals, custom khaki flight suits, and assorted other expenses were considerable by Depression-era standards. To help finance the flight, Chauncey's father Edward reportedly took out a small loan and forwarded the monies to his son, but the amount represented less than half the projected budget.

Chauncey, discussing the lack of funds with a friend, became so worked up that he broke down and cried—just as he had as a youth back home in Lynchburg, Virginia, when denied flying lessons on account of his race. The sight of the usually self-assured flyer with tears streaming down his cheeks was too much for his friend to bear. She directed him to the Jones brothers, black businessmen in Chicago whose varied ventures were said to include the city's numbers racket.

The hardened entrepreneurs of the city's South Side were unable to resist Chauncey's pitch. The Joneses chipped in $1,000. According to Janet Harmon Bragg, a licensed pilot and enthusiastic supporter of the planned flight, members of the NAAA "drained their pockets" to make up the rest of the budget.

While money was tight, Chauncey had an inexhaustible supply of the other ingredient indispensable to the flight: gumption, the moxie to believe that the status quo could be overturned. Chauncey's belief that conventions could come tumbling down like the walls of Jericho had been planted by his brilliant, compassionate, and tenacious mother, Anne. A school librarian, Anne was also the founder of the Lynchburg NAACP chapter and spent many waking hours laboring for equal rights.

Significantly, she had developed close relationships with the leading lights of the Harlem Renaissance and, writing in a room of her Lynchburg home that overlooked her meticulous flower garden, had proven herself a respected poet. Her verse was first published in the NAACP's magazine, *The Crisis*, in February 1920. Leading black poetry anthologies edited by Countee Cullen and other distinguished literary figures of the Harlem Renaissance would include her poems. Anne's parlor became a magnet for black intellectuals, entertainers, and activists like James Weldon Johnson, Langston Hughes, W.E.B.

Du Bois, Zora Neale Hurston, George Washington Carver, Marian Anderson, Paul Robeson, Thurgood Marshall, and, later on, Martin Luther King Jr.

The guest list at the Spencer home was a veritable who's who of the African American cutting edge, the black leaders forging change in the larger society. Growing up in the company of these luminaries, Chauncey felt the power of the movement for expression, self-determination, and dignity. When a barnstormer passing overhead in his youth kindled a passion for flight, he was primed to make his own contribution to the cause of freedom—in the arena of the sky.

■ ■ ■

Chicago was the natural launchpad for the Goodwill Flight because in the interwar years it had evolved into a hotbed of black aviation. The history of African American flight in Chicago started to build shortly after World War I, when a young hairstylist and manicurist on the South Side felt impelled to learn to fly. Twenty-three-year-old Bessie Coleman had arrived in Chicago's so-called "Black Belt" in 1915 as part of the Great Migration of blacks from the South. Fixing people's hair and painting their nails was more lucrative and less strenuous than sharecropping in the cotton fields of Texas, but Bessie felt there had to be more to life.

When her brother John returned from military service in a segregated infantry unit at the end of World War I, he had trouble readjusting to civilian life and regularly snapped at Bessie that women in France were far ahead of the women of the South Side. In one particularly humiliating tirade at Bessie's workplace, exacerbated by his drinking, he added that French women could even fly. According to Bessie's biographer Doris L. Rich, Bessie took it as a dare. Even when all the flight schools in Chicago refused to give her lessons, she would not be deterred. Her cause was championed by the *Chicago Defender*, and in late 1920—with donated funds helping to cover the tab—she traveled to France for flight training.

On June 15, 1921, Bessie was issued a pilot's license by the Fédération Aéronautique Internationale, affording the ambitious beautician the distinction of being the first officially certified African American female pilot. After further flight training in France and Germany the next year, she embarked upon an exciting career as a barnstormer and air show performer in a war-surplus Jenny. For her flying exhibitions, she regularly appeared in a tailored military-style jacket with a Sam Browne belt, jodhpurs, knee-high boots, silk scarf, and an officer's cap decorated with custom wings incorporating her initials.

In connection with her roving aerial displays, she made a point to appear at black schools and churches to encourage students and parishioners to consider flight as an avenue of advancement. Her ultimate aim was to establish a flight school for African Americans, so that black women in America wanting to learn to fly would not need to travel abroad to get their training.

Bessie settled into the groove of the air show performer's life, perfecting her display routine and her public relations acumen. She thrilled crowds with her flying prowess and inspired children with her lectures. The newspaper that had promoted her aviation aspirations embraced her as a role model and bestowed on her the exalted title "Queen Bess."

Three and a half years into her air show career, Bessie's goal of opening a flight school seemed within reach. But during a practice flight at Jacksonville, Florida, on April 30, 1926, her airplane turned upside down when a loose wrench jammed the controls. Not buckled in or wearing a parachute, Bessie fell five hundred feet to the ground and died on impact.

It was a tragic end to a gifted life. Bessie's flight school never opened. But like the mythical phoenix that rose renewed from the ashes, Bessie's memory lived on, giving succor to those of her race seeking to enter the domain whose door she had cracked open against insuperable odds.

Bessie was buried in Chicago's Lincoln Cemetery at Kedzie Avenue and 123rd Street. The black press eulogized her rhapsodically. Soon aviation clubs named after Bessie started to sprout up in black communities around the country. In death as in life, the trailblazing pilot caused African Americans to look to the skies.

A year after the fatal accident, a memorial stone was unveiled at her grave. The inscription aptly described Bessie as "one of the first American women to enter the field of aviation." The absence of any reference to her race spoke volumes about the ideal dear to her heart—that the world of flying should be color-blind.

The grave became a shrine of the city's black community, especially the flyers and would-be flyers within it. In 1931, African American pilots in Chicago began an annual tradition of flying their aircraft over the cemetery for the express purpose of dropping flowers on Bessie's grave to commemorate her life. Three years later, William J. Powell, a former Chicagoan, published a landmark book to spark interest in aviation among blacks and, fittingly, dedicated it to the memory of Bessie.

Powell, like Bessie's brother, was a veteran of one of the segregated infantry regiments that had seen action in World War I. During an August 1927 reunion of veterans in Paris, he visited Le Bourget Airport, where Charles Lindbergh had been swarmed by tens of thousands of fans at the end of his solo transatlantic flight only a few months before. Caught up in the lingering excitement while at the airport, Powell purchased a plane ride over the city and instantly became hooked on flight.

Upon his return to Chicago he sold his chain of successful gas stations and packed up for California to launch a new career in aviation. He knew the Golden State's weather would be more conducive to his new ambitions, and he could only hope the racial climate would also be an improvement. Soon after he reached the West Coast, he set up a Bessie Coleman Aero Club.

Powell saw aeronautics as ripe for participation by African Americans. He believed that compared to established industries like oil and steel, the aviation industry was new and its major growth lay in the years ahead. He argued that by getting in on the ground floor blacks would be able to play prominent roles.

A full-time proselytizer, he organized the first all-black air show in southern California for Labor Day 1931. Powell was encouraged by the results and sought to build on that success. As aviation writer Phil Scott related in *AOPA Pilot*, Powell scheduled another air show for December 6 and endeavored to boost attendance by fielding an air-demonstration team comprising five black pilots.

The team, called the Five Blackbirds, flew different light aircraft of varied paint schemes. One of the pilots was a woman, Marie Dickerson Coker. The Five Blackbirds performed to boisterous approval from the audience of forty thousand and to rave reviews in the black press, but funds simply dried up. Powell's formidable plan for a hundred-city national tour was shelved, and the Five Blackbirds faded into a historical footnote.

In 1934, when Powell came out with his book, titled *Black Wings*, those who knew him could easily see that it was a thinly veiled autobiographical account of his own introduction to flight. More important, it served as a manifesto calling for blacks to enter careers in aviation or, as he phrased it, "to fill the air with black wings." By carrying forward and refining Bessie's message and putting it into printed form, Powell's book represented a milepost in the espousal of aviation for African Americans.

The book made clear that Powell saw flight as possessing the intrinsic power to liberate those who engage in it. He asserted that for blacks to get into the sky they had to be bold in both thought and deed. He predicted that black involvement in aviation could produce "one million jobs for Negroes." His outlook was encapsulated in this statement: "Negroes will never ride as free men and women below the Mason and Dixon Line ... until they ride in airplanes owned and operated by Negroes."

Despite Powell's unstinting optimism, the Depression was in full swing, and nothing he did, including publishing a newsletter and offering classes, attracted the financial support he needed to actualize his objectives. In the late 1930s, heavyweight boxing champion Joe Louis visited Powell's modest aviation workshop in Los Angeles, but even the endorsement of such a celebrity made little difference given the extent of economic hardship.

By 1942, Powell was in failing health from complications of a poison gas attack he had suffered in World War I. He died that year, only forty-three years old. Like Moses, he did not reach the Promised Land, but he got to glimpse some of his adherents crossing into a more hopeful sphere, as barely a year before his death the long-intransigent War Department finally opened the Army's flight training to blacks.

Meanwhile, back in Chicago, the strongest advocate of Bessie's vision in the 1930s was pilot and mechanic Cornelius R. Coffey. Bright and industrious, Coffey graduated from the first all-black class at the city's Curtiss-Wright Aeronautical School, a trade school noted for its instruction in aircraft maintenance, which before 1931 had excluded blacks. As a measure of his raw smarts and mechanical aptitude, he ranked at the top of his class.

The early 1930s brought an existential threat to black aviation in Chicago, when the one airport in the area that had allowed flying privileges to blacks permanently shut its doors. In 1933 Coffey and his friend John C. Robinson, who had graduated second in Coffey's class at the Curtiss-Wright school, led the fledgling Challenger Air Pilots Association in the purchase of land for an airport in Robbins Township, southwest of the city.

But their hopes were dashed when, within a year, a severe storm with fierce winds tore through the property, collapsing the hangar and wrecking the light planes based there. It was a devastating setback. Yet, according to information reported by *Air & Space/Smithsonian* contributor Giles Lambertson, in the wake of their despair, the group's members were given a new home on the south end of Harlem Airport, a few miles to the north of Robbins at Eighty-Seventh Street and Harlem Avenue in Oak Lawn, thanks to the airport's enlightened operator. Coffey, who had led the first flower drop over Bessie's grave, opened his own flight school at the new location. He had never met Bessie, but his school represented the fruition of her dream.

It was only logical that Chauncey Spencer, seeking to realize his long-repressed dream of flight, should journey to Chicago to get his start. In 1934, at twenty-eight years of age, thinking that "time had perhaps passed me by," it was a now-or-never moment for the Lynchburg native. He had been a truck driver, social worker, and manager of the Harrison Theater back in his Virginia hometown, jobs of no particular interest to him except insofar as they supported his marriage, which had now soured.

Oscar S. De Priest, Chicago's black congressman and a Spencer family friend, was proud that the city's blacks had begun to build a presence in aviation. Many of those involved lived within his South Side district. He personally counseled Chauncey to come to the city to learn to fly.

In Chicago Chauncey was stewarded by Earl W. Renfroe, a local dentist and budding flyer in the black community. Renfroe introduced

Chauncey to the Coffey Flying School, where his flight training commenced. Also through Renfroe, Chauncey struck up a friendship with Dale White, a black mechanic and pilot who had been certificated four years earlier.

Like many aspiring aviators, Chauncey had a hard time making ends meet. To supplement a stipend from his father, he got a job washing dishes at a restaurant in downtown Chicago. Later he would write that he "was willing to eat the cheap meals" because the sacrifice enabled him "to get off the ground."

While a student pilot, Chauncey became an exhibition parachutist. The sideline represented an extra source of income, but more than that, the free falls exhilarated him. Not since his childhood escapades sliding down hills headlong in a makeshift airplane had he experienced such visceral thrills.

He continued public skydiving after he obtained his pilot's license; it was a way to spread the word to fellow African Americans about the personal gratification that could be theirs. Photos from 1938 and 1939 show Chauncey attired in full aeronautical regalia and beaming, surrounded by admirers at Harlem Airport and clearly in his element. One of the black air shows in which he performed as a jumper had an estimated twenty-five thousand spectators.

It occurred to members of the black flying group that a publicized flight to targeted cities would bring the talents of African American pilots to the attention of a much larger audience. Newspaperman Enoch Waters, in keeping with the ideals of the *Chicago Defender*'s founder Robert Sengstacke Abbott, suggested that the flight should culminate in the nation's capital with an overt plea for a nondiscriminatory future in aviation. The obvious choices to make the proposed flight were Dale White and Chauncey Spencer.

Dale, with his accumulated flight experience and an ever-serious Rock of Gibraltar steadiness, was a natural for the project. Chauncey's irrepressible charm and good looks—some in the NAAA compared him to film idol Clark Gable—would make him the perfect companion. One would be the solemn operator of the machine, the captain of the ship, while the other would be the affable schmoozer between hops.

Though opposites in style and demeanor, both men were indispensable to the flight. Each contributed his skill set. Dale was the more seasoned pilot, the one who could get through any contingency in the air, while Chauncey, serving as navigator and public relations coordinator, was the supreme communicator, able to disarm anyone with his broad smile and winning personality. In time Dale came to resent being the foil for his more gregarious partner. But much later, after both had had distinguished careers as civilian employees at Wright-Patterson Air Force Base in Ohio, they resolved their simmering post-flight rivalry.

■　■　■

The Lincoln-Page joggled along at a respectable eighty-five miles per hour, its five-cylinder Kinner radial engine clanking out its trademark "ka-put-ta-ta." From Chicago, the two flyers needed first to round the drooping coast of Lake Michigan, with the smokestacks at Gary billowing to one side and the greening expanse of spring's recrudescent cropland to the other. Flying low in the open air, silk scarves flapping in the slipstream, the pilots could whiff a fortifying mix of fragrances rising into the air.

The pastures of the Midwest opened up beneath them, with their simple gridwork of north-south and east-west section lines. Conveniently for navigation, there were also the great railways connecting the nation's centers of commerce, punctuated by little whistle-stops with names like Walkerton, Nappanee, Cromwell, Kimmell, Albion, and Avilla—each of them a dot to be noted or perhaps checked off the chart to confirm the integrity of the navigational plot, for the aircraft had only the most rudimentary instrumentation.

But the Chicago-to-Washington flight never really went according to plan. Dale had to set the plane down in Avilla, a tiny hamlet in northeast Indiana, to fix leaking fuel lines. The pilots had traveled a mere 150 miles in what was planned as a trip of more than ten times that distance. The unexpected stop lasted six hours. Because of the loss of fuel, once the intrepid travelers were airborne again they had to go "off course to get gas," as Dale jotted in his logbook. The duo landed on a dirt road in Fort Wayne, Indiana, hand-pumped gas into the upper wing's fuel tank, and resumed the adventure.

But no sooner had they crossed the state line into Ohio than trouble struck again. This time the engine's crankshaft broke, causing the plane to buck violently. Dale had to draw on his every resource as a pilot to get the Lincoln-Page down in one piece.

The plane's ordinarily gentle handling characteristics and control responsiveness, owing to its long moment arms and aileron connector struts, were welcome attributes. Dale picked out a farm pasture within gliding distance as the Lincoln-Page gradually sank closer to the ground. He held it steady in the descent, touched down, and rolled out until, according to Chauncey, the plane "finally rested within a hundred yards of the farmer's barn."

The plane was a relic, having been designed in 1929, a decade earlier. It had no brakes and instead of a tailwheel only a spring-leaf tailskid, which drastically limited ground steering. Both men eased themselves out of their respective cockpits with a huge sense of relief that they had dodged the worst possible consequences of their latest mechanical mishap. Except for the engine, their ship remained intact and viable as a flying machine.

Not sure how they would be received by the owner of the farm where they had just landed, the men were further relieved when

Edward Miller, in plaid shirt and coveralls, overcame his initial shock upon surveying the scene and welcomed them, saying, "We're glad you're okay." Miller, a descendant of German immigrants, drove the black airmen to a tavern for a meal and arranged for their lodging in a rented room on the second floor.

As word spread about the two goggled visitors who had literally dropped from the sky, Chauncey would write, "most of the towns-people came to the cornfield to see us and our plane." The black pilots were such a novelty in the little village of Sherwood, Ohio, that they became instant celebrities. For the two days it took the NAAA to raise the fifty-four dollars for the parts to repair the engine and to dispatch Cornelius Coffey to make the repair, Chauncey and Dale feasted with the Millers and their neighbors.

By the time Coffey drove onto the property, a small army of villagers was there to help. Meanwhile, Miller's wife made fried egg sandwiches for the men. A couple of the Miller children became so attached to Chauncey and Dale during their short stay in Sherwood that when it came time for them to leave, the kids wrapped string around the Lincoln-Page and tied it to the granary, hoping that it would secure the plane in place.

The pilots gave one of Miller's daughters a plane ride in their rented biplane, but the weather precluded their taking up the other daughter, twelve-year-old Ann. Sixty-four years later, in a poignant interview by Michael Laris in the *Washington Post*, Ann described her interaction with the air travelers who unexpectedly came into her life. "The experience with Chauncey is the most wondrous thing that happened to me in my whole life. It gives you a good heart."

Three days after falling into the friendly fields of Sherwood, Chauncey and Dale were back on their Goodwill Flight, the slender fuselage of the Lincoln-Page cruising eastward again over the next town which, by some quirk of fate, was called Defiance. About the residents of Sherwood and their generosity, Chauncey wrote, "They were a gracious group of people who paid all our expenses while we were there."

One can only wonder if the men would have made their ultimate destination without the kindness of the strangers they had encountered by happenstance along their route when dire peril risked ending the whole flight—and how their absence from the halls of Congress might have delayed the entry of blacks into the Army Air Corps and aviation generally. The unforeseen pocket of understanding and tolerance at the flyers' most pressing time of need bolstered their spirits. If such goodness could be found at the country's core, there was hope that it might be reflected in the country's capital.

Not all their stops were so accommodating. At Morgantown, West Virginia, they were denied overnight parking. Forced not down but up and away into the impending darkness at sunset, they barely managed to find their way over the foreboding Alleghenies to Pittsburgh in the pitch black of night by following the lights of a Pennsylvania Central Airlines 247D passenger transport that just happened to be passing through the same airspace heading into the city's airport. On May 14, after several more stops, they finally arrived at Hoover Field on the banks of the Potomac.

In Washington the flyers were shepherded by the goateed Edgar G. "the Goat" Brown, the strong-willed founder of the United Government Employees Union and a noted advocate for civil rights. Up and down the halls of Congress, Brown opened doors for Chauncey and Dale. They met members of the Illinois congressional delegation, including the baritone-voiced Everett McKinley Dirksen, then a representative from Chicago and later the state's senior senator, who as leader of the chamber's Republican minority in the 1960s would throw his weight behind the era's historic civil rights legislation.

Chauncey did not take to Dirksen or Illinois's other politicos. He saw them as "interested in themselves," more concerned with photo ops geared to chalk up points with black constituents back home than with listening to him and his partner after they had surmounted incredible difficulties getting to Washington to make their case. In the words of the *Washington Post*'s Michael Laris, it was "a letdown." But in retrospect, Chauncey acknowledged that Dirksen deserved credit for introducing the nondiscrimination amendment to the House's civil aeronautics bill, a key measure that opened the Civilian Pilot Training Program to blacks.

With Chauncey feeling downcast, Brown knew the answer was to keep moving, so he ushered the flyers in the direction of the basement. From that point, a couple different accounts have been told about how things unfolded. According to one version, the three men were making their way down the staircase when a senator who was coming up extended a greeting to Brown. In the other version, the three men rode one of the underground electric trains that connect congressional offices with the Capitol; as they were exiting their car the senator in question could be seen walking towards them, and Brown reached out to him.

In either version of the chance meeting, the story thereafter plays out the same way. Brown introduced his associates to the senator, a little-known Missourian by the name of Harry S. Truman. Brown is reported to have told Truman that the two black flyers he was escorting wanted to get into the Army Air Corps. Truman was engaged and inquisitive.

Truman—being from the "Show-Me" state—wanted to see the plane that the two had flown to Washington. So that afternoon he met with the Goodwill Flyers at the airport. Chauncey invited Truman to go up for a ride, but he declined. Instead, he climbed up on the wing, peered into the cockpits, and then peppered his guides with one question after another about *Old Faithful*: its fuel capacity, rental cost, insurance.

In Chauncey's eyes, Truman was refreshingly genuine. He showed an interest without any photographer around to record the scene for publicity purposes and spent considerable time with a couple of guys who weren't even voters in his state. The plainspoken fellow could be gruff, but this only proved his authenticity.

The visit ended when the senator who would become known as "Give 'Em Hell Harry" brusquely declared, "If you have the guts to fly this thing to Washington, I have enough guts to back you up." The story became legend within the black community. Chauncey relished telling it countless times until he died in 2002 at age ninety-six. There were other events and considerations that had more to do with ending the prohibitions on blacks in military flying units, but Chauncey summed up his feelings about the flight in his autobiography: "By

Chauncey Spencer with his sister, Alroy Spencer Rivers, beside *Old Faithful*, the Lincoln-Page biplane, at Floyd Bennett Field in Brooklyn during a stop on the Goodwill Flight with Dale White from Chicago to Washington in May 1939. Note the names of the flight's sponsoring organizations, the National Airmen Association of America and the *Chicago Defender* newspaper, emblazoned on the rented aircraft's fuselage. Despite living in the adjoining borough of Queens, Harry would not know of the historic flight and its impact on opening up flying opportunities for blacks until years later. *National Air and Space Museum*

working within the legal structure, we had effected a change that would, ultimately, make a difference for all Americans. A new era in American history had begun, and we were jubilant."

■ ■ ■

Like Queen Bess, the Goodwill Flyers spread the gospel of aviation at every stop on their flight. One of those stops, the day before they landed in Washington, was New York City. They had originally been scheduled to arrive at Flushing Airport in Queens to be near the World's Fair, but flooding at the airport forced them to divert to Floyd Bennett Field in southeast Brooklyn.

Chauncey was no stranger to New York. He had lived there for a short while in the 1920s, even acting part-time at the Lafayette Theater in Harlem. Back then his older sister Alroy was a student at Hunter College. She had subsequently settled in the city, and when her brother arrived by air amid much hoopla she went to meet him.

As had been planned at the flight's outset, Chauncey and Dale would be whisked through a series of appearances and interviews to maximize their limited time in New York. They were greeted in the morning by the wife of tap dancer and honorary Harlem mayor Bill "Bojangles" Robinson. Soon they were off to the Mimo Club in Harlem for a grand soiree celebrating Joe Louis's twenty-fifth birthday to the harmonious strains of Duke Ellington and his band. Later came more jazz music and Lindy Hop dancing at the Savoy Ballroom on Harlem's main drag, Lenox Avenue.

The black newspapers ran photographs of the Goodwill Flyers and the celebrities they met during their layover in New York, using news of their flight's progress to dramatize the desire of African American men to be pilots in the Army Air Corps. In pointed language, one of the newspapers opined, "the military leaders of the

United States ignore the intrepid black men who would serve their country in the air." References were made to expatriate Eugene Jacques Bullard, who had joined the French Aeronautique Militaire during World War I; Jimmie Peck, who flew for the Loyalist side in the Spanish Civil War; and Chicago's own John Robinson, who advised Ethiopian emperor Haile Selassie on the formation of an air force as the army of Italian dictator Benito Mussolini threatened the African nation's independence. It was a powerful message, but at the time only a narrow sliver of the population was on the receiving end.

In a working-class neighborhood of Queens, one borough removed from where *Old Faithful* had landed, an African American teenager who was completely unaware of the Goodwill Flyers had independently developed a burning passion for flight and begun to fantasize about flying the U.S. Army's frontline combat planes. Harry T. Stewart Jr. had heard nothing of the Spencer-White flight despite his proximity to it. Because the Stewart family lived in an integrated neighborhood and had neither a subscription to a black newspaper nor membership in an activist black church, young Harry might as well have been a world away when the Lincoln-Page came to New York and its two pilots spent the day doing up the town.

It would be a while before Harry became aware of the Chicago pilots' journey and its significance for him and other blacks infused with the dream of flight. One day Harry would meet an aged Chauncey Spencer and thank him for helping to pry open the gateway to the skies. But that was many years in the future.

Meanwhile, Harry would face his own challenges rising up into this alluring and still barely accessible domain. He did not know it yet, but he and others would together take the proverbial baton from Chauncey and Dale to ride the wind in battles to come and, in a manner that would make his aerial antecedents proud, unblock the gateway several notches more.

With the glamorous parts of their extraordinary eleven-day adventure behind the Goodwill Flyers as they thrummed their way back towards their Chicago home, they purposely angled off the straight-line course of their flight between Lima and Fort Wayne. Dale recorded the reason for the course deviation in the "Remarks" column of his logbook: "Via Sherwood O. to salute the Millers."

In the process of bringing change to their profession, Chauncey and Dale had been touched by the selflessness of the ordinary citizens they chanced upon during their flight. The next chapter in the history of black aviation would be written by young men of color yearning to get their hands on the country's latest military pursuit ships—dreamers like Harry Stewart.

Chapter Two

THE SKY BECKONS

New day has begun.
—Langston Hughes, "Black Maria"

If Harry Thaddeus Stewart Jr. was a dreamer, it was at least in part because his father was too. The elder Stewart had been born in 1903 in Phoebus, Virginia, now a historic district consolidated into the city of Hampton. Harry's grandfather, Preston James Stewart, worked as a wheelwright in the local blacksmith's shop, and his grandmother Bessie Maude Gathwright Stewart was a seamstress. Their circumstances were humble yet adequate to provide for Harry Sr. and two other sons, Preston Junior and Conrad.

Growing up in coastal Virginia in the early twentieth century as the son of a man who had been born into slavery in Alabama during the Civil War, Harry Sr. felt hemmed in by his surroundings. By the middle of the 1920s, as he pondered his future, he did not want to resign himself to a life circumscribed by the prevailing baneful mix of skewed law and spiteful custom. Trapped in menial dead-end jobs, he reasoned that his only alternative was to leave home in search of something better. Casting about might lead nowhere, but he would never know unless he tried.

It was not something he considered cavalierly, for he had already married his sweetheart Florence Bright and together they had begun to raise a family. Florence, perky with an elfin smile, was game for the move. Like her husband, she thought not only of her own future, but of the future her children would have in the South, where Jim Crow still reigned.

Florence's lineage could be traced back to the Bubi people, an ethnic offshoot of the West African Bantu tribes who in the seventh century had settled on Bioko Island in what is now Equatorial Guinea. Like her ancient ancestors, she hankered for a place that offered greater independence, and she possessed the energy to get there. If her husband wanted to break from the community he had been a part of since birth for the prospect of a better life for himself and his family, she would willingly follow him.

Harry Sr. wanted his parents and brother to join him too. At first his parents were reluctant to agree to the move; they were set in their daily routine, and though it was against the backdrop of a suffocating social order, they had long since reconciled themselves to their circumstances. It took a lot of prodding, but eventually they were persuaded to follow their son, whom they could hardly fault for seeking to expand his opportunities. Harry Sr.'s older brother, Preston Jr., had died in an accidental drowning when he was fourteen years old, but his younger brother Conrad was eager to go and, when the time came, would accompany his parents for a reunion in a new city away from the South.

Luckily, the means for Harry Sr. to literally sail to new shores was readily available. Nearby Newport News serviced a shipping line that made regular runs to cities up and down the sea lanes along the East coast, including New York. Believing that anywhere else, perhaps even the voyaging itself, would be an improvement, in 1925 Harry Sr. hired on with the company and climbed aboard one of its passenger liners.

It was a gutsy call, but in launching onto the sea, ultimate destination unknown, the young man was lifted by the idea that his new life would have a greater measure of dignity and potential for fulfillment.

Work as the assistant galley cook was less than gratifying. Harry Sr. spent his time below decks in the sweltering recesses of the hull preparing meals for the passengers and crew. Paradoxically, he thought in the early going, his chosen instrument for deliverance was hardly an improvement over the hardscrabble reality he had left behind. Nevertheless, he clung to the hope that the arduous journey would be worth it. In his dreams a better place awaited him, possibly just over the horizon at the next port of call.

Transiting into New York Harbor for the first time, Harry Sr. saw the city's remarkable skyline rising from the water like the magical kingdom in a fairytale. The Virginian, like the émigrés arriving in an endless stream from the other side of the Atlantic, passed slowly before the imposing Statue of Liberty, with words of welcome at its base and a symbolic torch in upraised hand, and felt the warmth of enfranchisement. The temptation to make a new life here, in this most cosmopolitan city, was irresistible.

On his return home he talked it over with Florence and others in the family. They would try it; they calculated that they had nothing to lose. Several additional trips to New York ensued, on which Harry Sr. made inquiries and did his best to prepare for the move. On the fateful voyage in 1926, when the passenger liner slid alongside its pier in New York once again, the improbable mariner consummated his exodus. He walked off the ship and kept going, not bothering to look back.

The story has been handed down by word of mouth through the subsequent generations of Stewarts. They relish telling the tale, for it speaks to the daring of their patriarch. He didn't just imagine a change in venue and circumstance; with only his fortitude and the supportive wishes of his inner circle, he went out in pursuit of his dream.

According to the account that has been told and retold for nearly a century, when Harry Sr. made his immensely consequential turn away from the ship his eyes pointed forward, resolutely forward, exclusively in the direction of his new beginning.

In the fragment of time that it took Harry Sr. to traverse the plank connecting vessel to dock, he exchanged the drudgery of seagoing mess hand for the infinite possibilities of the intimidating metropolis. The newcomer savored the chance to start anew in this vast, bustling city full of new arrivals from lands far away. He soon sent for his wife and children, as well as his parents and brother, as he plunged into the maze of New York, glad to have escaped the limitations that had hemmed in his family's life in the South.

Slim and slightly taller than average height with a courtly bearing, Harry Sr. began the next phase of his odyssey as a doorman. The city's expanding population of apartment dwellers needed all manner of service personnel, and a black man who exuded deference, who possessed that gingerly deftness to be demure in the presence of tenants in the silk-stocking districts, fit the criterion perfectly.

The transplanted Southerner could have made a lifelong career of swinging open doors and carrying up packages for his building's tenants. Like Pullman car porters and White House ushers, black men who faithfully served upscale apartment dwellers in New York could expect a driblet of benefaction, a pinch of patronage to soften their twilight years. But there was a glint in Harry Sr.'s eyes betraying a prodigious ambition that would not be satisfied by a few coins dropped into his palm as rich patrons rushed past, too busy to learn his last name.

Meanwhile, not all was well in the family. Almost as soon as Harry Sr.'s parents arrived in New York with Conrad, it became obvious that Preston was not adjusting to life in the big northern city. The rural surroundings Harry Sr.'s father had always known were now supplanted by the most urban of settings; instead of the tranquility of open spaces, he was having to cope with a high-density habitat. Even worse, there was no work for him as a wheelwright, which made him feel useless.

Knowing that there was no going back, Preston felt trapped. He began to see himself as a burden on Harry Sr., who was trying to provide for his wife and children. Preston quickly plunged into a deep depression and one morning he took a gun to his head, tragically ending his life.

It was an awful blow to Harry Sr., but he would not let his father's suicide upend his life. Soon a gainful offer from a newly-founded company in the city's garment industry lured him away from the doorman's job. The factory, which produced a line of outerwear, presented a more lucrative career path. The best part of it was that Harry Sr. and his new boss, a fair-minded white businessman, developed a mutually respectful working relationship.

Harry Sr. and Florence were content if not overjoyed with the home they made in Harlem for their growing family. They had moved from a first-floor apartment on 126th Street at Third Avenue into an apartment on the top floor of a five-story tenement at 129th Street and Fifth Avenue. The streets below teemed with activity and, in the middle of summer, mother and father

When Harry was two years of age, his father moved to New York City and soon afterwards brought his extended family from Virginia to join him. Seen here is Harry with his parents on the fifth floor of a tenement building at 129th Street and Fifth Avenue in Harlem, 1926. *Harry Stewart Jr.*

would carry their children out onto the fire escape for relief from the heat. Like many black families that had migrated from the rural South to northern cities, the Stewarts were adapting to urban life.

■ ■ ■

In 1928, when Harry Sr. believed that things were falling into place and he could begin to relax, young Harry came down with a severe fever compounded by respiratory complications. Having been born back in Virginia on July 4, 1924, Harry was only four years old at the time, and his parents were worried that they might lose their firstborn child. As his temperature spiked and his breathing became more labored, they rushed him to the hospital.

After a day of observation in the children's ward, paralysis set in affecting the little boy's right leg. The doctors had the sad task of informing Harry Sr. and Florence that their son had polio. While treatment options were limited, the four-year-old managed to bounce back on his own.

But young Harry's leg did not fully heal. The hospital prescribed a leg brace for daily use. Harry, frustrating his mother and father, showed his precocious streak by constantly shaking out of the brace and maneuvering without it. In later years, he conjectured that he had done himself a favor by exercising without the mandated support.

As Harry got a little older, it became clear that he had lost reflex sensitivity in his right leg and that it would never have the circumference or length of his left leg. The muscle in the calf of his right leg had permanently atrophied. Despite the bad hand dealt him by polio, he learned to work around the handicap, raising himself from a sitting position by leaning into his left leg before putting weight on his right side. The technique became second nature to him, so that those who didn't know Harry's medical history had no idea of his disability.

Later still, when Harry was about to enter elementary school, a physical examination detected a systolic heart murmur. It was theorized that the condition had developed as a complication of the polio. The diagnosis caused his doctor to recommend that he not participate in athletics at school. But the disability only drove Harry to strive ever harder, determined that the kinks in his body would not hold him back.

■ ■ ■

Harry's parents knew from the struggles they had experienced both before and after setting foot in New York that life is not a linear progression always heading up. Sadly, after a few years, the garment business that employed Harry Sr. began to falter. The clothing company's owner, who had become Harry Sr.'s friend, invited his loyal employee into his office. The owner expressed his deep regret that, despite the best entrepreneurial exertions, the firm was in an irreversible slump. With closure imminent, the owner volunteered to provide a glowing recommendation to prospective employers.

Now with Florence and four children to feed, Harry Sr. wasted no time making the rounds. A clerkship at the Brooklyn General Post Office looked agreeable; it promised security, and so he grabbed it. Later he learned that his former boss's strong endorsement persuaded the post office's personnel board to hire him. The timing was impeccable. The stock market crash of 1929 occurred soon afterwards, signaling the onset of the Great Depression.

The post office job shielded the Stewart family from the worst of the hard times. Desirous of more space and good schools, the family settled in the austere, unpretentious, and proud Corona section of Queens, noteworthy for its ethnic mix, with a decidedly Italian influence. Indeed, the word "corona" is Italian for "crown."

Corona grew as working families moved from the city's populous core in an eastward migration to sections of Queens. The Stewarts' home was a brick walk-up at 3142 104th Street. Out on the far side of the East River and south of Flushing Bay, residents lived in the shadow of Manhattan's skyline of soaring neo-Gothic and art deco towers on one side and with a view of the bedroom communities stretched out across Long Island's uncluttered acreage on the other side. Corona was not so much a destination in its own right as a contiguity of row houses interspersed with rail lines and roadways to accommodate the workday commuting of the upscale suburbanites in Great Neck and beyond.

In its most conspicuous accommodation to the city, Corona's shoreline was, in historian Robert Caro's words, turned into "foothills of filth," and the squiggly fingers of the Flushing River became "an open sewer." In 1909, the Brooklyn Ash Removal Company, controlled by a crafty figure named John "Fishhooks" McCarthy, who had ties to the Tammany Hall political machine, had begun to use the coast's pristine salt marsh and meadows as its dumping ground. A steady succession of railcars unloaded massive amounts of cinders and ash collected from the coal-fired furnaces that were common for heating homes and businesses in the early part of the century.

F. Scott Fitzgerald referred to the low-lying coastal waste dump as "a valley of ashes" in his 1925 novel *The Great Gatsby*. It was, he wrote, "a fantastic farm where ashes grow like wheat ... through the powdery air." The novelist latched onto the ash heap as a literary device to connote the effect of unrestrained greed and the chronic predicament of the less fortunate. The neighborhood where the Stewarts lived was far enough away from the notorious site that they did not feel its adverse effects, but close enough for them to know of the harmful fallout.

Eventually the ash mounds proliferated; the tallest one rose a spectacular ninety feet and was nicknamed "Mount Corona." The area came to be known as the "Corona Ash Dumps," "Corona Dumps," or simply the "Dumps."

In the early 1930s the city's imperious parks commissioner, Robert Moses, envisioned transforming the blighted area and surrounding land into a vast park to rival Central Park. He hatched a plan to clear 1,346 acres in connection with the siting of the 1939–1940 World's Fair. Development of the parklands would follow the fair, while landfills elsewhere would be used for future waste disposal.

In 1934, with newly elected reformist Mayor Fiorello La Guardia on board, New York bought the dumping ground from the private company that had been accused of scalping the city. Neighborhood residents recognized the logic of the proposed beautification; converting the dirty, smelly mass of waste and decay, blamed for a polio outbreak in 1916, into a green esplanade unquestionably made sense. But young Harry, who grew up as this project unfolded, remembers an uproar over the city's rush to condemn properties east of Corona's 111th Street.

The displacement of families to make way for the appurtenant parkway and bridge miffed many in the neighborhood. Adding to their ire was the renaming of the dumps. Henceforth it would be known as Flushing Meadows Park, as though the Corona name could be expunged like the ashes.

Harry observed the controversy play out in the neighborhood where he came of age. The parents whose children he sat with in school and played with in extracurricular activities had exhibited the will to stand up to the priggish steamrollering of a detached officialdom. A seed was planted; Harry himself would later refuse to accept the world as he found it. Even though the tides of war and economic necessity would carry him far from the landscape of his youth, Harry remained anchored to the ethos rooted in the place he would always remember as home.

■ ■ ■

For young Harry, life in the Corona section of Queens was next to idyllic. On his first birthday after the move to Corona, he got a cowboy outfit and cap pistol as presents. He went out into the street to show off and, to his surprise, was met by another neighborhood kid attired in an Indian costume and brandishing a bow and arrow. The two staged a shoot-out that cemented a friendship destined to last, on and off, for years to come.

The "Indian" was Joseph E. Gordon, a classmate the same age as Harry. About five years later the Gordons moved to Brooklyn. In a twist of fate worthy of a Dickens novel, the two boys would meet again as young men in vastly altered circumstances where guns were not for play but for real, and where they would not be opponents but comrades.

Harry's father took a deep interest in the quality of his children's education. He developed a passion for early-childhood development that led to his devoting much of his free time to youth counseling and extracurricular field trips. When his Corona neighborhood's elementary school, P.S. 92, fell into disrepair late in his life, he used his position as a highly respected member of the community to champion the construction of a replacement. In February 1993, the new school went up—bearing Harry Sr.'s name!

Thanks in part to the involvement of Harry's father and other similarly driven parents, the neighborhood's public schools in the prewar years offered an impressive education and, at the same time, melded the diverse student body into a surprisingly workable and arguably cohesive whole. Harry thrived in this enclave of tolerance and mutual respect. He joined his fellow students in a Boy Scout troop and got his biggest thrills when he and the Scouts steered hand-crafted go-carts down city streets blocked off expressly for the exhil-arating speed dashes. But Harry's sights would soon turn skyward.

Aviation was all the rage, as an increasing stream of ever more advanced airplanes arrived on the scene. In August 1931, the Dornier Do X, a gargantuan German flying boat, touched down in the waters off the city. It had made news crossing the South Atlantic and then hopscotching north from Brazil.

The unwieldy airliner, one of only three ever built, could carry up to 150 passengers. It had a dozen engines arrayed in a push-pull configura-tion atop a wing that hung over a massive whale-like hull. The monstros-ity turned heads wherever it went, showing how far aviation had come in the few years since Lindbergh's record solo flight across the ocean.

It was moored within view from the shore for part of a nine-month layover that included heavy maintenance and engine over-hauls, and the public was invited to take a closer look. Harry remembers being taken aboard by his curious dad, who paid the considerable price of a dollar each to be motored out to the leviathan. Not only did the walk-through make an indelible impression on both father and son, the plane's design presaged the cutting-edge technol-ogy and advanced engineering that would vie for global dominance in a life-or-death aerial faceoff fated to ensnare Harry just a bit more than a decade later.

The early 1930s was a time when the U.S. Navy believed in the utility of huge, rigid airships. Theory held that dirigibles could stay aloft for extended periods, cover vast swaths of ground, surveil dis-tant locations, and might even carry "parasite" fighters. From time to time Harry saw the expansive sausage shapes floating surreally across the sky.

The Navy's *Akron* and *Macon* airships occupied a disproportionate share of the skyscape above New York, projecting design creativity and technical innovation. But both airships came to grief in mid-decade, and in May 1937 the *Hindenburg*, Germany's foremost commercial dirigible, exploded in a much-photographed fireball at Lakehurst, New Jersey, horrifying the world and bringing an end to the airship era. Like the Dornier, the airships were doomed, but they had lit imaginations and foreshadowed the coming revolution in flying machines.

Meanwhile, the matinees that featured box office headliners as swashbuckling heroes in dueling biplanes further excited Harry's interest in flying. At home he built model airplanes with his friends. Gluing the pieces together fostered a basic knowledge of the workings of actual aircraft.

Harry also devoured aviation-themed pulp magazines. His favorite was *Flying Aces*. Others included *Sky Birds*, *G-8 and His Battle Aces*, and *Popular Aviation and Aeronautics*. The exaggerated stories of danger and adventure in the sky, illustrated in gaudy comic-book style, only partially satiated his appetite—for the more he read, the more he longed for the real thing.

Throughout the 1930s, the sky over New York was abuzz with rakish designs testing the limits of the preponderant aeronautical conventions. The area's active military airfields and the burgeoning aviation industry were energized by talk of war. Military contracts for new designs were going to plants in the area, such as Grumman's Long Island facilities. Of course, commercial airlines were modernizing their fleets too.

Harry's favorite aircraft in the mix of traffic he observed passing over his home was the Army's B-10 bomber. Sometimes seen in formation flight, the bulbous twin-engine aluminum-frame warplanes shimmered in the high sun. Though slow and otherwise unsuited for emergent air warfare, they represented a bridge to the sophisticated four-engine bombers that were in the development and production pipeline.

Air Corps doctrine at the time was that the bomber behemoths would be able to defend themselves against interceptors while delivering knockout blows to an enemy nation's industrial infrastructure. The pummeling from these untouchable bombers would force even a heavily fortified opponent with a dynamic economy into submission. It was a seductive thesis.

The B-10 bomber was an evocative symbol of a rising vanguard, as well as a catalyst for Harry. The shiny aircraft, accented in the Air Corps' blue-and-yellow color scheme with barber-pole red-and-white striping on the rudder, inspired visions of hazard, drama, and glory. Little did Harry know that in just a few years he and similarly motivated schoolboys would disprove the air power theory that extolled the primacy of the bomber. When barely beyond their teens, they would upstage the high-ranking conceptualists by demonstrating on harrowing missions that the hulking bombers succeeded only when protected by swarms of "little friends," the long-range escort fighters.

As much as Harry wanted to go up for a plane ride, he did not press the point with his father. He knew that the harsh realities of the Depression precluded his father from plunking down a five-dollar bill for a local scenic flight. But Harry kept his eye on the winged wonders cruising over his section of Queens.

In 1936, the Stewart family moved to a roomier house a few blocks south at 105-11 Thirty-Fourth Avenue. Harry's frequent walks to the neighborhood airport would still take only about forty-five minutes from the new location. He could hike up 105th Street to East Elmhurst and then cross diagonally on Astoria Boulevard to any of the north–south streets, like Ninety-Fourth Avenue, which cut through North Beach and got him to the airport's perimeter for views of the private planes and flight school trainers.

The airport had been built in 1929 on the grounds of the Gala Amusement Park, which had been owned by a partnership that included the Steinway piano family. At that time, it was named after the famous aviator and inventor Glenn H. Curtiss. In 1935, the year after Fiorello La Guardia assumed office as mayor of New York, the city bought the site and renamed it North Beach Municipal Airport. La Guardia, who was an accomplished World War I Army aviator and champion of commercial air service, worked from that point to transform the sleepy little airport on Bowery and Flushing Bays into a modern hub.

New runways, hangars, and a circle-shaped administration building with an observation deck in the back and a control tower on top were built to handle commercial air traffic. On October 15, 1939, the enlarged and revitalized airport was opened and rechristened New York Municipal Airport–LaGuardia Field in honor of the hard-driving and flamboyant mayor. Among the more than 325,000 people who turned out for the dedication was Harry Stewart.

Only fifteen years old, but already knowledgeable about the distinguishing features of contemporary aircraft and able to differentiate among the various types, Harry was drawn to the gleaming aluminum DC-3 parked on the ramp; it seemed to tower over the many onlookers. The lustrous transport evinced air travel's entry into the modern age, the leap from handcrafted wood-and-wire contraptions to production-line wonders that could outperform even the Army's previously touted B-10. The DC-3 on display had been flown in expressly for the ceremony by Transcontinental & Western Air (later to become Trans World Airlines with continued use of the acronym TWA), which would begin regularly scheduled passenger service from the airport in December.

Harry knew from the aviation magazines that the DC-3 accounted for almost all domestic commercial air traffic and that TWA had spurred the development of its precursors, the DC-1 and DC-2. It was a sign of TWA's prestige that Charles Lindbergh had gone to work for the company as a consultant. Capitalizing on the flyer's celebrity, the airline emblazoned "The Lindbergh Line" across the upper fuselages of its planes and used the tagline in advertisements.

Harry, trim and dapper in suit and tie, cracked an effervescent smile as he posed for a few pictures with the TWA DC-3. His elation is evident in the photos. There was little doubt that the teen was on his way, somehow, to piloting planes.

Further inspiration came next spring when Pan American Airways inaugurated the first scheduled transatlantic passenger airline service from LaGuardia's new Marine Air Terminal. Luxurious Boeing 314 flying boats launched from a dock with a long copper-roofed walkway that sheltered the air travelers as they boarded. The Clippers lifted off from Long Island Sound for the exotic destinations of Lisbon and Southampton.

Harry's dream of flight was kindled by airplanes operating out of local airports. On October 15, 1939, North Beach Municipal Airport, within walking distance of Harry's home in the Corona section of Queens, was rededicated as New York Municipal Airport–La Guardia Field. Harry, then fifteen years old, was one of more than 325,000 people who came to celebrate. The teenager wanted to grow up and fly the DC-3 airliner on display. The slogan on the plane's fuselage—"The Lindbergh Line"—identifies it as belonging to Transcontinental & Western Air, the precursor of Trans World Airlines or TWA. Eleven years later, Harry tried to apply for a flying position with the airline but was rejected out of hand. Sixty-nine years after the rejection, the successor company, American Airlines, awarded him status as an honorary captain. *Harry Stewart Jr.*

One day, Harry recalls, he snuck past the fence at LaGuardia and began to climb on a derelict plane parked in the grass. A New York City policeman showed up and yelled, "What are you doing?" When

Harry explained, the policeman responded, "Who can blame you?" The two of them went into the plane's cockpit, sat down, and pondered what it would be like to actually go up in it.

On days that Harry visited the revamped airport, as the sun blazed down on beautiful airliners and a fresh breeze blew in from the bay, he believed that the possibilities before him were infinite.

■　■　■

By coincidence, the students at Harry's junior high school, P.S. 16, had to sit for one-on-one interviews with their guidance counselors soon after the dedication of the airport. Harry's counselor was his history teacher, Grace McLaughlin. She had high expectations for Harry because, among other things, he had won the Theodore Roosevelt Oratorical Medal, the award in a district-wide public speaking competition.

But the interview was rather perfunctory until it got around to the question of future plans. When Mrs. McLaughlin asked Harry what he wanted to do, he answered, without hesitation and with gusto, "I want to be an airline pilot."

Caught off guard by the innocence of her student, Mrs. McLaughlin started to tear up. Hadn't anyone told the fifteen-year-old that the airlines didn't hire blacks to fly their planes? She felt sorry for Harry and fought back the tears as she spoke to him candidly about his prospects. "Colored people aren't accepted as airline pilots," she said. Trying to soften the harsh reality, she told Harry that there were other avenues open to blacks and urged him to set his sights on something more attainable.

Harry listened politely, but took a dim view of his counselor's well-intended advice. He had just seen one of the world's leading airliners and even touched its smooth metal surfaces. With the plane so close, he asked himself, how could the possibility that he might fly it be so far away? The plane would fly the same regardless of the color of the person at the controls.

Harry's unjaded vision of a bias-free world aloft was essentially the vision being advanced by civil rights leaders and the handful of black aviators. But in Harry's case the vision was self-derived; up to that point in his life he had no knowledge of the strenuous undertakings of the first generation of African American flyers.

In prewar America, the white press turned a blind eye to the aerial achievements of black airmen. Only black reporters were on the beat, and the Stewart household did not subscribe to the local *New York Amsterdam News* or any other black newspaper—by the decision of Harry's mother Florence, who Harry described years later as "puritanical" and "our censor." She thought the black press was too often risqué in its reportage and had decided that such sensationalism had no place in her home where her children might be exposed to it.

Also, Harry was coming of age in a predominantly white neighborhood, and news of black pilots attempting to open up the airways wasn't on the lips of his mostly white classmates. Even in church, Harry didn't hear about the exploits of trailblazers like Bessie Coleman and William Powell, let alone the Spencer-White flight. The Stewarts attended the Chapel of the Resurrection, a black congregation in the Corona section of Queens affiliated with the Episcopal Diocese. The pastor, Elijah H. Hamilton, was a traditionalist. Unlike other black ministers, who used the pulpit to relate current events and stake out opinions on them, the Reverend Hamilton preached church doctrine in sermons heavily laden with quotations from scripture and nearly devoid of commentary on social justice, community activism, and the issues of the day.

One black figure in prewar aviation did come to Harry's attention, in a fluke encounter. Harry and a friend were talking to an adult acquaintance on a busy sidewalk in Harlem when, quite by coincidence, a flashily dressed African American, walking stick in hand, stopped to say hello to the adult, whom he knew.

Thus Harry met Hubert Fauntleroy Julian, a born showman who had combined his talent for grabbing headlines with flying. Once a performer in one of William Powell's California air shows and later, like John Robinson, a short-lived volunteer in Haile Selassie's Ethiopian air force, the reputed Black Eagle of Harlem was more self-promoter than pilot. Julian was theatrical and prone to exaggeration, and his braggadocio was an instant turnoff for Harry.

But, refusing to be discouraged, Harry dismissed the character on the sidewalk as an anomaly, sure that the flying fraternity generally was made up of individuals of a higher caliber. Harry's dream of flying never waned. And one day, reading a magazine in the Flushing High School library, he came across a short article that reinforced his dream as never before. It reported that in March 1941 the Army would start to train—in the terminology of the day—an all-Negro flying unit: the 99th Pursuit Squadron.

Suddenly, Harry had something tangible he could embrace, a flying organization that would actually accept blacks. With war clouds billowing, this is where Harry wanted to serve, in the new black flying unit. It had "the glamour, the polish, the elite," as he would say.

Harry's wish got a boost on December 7. Walking home from Sunday school in the afternoon, he saw three fighter planes circling overhead, as if on patrol. Closer to home, he caught a glimpse of his neighbors huddled in the street, clearly discussing a topic of intense interest.

Listening to his animated neighbors, he heard how in the early morning hours the Japanese had attacked U.S. forces at Pearl Harbor. America was at war. Emotions were running high: Harry overheard one of the older neighbors say, "We'll have the Japs under control in two weeks!"

Harry was excited at the prospect of being in the Air Corps, so a few weeks after Pearl Harbor he went to the Army recruiting station on Lexington Avenue. He sashayed in and announced that he wanted to join the 99th Pursuit Squadron. The recruiters chuckled and told him that the Army didn't work that way; for one thing, at seventeen years of age, he was too young. Embarrassed but determined, he then carefully laid out his plan for enlistment to coincide with his eighteenth birthday. He returned to the recruiting station the day after Independence Day in 1942.

There would be written and physical exams, and then the Army would decide what it wanted to do with the eager volunteer. Harry nodded his acknowledgment, hoping that his choice of service would be honored. He filled out the paperwork, assiduously noting his preference for the Air Corps, and then sat for the written exam in a room filled with hopeful young men.

The presiding sergeant scored the tests and announced the results to the applicants, most of whom appeared to have at least a high school diploma. In a tremendous blow to his plans, Harry had failed. There would be one more chance to take the exam, in thirty days. If he didn't pass then, his dream would fizzle and die.

Harry bought a study guide and spent the next month practically memorizing its contents. He did everything the study guide recommended, including going to bed early with a glass of milk the night before the second written exam and waking early with a hot shower. And it worked: Harry passed! From that point, it would be a waiting game to see if the Air Corps got to him before the draft board did.

While waiting, Harry made a decision that he lived to regret. With war raging and his future subject to word from the War Department, school seemed irrelevant. Eight or nine of his classmates, both black and white, had already dropped out of Flushing High, lured by the plethora of jobs and the improved wages in the suddenly booming wartime economy. Feeling the peer pressure, Harry disregarded his parents' advice and dropped out too.

He started as a laborer at nearby Camp Kilmer in New Jersey and then took a job as a shipping clerk with the Chase Bottle and Supply Company, a wine importer in the city. In March 1943, eight months after he had turned eighteen, he received an official notice with orders to report for induction at Camp Upton in east central Long Island. This is what Harry had dreaded: he was being drafted with the likelihood of an assignment to the infantry, usurping his preference for the air arm.

Each day that passed as he waited for the March 20 induction date, Harry bemoaned the likelihood that he would be tasked to the infantry and miss out forever on the chance to fly. Then, just two days before his scheduled induction, by the caprice of the bureaucracy, he received a telegram from "H. H. Arnold." Though Harry didn't know it at the time, he would learn soon enough that "Hap" Arnold was the commanding general of the Army Air Forces.

The telegram ordered Harry to report to Keesler Field in Mississippi. Holding both notices in opposite hands, Harry—not knowing what to do—looked to his father for advice.

Harry Sr. sized up the situation with the conflicting orders and he counseled his son to report to Camp Upton with the Arnold telegram in his pocket. At the right time, he said, pull it out and hand it to one of the induction center's officers.

The advice was prescient. The officer in charge determined that the latter orders superseded the earlier notice. Harry was ecstatic.

A few days later, as Harry packed and readied himself to leave home, the mood was bittersweet. His father and siblings were immensely proud of him. But Florence was in a state of despair at the thought of her firstborn going to war. It was the same anguish that was befalling so many other families facing the same circumstance. Harry's mother, simply unable to bring herself to say goodbye, stayed in her room with the door closed, fretting over the dangers awaiting her son.

Harry climbed down off the front porch with a lump in his throat, glanced back momentarily, and waved adieu to his dad, two brothers, and sister. He swung around and stepped to the waiting car, not knowing if he would ever see his family again. It was the hardest step in his passage from Corona to Army fighter planes, from dreams of glory to touching the sky.

Chapter Three

AIMING HIGH

Kites rise highest against the wind—not with it.
—Winston S. Churchill

Finally on a path to earning the coveted silver wings of an Army aviator, Harry did not know how spine-chillingly close the flight training program for blacks had come to dissolution. The larger-than-life individual chiefly responsible for rescuing the program would become his commanding officer—and in the waning days of the war they would brave treacherous skies together as friends, colleagues, and wingmen.

This extraordinary leader in Harry's future was noted for projecting an unforgettable earnestness. From the way he carried himself, you could tell this was a man who aimed high. He stood tall and stately, averse to small talk and impervious to the tyranny of petty things.

His answer to the racial snubs directed his way was not reciprocation but pity. Polite but formal, he possessed an indefatigability that bordered on stubbornness. A profound morality and a belief that righteousness has the upper hand over injustice undergirded his outlook. A thinker and doer, he was guided by a deep sense of honor and he remained unceasingly conscious of the need to produce tangible results.

He was not someone to be trifled with, and he did not take kindly to being identified by something as superfluous as skin color. Depth of character was what mattered to him, and if color came into it at all, then he would choose the distinctive pinks and greens woven into the threads of his proudly-worn Army Air Forces uniform to be the ones that defined him. His life was driven by service to the country, the sense of duty in leading high-flying formations in a noble cause. In his own words: "The privileges of being an American belong to those brave enough to fight for them."

Benjamin O. Davis Jr. was a man's man. Some would say a super-man. The son of the Army's first black general, Davis had been groomed from birth to attend West Point, a pathway into the officer corps that had eluded his father. At the academy Davis was shunned by his white classmates. Somehow, in the face of this silent treatment, he managed to hold his head high and to graduate thirty-fifth in a class of 276.

Itching to get into flying ever since he was fourteen years old and his dad had paid for a flight in a barnstormer's biplane, Davis applied for an aviation billet as his West Point graduation neared in 1936. Predictably, his application was rejected: at the time it was Army policy to restrict flying slots to whites only. Davis later described the decision as "shameful" and "unworthy of the great democratic nation in which we lived." Refusing to let go of his ambition to fly Army airplanes, he bided his time as an infantry officer and ROTC instructor until, at last, the Roosevelt administration relented to the political pressure of civil rights organizations.

In late spring 1941, five years after receiving his commission, Davis went to Tuskegee and entered the Army's first class for blacks seeking to be military pilots. Davis described flying as "a complete, unadulterated joy" and cruising over Alabama farmland as "more exhilarating than anything I could have imagined." While by most accounts he was not a natural pilot, he was a natural leader. Accordingly, when he earned his wings on March 7, 1942, it was a given that he would be the one to take charge of the black pilots winged at Tuskegee.

The initial class of thirteen cadets had been winnowed down to only five by graduation day, a sign that there would be no special favors in this flying program. In fact, the students would have to perform at least to the standard of white cadets or suffer the dreaded fate of being "washed out." In May, dual orders came promoting Davis to major and just as quickly to lieutenant colonel. Soon afterwards, he was formally designated the commander of the first all-black air combat unit, the 99th Pursuit Squadron (shortly, with the service-wide change in nomenclature, renamed the 99th Fighter Squadron).

By July, subsequent classes had graduated enough pilots and support personnel to fill all positions on the squadron's roster. Preparations were made for combat operations, and after passing inspection the squadron achieved its approval for deployment in September. Davis expected that the squadron would ship overseas the next month, but that did not happen.

Month after month passed with no word on when the 99th would deploy. The wait grew "tiresome" for Davis, and his men were unhappy with the segregated environment in Alabama, the uneven treatment they were receiving at the hands of Tuskegee's early cadre of white officers, and the fact that the skills of the 99th's combat pilots were not being put to use as the war raged. Some chalked the delay up to logistical problems, while others blamed it on ulterior motives of higher command authorities. According to historian Alan L. Gropman, at the time the unit had completed its combat training, the Army Air Forces "could find no commander in a combat zone who would accept the unit."

■ ■ ■

After a six-month wait, in April 1943, the 99th was finally on its way. The destination was North Africa. The black airmen sailing to the war zone were a small fraction of the four thousand troops onboard the converted luxury liner SS *Mariposa*, and Davis, reflecting on what it felt like to be in close quarters with an overwhelmingly white complement of troops, would write that he and his men were released "at least for the moment, from the evils of racial discrimination. Perhaps in combat overseas, we would have more freedom and respect than we had experienced at home."

The squadron arrived at Casablanca and from there took a slow train to an isolated location not far from Fez in the Moroccan desert for training with new Curtiss P-40L Warhawk fighters. The highly accomplished and independently minded Philip Cochran of the 33rd Fighter Group taught the 99th's pilots the tricks of the fighter pilot's trade. Also, instruction included mock dogfights with the 27th Fighter Group's North American A-36 fighters, which were dive-bombing versions of the P-51 Mustang. It was an invigorating experience for Davis, and he considered relations with the other units in the area as excellent.

At the time the 99th had to be attached to an existing white fighter group because not enough blacks had graduated from Tuskegee to form the three squadrons that would normally make up a fighter group. How the black and white pilots related to each other in this arrangement would depend in large part on the attitude of the host group's white commander, and Davis's high hopes were soon deflated.

He got the first inkling of what that commander's attitude would be when he reported to the headquarters of the fighter group. Davis was greeted by Colonel William W. "Spike" Momyer, the 33rd Fighter Group's commander, "not in a friendly manner, but quietly official." According to the account of the meeting in Chris Bucholtz's history of the unit, Momyer did not return the salutes of Davis or the 99th's deputy commander.

The snub would be a harbinger of things to come. But Davis had responsibilities to carry out, so he put aside the condescension that he had encountered. Performing satisfactorily in the coming real-world test was what mattered to him.

According to Dr. Gropman, Davis gathered his men before their baptism of fire and told them, "We are here to do a job, and by God, we're going to do it well, so let's get on with it." Led by Davis, the 99th went into action on June 2, 1943, flying from a former Luft-waffe base at Fardjouna on Tunisia's Cap Bon Peninsula and target-ing enemy positions on the island of Pantelleria in dive-bombing raids, as part of Operation Corkscrew.

On June 9, the 99th came into contact with Luftwaffe fighters for the first time. While escorting a dozen Douglas A-20 bombers back from a raid over Pantelleria, five of the thirteen P-40s broke away from the formation in hot pursuit of the attacking Messerschmitt Bf 109s. Led by Charles W. Dryden, these five P-40s scattered as they chased the faster enemy planes in a futile attempt to knock them out of the sky.

Such aggressiveness was not fundamentally undesirable; after all, fighter pilots were expected to be pugnacious in the air. But staying with your squadron mates was a cardinal rule in air fighting. While peeling off to give chase was not an uncommon reaction of greenhorn fighter pilots, in the coming months the failure to maintain the forma-tion's integrity in this one instance would feed a narrative that almost unraveled the black flying program.

Overall, Davis was pleased with the squadron's performance, and on June 11 Pantelleria fell, becoming, in Davis's words, "the first defended position in the history of warfare to be defeated by the application of air power alone." Davis felt validated when he received a note from the colonel serving as the Allies' area commander saying, "You have met the challenge of the enemy and have come out of your initial christening into battle stronger qualified than ever."

Missions in mid-June included providing cover for shipping in the Mediterranean. Then, on July 2, Davis led a dozen of his squadron mates on a bomber escort mission to Castelvetrano in southwest Sicily, where the formation was jumped by enemy fighters from above. In the ensuing encounter the 99th lost two of its pilots, Sherman W. White and James L. McCullin, but the squadron also scored its first aerial victory, with Charles B. Hall's shootdown of a Focke-Wulf Fw 190.

The events affected the squadron's psyche. For the first time the men of the 99th felt the mixed emotions of losing close friends in combat and the elation of downing an opponent. The latter prompted a congratulatory visit by supreme Allied commander General Dwight D. Eisenhower, accompanied by senior air commanders Major Generals James H. Doolittle and John K. Cannon and Lieutenant General Carl A. Spaatz.

The invasion of Sicily proceeded apace, and the 99th moved to the island, setting up operations at Licata on July 19. The squadron flew a variety of missions but did not have much contact with enemy fighters. Fighting continued until the German and Italian forces completed an evacuation on August 17. Early the next month, Davis was surprised to be recalled to the United States to take command of the newly-formed, all-black 332nd Fighter Group.

Each mission flown by the 99th had honed the skills of its pilots. But according to historian J. Todd Moye, "The black pilots received minimal guidance from Momyer's outfit." The 99th's Spann Watson recalled that the only preflight instruction he ever got from the 33rd prior to a combat mission was "You boys keep up." The tension within the group was unnecessary and counterproductive, exposing Momyer's racial intolerance as a weak spot in the character of an otherwise superb officer who became an ace and who proved his skill as an air tactician.

■ ■ ■

Within a matter of months after the 99th had arrived in North Africa, Momyer indulged his true feelings and cut the rug out from under Davis by clandestinely filing a field assessment of the 99th's performance that panned the squadron's air combat results. Of the black pilots, Momyer wrote, "It is my opinion that they are not of the fighting caliber of any squadron in this group." He extrapolated unfairly from the June 9 mission, claiming that the pilots would hold formation only "until jumped by enemy aircraft, when the squadron seems to disintegrate."

Momyer's boss, Major General Edwin J. House of 12th Air Support Command, added his own commentary, in which he claimed that the consensus among his fellow officers and medical professionals was "that the negro type has not the proper reflexes to make a first-class fighter pilot." These aspersions echoed overtly racist passages from the infamous 1925 Army War College memorandum, which had asserted that blacks are "by nature subservient" and "mentally inferior." House went so far as to recommend that the 99th have its P-40s exchanged for the less maneuverable Bell P-39 Airacobras and be reassigned to the northwest coast of Africa. House further recommended that if and when a black fighter group was formed, it should be held back for homeland defense.

Virtually the entire chain of command, including Northwest African Tactical Air Force commanders Lieutenant General Spaatz and Major General Cannon, endorsed the Momyer document.

Cannon added his own comments, in which he asserted that the 99th's pilots lacked the stamina and lasting qualities of white pilots, concluding that the black airmen had "no outstanding characteristics" when operating in wartime conditions and when compared with their white counterparts.

The assessment received its potentially most damaging endorsement when it hit the desk of Army Air Forces Chief Henry H. "Hap" Arnold, whose doubts about the black flying experiment were long-standing. Arnold sent a series of recommendations to Army Chief of Staff George C. Marshall calling for the 99th and the three new squadrons of the 332nd to be moved to a "rear defense area" and urging that the air combat training program for blacks be abandoned. The Arnold recommendations, if implemented, would have been the death knell for African Americans in frontline military aviation for years to come.

Since Momyer had gone behind his back, Davis knew nothing of the negative assessment until his return to the United States. Furious at the unfair charges and at being totally blindsided, Davis would answer Momyer's accusations before a government panel the next month. It would be a make-or-break moment for the 99th Fighter Squadron, the 332nd Fighter Group, the 477th Bombardment Group (an all-black medium bombardment unit receiving stateside instruction at the time), and the pilots-in-training at Tuskegee.

Chapter Four

SAVING THE
EXPERIMENT

Do what you think is right and let the law catch up.
—Thurgood Marshall

The experiment in black military flying was never in more danger than when William Momyer's accusations had gained traction in the Army Air Forces' hierarchy. Saving it was largely up to Benjamin Davis Jr. He would have to shoulder the heavy burden of defending the 99th Fighter Squadron. For starters, on September 10, 1943, Davis held a press conference in Washington in which he calmly described the progression of the 99th from the time he had assumed command and then made the case that blacks were proving that they could indeed be effective combat pilots. He spoke highly of the men serving with him. It seemed to go well.

But *Time* magazine had gotten wind of Momyer's critique and the Arnold recommendations. In a September 20 article, the magazine insinuated that the Tuskegee Airmen were not up to the job. Davis was furious—as was his wife, Agatha Scott Davis, who sent a letter to the editor chastising the magazine for having "created an unfavorable public opinion about an organization to which all Negroes point with pride." Doing so, she said, risked impairing "one of the strongest pillars upholding Negroes' morale in their effort to contribute to the winning of the war."

Davis was facing decision-makers who wouldn't be easy to sway. Secretary of War Henry L. Stimson was steeped in the establishment, a product of Phillips Academy, Yale College, and Harvard Law. In 1891, fresh out of law school, he had joined the New York law office of Elihu Root, whose client list would eventually read like a who's who of the New York social register, including names such as Carnegie, Gould, Whitney, and Harriman. When Root left his law practice to become a member of William McKinley's cabinet, Stimson became one of the firm's name partners and maintained the firm's tradition of public service by rotating in and out of government.

As a lifetime Republican and staunch opponent of the New Deal, Stimson was flabbergasted when Franklin Roosevelt offered him the position of secretary of war in 1940. But domestic policy issues aside, Stimson concurred with the broad outline of Roosevelt's foreign policy, and the president, for his part, respected Stimson's prior service as William Howard Taft's secretary of war, especially his efforts at modernizing the Army. Stimson did not take long to accept the appointment.

Stimson's official postwar biography, written in collaboration with McGeorge Bundy, states, in a section subtitled "The Army and the Negro," that he proudly considered his "convictions were those of a northern conservative born in the abolitionist tradition." Indeed, "he believed in full freedom, political and economic, for all men of all colors." Still, Stimson refused to accept what he called "social intermixture" of the races.

It was a paradox: while the secretary of war fiercely scorned the view that African Americans should be held back because of their race, he rejected the idea of full-blown and immediate racial integration, which he called a "jump at one bound from complex reality to unattainable Utopia." In other words, Stimson, like many elites in the decade before the landmark Supreme Court ruling in *Brown v. Board of Education*, adhered to the doctrine of "separate but equal," to quote the court's 1896 ruling in *Plessy v. Ferguson*.

In Stimson's view, "the persistent legacy" of the separation of the races meant it was "hardly constructive" to promote the sudden undoing of segregation, as some "radical and impractical" African American leaders were doing during the war. Although these leaders are not named in Stimson's biography, he surely had in mind passionate civil rights advocates such as Walter White and A. Philip Randolph, heads of the NAACP and the Brotherhood of Sleeping Car Porters, respectively.

Stimson was at best ambivalent about the employment of black troops on a large scale. Theater commanders were "not enthusiastic in accepting Negro units; in each theater there were special considerations which made Negro troops a problem. But," as his biography notes, "fair-minded soldiers agreed that the Army must make full use of what Stimson called the 'great asset of the colored men of the nation.'"

If there was a soft spot in Stimson's attitude on race, it emanated from his experience in battle during World War I. As someone who had spent years championing military preparedness and months calling for intervention, he had felt compelled to join the Army. On May 31, 1917, at forty-nine years of age, Stimson went in at the rank of major and spent the summer acquainting himself with the workings of artillery units at Fort Myer in Virginia. After a personal appeal to the then secretary of war Newton D. Baker and Army Chief of Staff Major General Hugh L. Scott, Stimson's formal assignment came through—second-in-command of the New York-weighted 305th Regiment, 77th Division, in the field artillery at Camp Upton on Long Island.

He was sent to France in advance of his unit. After further training, he was reunited with his fellow New Yorkers and led them into battle near the Baccarat Sector on July 11, 1918. Stimson's frontline service lasted three weeks before he received a transfer order back home to lead the 31st Artillery in a workup at Camp Meade in Maryland. He had spent nine months abroad and had briefly tasted combat.

Before he and his new unit could deploy to the front lines, the Armistice was signed. Suddenly Stimson was a civilian again. Though he later joined the Reserve and attained the rank of brigadier general, his rank upon discharge from his last active-duty assignment is how he is remembered. From the end of World War I, he was referred to by close friends as Colonel Stimson.

Significantly, the experience of leading men in battle revealed to Stimson what he and Bundy described as "the quality of the enlisted men of the regiment." These men, "drafted soldiers of New York City and its environs," though possessing "little formal education" and seeming to be "underfed," represented "almost every national strain in the American melting pot" and proved to be "quick, resilient, and endlessly resourceful." Stimson "was joyfully astonished" by the industry of the diverse troops under his command.

His service in uniform had, above all else, "taught him the horror of war." But he also "learned as he worked with the men of his own Army that the strength and spirit of America was not confined to any group or class." Stimson called the experience "my greatest lesson in American democracy."

After the war, Stimson admitted to "having at first opposed as unwise the training of colored officers." He had an "early mistrust of the use of the Army as an agency of social reform." But once he changed his mind, no doubt under pressure from the White House and owing to the exigencies of the manpower shortage, he "found his own sympathies shifting." Stimson made three inspection tours of

African American units in training and "each time he was impressed by the progress achieved by intelligent white leaders and colored soldiers working together."

His biography recounts one such visit, describing the message he gave to the members of the 99th Fighter Squadron. The secretary of war told the black unit that "the eyes of everybody were on them" and "their government and people of all races and colors were behind them." Looking past World War II, Stimson felt the future success of blacks in the military depended on "such an officer as Colonel Benjamin O. Davis Jr." who, according to Stimson, stood as "direct refutation of the common belief that all colored officers were incompetent." Stimson further stated, "Davis was exceptional."

It was high praise for the leader of the all-black flying unit. But Stimson betrayed a disquieting personal belief when he added that "in the development of more such exceptions lay the hope of the Negro people." It was as if he was saying that to be successful African Americans had to be "exceptions." This patronizing attitude, or worse, infused the War Department's mind-set on the matter of race. It was this thinking that African Americans were up against during their wartime service and that Davis had to overcome in the defense of his squadron at home.

■ ■ ■

Davis knew that the stakes were high when he sat down on October 16 to testify before the War Department's Advisory Committee on Negro Troop Policies, a panel that had been created a year and a half earlier to handle issues revolving around the Army's employment of blacks. There were sympathetic members on the committee: Truman Gibson, a black attorney from Chicago who served as Secretary Stimson's civilian advisor on Negro affairs, and Benjamin O. Davis

Sr., the beleaguered squadron commander's father. But it was chaired by an assistant secretary of war whose fairness in the treatment of minorities could reasonably be suspect.

Stimson described John J. McCloy as a "great find." Like Stimson, McCloy had commanded a field artillery battery for a few weeks in France during World War I, graduated from Harvard Law School, and temporarily given up a lucrative blue-chip legal practice in New York to work in government. McCloy served as one of Stimson's four key aides at the War Department throughout the entirety of World War II.

As Bundy would put it, "For five years McCloy was the man who handled everything that no one else happened to be handling.... He became so knowing in the ways of Washington that Stimson sometimes wondered whether anyone in the administration ever acted without 'having a word with McCloy.'"

Considerably younger than his boss, McCloy would return to New York after the war and parlay his public stature into a small fortune, beginning with the negotiation of his name onto the shingle of the law firm best known for its representation of the Rockefellers. Then he headed the World Bank and served as the American high commissioner for Germany. His professional life culminated in his appointment as chairman of the Chase Manhattan Bank.

McCloy's involvement in the nonprofit sector included longtime service as a trustee of the Rockefeller Foundation, followed by a stint as head of the Ford Foundation. In later years he would chair the Council on Foreign Relations. In private life he had great influence in legal, business, and government circles and was widely viewed as a pillar of the foreign policy establishment. He and a handful of other former high-ranking officials with similar Ivy League pedigrees—men like George Kennan and Dean Acheson—came to be called the "Wise Men."

But the admiration for them was not universal. Various minority groups had grave doubts about McCloy—in the early war years, none more so than Japanese Americans.

McCloy used all of his lawyerly skills to help draft Executive Order 9066, which stripped Japanese Americans of their constitutional rights and authorized their wholesale detention during the war. President Roosevelt signed the order on February 19, 1942. It was written and signed after it was known that the small percentage of Japanese Americans who might pose a national security risk in the aftermath of the attack on Pearl Harbor were already either in custody or under surveillance.

McCloy feared that the Supreme Court would declare the internment program unconstitutional. With oral arguments pending in May 1943, McCloy withheld a military report on the West Coast evacuation that would have undercut the government's case. While most of the justices expressed reservations about the roundup of a whole class of citizens, in military matters they were inclined to defer to the judgment of the commander in chief and his officers. They decided the defendants in two cases could be detained on the narrow grounds of having violated curfew orders. The third case, *Korematsu v. United States*, was remanded to a lower court.

By spring 1944 there was growing sentiment that the internments should end, and McCloy seemed willing to bend and allow greater numbers, though not all, of the internees out of detention. According to Kai Bird, McCloy's biographer, Roosevelt himself "put thumbs down" on the proposal to allow a "substantial number" of Japanese Americans to return to California. It was an election year, and McCloy attributed the president's decision to political advisors who expressed concerns about how perceived weakness on Japanese American internment could jeopardize the California vote.

Bird wrote, "McCloy now almost single-handedly blocked every step toward early release." Indeed, McCloy would stop at nothing to prevent the executive order from being overturned by the Supreme Court—in the full knowledge that continued detention was not for national security reasons but rather for political expediency.

With Machiavellian cunning, McCloy quietly released the report that he had previously withheld, thinking now that its scurrilous charges against Japanese Americans would alarm the justices sufficiently to win them over. As Bird pointed out, "the report contained false information." On December 18, 1944, the Supreme Court issued its opinions in the remaining cases. In one of them, the justices unanimously decided to free a Japanese American while avoiding the central constitutional issue. But in the *Korematsu* case, the court ruled in a six-to-three decision to uphold the conviction, thereby affirming, albeit on narrow grounds, the constitutionality of the executive order.

McCloy had gotten his way, but his success in eking out a legal win was eventually seen, almost uniformly, as a travesty of justice. In rulings that came well after McCloy's role in the sordid affair had faded from memory, the Supreme Court reversed itself.

The cynicism on display in McCloy's role in the wartime internment of Japanese Americans was equally apparent in his actions with respect to Jewish refugees during the war. In March 1944 the War Refugee Board's John Pehle presented a plan to the administration suggesting that an executive order be issued to grant refugees temporary haven in the United States, given the reluctance of Congress to liberalize immigration laws. McCloy weighed in, urging caution.

While McCloy had been quick to embrace an executive order to put Japanese Americans in detention centers, he argued against adoption of an executive order to open up the country to fleeing Jewish refugees. His reasoning was that national security was at stake in the former case but not in the latter; humanitarian considerations played little if any part in his deliberations. Stimson agreed with McCloy.

McCloy's objections to opening doors for Jewish refugees extended beyond just the United States. In the same month that he argued to restrict refugee settlement on American soil, McCloy testified zealously on Capitol Hill to block Jewish refugees from settling in Palestine, so as not to offend the region's Arab population and to retain the United States' access to wartime oil supplies. His testimony was in response to a resolution introduced in Congress calling for the "free entry of Jews" into Palestine and the eventual formation of "a free and democratic Jewish commonwealth." McCloy's persuasive words nipped the humanitarian plan in the bud, and the Jews who might have been saved became statistics, as the death toll at extermination camps continued to rise.

In a separate matter related to Hitler's Final Solution, starting in late June 1944 Jewish and humanitarian leaders made repeated requests for the Allies to bomb the rail lines leading to Auschwitz, the infamous Nazi concentration camp. The month before, the Germans had begun deporting the first batch of Hungary's Jews to Auschwitz in a plan to annihilate what was the last remaining large Jewish community in Europe. There could be no mistaking what awaited the transferees because, almost contemporaneously with the deportations, two Jewish inmates at Auschwitz, Rudolf Vrba and Alfred Wetzler, escaped and wrote a thirty-page report describing the camp's daily horrors in great detail.

Their report on Auschwitz made no difference to McCloy. The fact that hundreds of thousands of innocents faced certain death without some kind of intervention failed to move him; his letters of refusal included a dispassionate argument that ending the war had to take precedence and the false assertion that the requested bombing would require the diversion of "considerable" resources. Hungary's eight hundred thousand Jews were abandoned with more than half left to die in the Auschwitz gas chambers.

■ ■ ■

In the first year of America's involvement in World War II, blacks experienced little to assuage their concerns about the Army's racial policies. On January 15, 1943, Secretary Stimson's first civilian advisor on Negro affairs was so frustrated by the Army's slow-to-change treatment of blacks and the delay in deploying the new all-black fighter squadron that he quit. The resignation by William H. Hastie Jr., a Harvard Law graduate, former federal judge, and dean of the Howard University Law School, prompted the Army to finally commit to send the 99th Fighter Squadron into combat.

But now, nine months after Hastie's departure, the commander of the squadron was having to defend his pilots' in-theater performance. Benjamin Davis Jr. was the public face of the black squadron. As the senior black officer in the Army Air Forces, he carried a greater share of the weight in the fight for the so-called "Double V": the hoped-for dual victories in the wars against 1) totalitarianism abroad and 2) racism at home.

It was a marathon series of battles on two fronts. Davis had left the fighting in Sicily to confront the internecine skirmishes within the War Department, having recently turned over command of the 99th to his capable deputy, Major George S. "Spanky" Roberts. The load on his shoulders was immeasurable, but if anyone could stand up to the likes of McCloy and reverse the coldhearted governmental inertia it was Davis, for he had exactly the right combination of strengths: intellect, courage, perseverance, poise, moral rectitude, and an old-fashioned style of charisma that did not necessarily play well on camera but that could be mesmerizing in person.

Like other hard-driving air commanders of his time, Davis would not have won a popularity contest. But he could rally and spearhead his men to ultimate success in contested skies. And behind the scenes in Washington, when in the company of officers and policy-makers unaccustomed to sitting across the table from a black man, Davis's character, intensity, performance record, and focus on the facts could carry the day.

Davis knew that the fate of the "experiment" in black military aviation hinged on his presentation before the McCloy Committee, as the advisory panel was commonly called. Rather than succumb to the temptation to let off steam, he employed "the utmost discretion." As he would confide in his autobiography, "It would have been hopeless for me to stress the hostility and racism of whites as the motive … although that was clearly the case. I had to adopt a quiet, reasoned approach, presenting the facts about the 99th in a way that would appeal to fairness…."

In defense of the 99th, Davis pointed out that it "had performed as well as any new fighter squadron, black or white" in similar circumstances. He conceded "some mistakes in the first missions," but, he explained, "[t]his would have been true of any squadron handicapped by a lack of experienced pilots." He pointed out that the squadron's pilots had matured quickly "from inexperienced fliers to seasoned veterans."

In refutation of Momyer's claim that the black pilots lacked composure under fire Davis pointed to the bomber escort mission he had led on July 2, detailing how "we had stayed right with our bombers and absorbed the attacks of the enemy planes." Significantly, Davis explained that the 99th had not shot down more than a single enemy plane up to that point because the squadron's missions were mostly dive-bombing and support of ground troops, and in those missions "encounters with enemy aircraft were practically nonexistent." Davis added that the 99th had also suffered from "a manpower disadvantage," operating with from four to nine pilots below the squadron norm during the deployment's first two months because of delays in the expected replacements. He told the committee that the black squadron "would go through any ordeal that came our way, be it in garrison existence or in combat, to prove our worth."

Davis brought up the absurdity of blacks and whites fighting together "in a common cause on the battlefront" but being prohibited from training together back in the United States. Speaking from the heart, he recounted how when the squadron shipped out aboard the *Mariposa*, "segregation and discrimination had ceased." Then, reversing the roles of witness and questioner, he gave those around the table something to think about, asking, "Why did [segregation and discrimination] have to be perpetuated in the armed services at home?"

It was a masterful presentation, and the black press seized on it, helping to build support for the 99th within the black community. Davis's strong defense of the black flyers and the support of the country's black population made it doubly difficult for McCloy to come down against the Tuskegee Airmen. The assistant secretary knew that an election year was on the horizon and the president was trying to court black voters.

Davis's well-reasoned case and Judge Hastie's abrupt resignation earlier in the year appeared to be turning points in McCloy's attitude on race in the military. Moreover, Eleanor Roosevelt's sympathy for the black flying program was a matter of record. Despite his demonstrated propensity to side against minorities, McCloy was not comfortable undermining the black flyers.

He resorted to the bureaucrat's classic dodge. The issue was left on the doorstep of the Army's chief of staff. General Marshall had already received a draft letter prepared by the Air Staff that, if signed and sent to Roosevelt, would permanently ground the Tuskegee Airmen and end the whole experiment.

But, it should be noted, the draft letter's content was not universally backed by the Air Staff; in fact, one of Hap Arnold's most trusted advisors strongly dissented. Colonel Emmett E. "Rosie" O'Donnell Jr., a native of Brooklyn and a 1928 graduate of West Point, argued against sending the letter—not because he disagreed with Momyer's view, but because he felt the blowback from the black community and elements of the press would be too costly. He argued, "Every country in this war has had serious trouble in handling disaffected minorities ... to recommend at this time any action which would indicate the relative inferiority of the colored race would be really 'asking for it.'" According to O'Donnell, "Further, I feel that such a proposal to the President at this time would definitely not be appreciated by him. He would probably interpret it as indicating a serious lack of understanding of the broad problems facing the country." The colonel concluded that "it might be far better to let the entire matter drop, without any letter to the President." Though O'Donnell's argument was laced with the era's prevailing prejudice, his recommendation was the right one.

Given the sensitivities on all sides of the issue, General Marshall commissioned a study to compare the 99th's performance with that of other P-40 squadrons in the Mediterranean theater. The study covered the eight-month period from July 1943 through February 1944. In the end it validated Davis's position, concluding that there was "no significant general difference" in performance between the black and white fighter squadrons.

By the time the report was rolled out, the 99th had already definitively debunked the accusations and rendered them moot. In two successive days in late January 1944, the squadron scored a dozen air-to-air victories in support of the Allies' landing near Anzio,

Italy. There could be no further doubt about the fighting prowess of the all-black 99th.

Even Hap Arnold was moved to congratulate the squadron, calling its performance "very commendable." *Time* magazine backed off its previous criticism, publishing an article that hailed the Anzio aerial kills as having "stamped the final seal of combat excellence" on the 99th. The *New York Times* quoted one of Davis's Tuskegee classmates, Lemuel Custis, who had been credited with one of the aerial victories at Anzio. Referring to the perception of the squadron as an experiment, Custis said, "Now I think the record shows that it was a successful experiment."

In the wake of the uproar instigated by Momyer, the 99th was transferred to Foggia near the Adriatic coast and then to Capodichino near Naples on the Mediterranean coast, attached to the 79th Fighter Group. The 79th, commanded by Colonel Earl E. Bates, offered a welcoming environment for the black pilots. In the words of Professor Moye, Bates "saw to it that the officers of the 99th were integrated into the work of the group and treated them as equals."

There was even a newspaper dispatch reporting that the men of the 79th had disobeyed an order from Lieutenant General Jacob L. Devers, then the Army Air Forces commander in the Mediterranean theater, not to fraternize with their black comrades. It was reported that the white pilots had "held a desegregated dinner party with dancing to celebrate the anniversary of the 79th's entrance into combat."

It was a glimmer of the beginnings of a new way of doing things in the American armed forces—and a clear sign that Davis and his black flyers had fought off the existential threat posed by the Momyer report, which could so easily have killed the "experiment." Referring to Davis, Dr. Gropman, the historian, wrote, "His innate dignity, intelligence, and measured judgment saved [the experiment] from early disaster." Years later Davis, reflecting on events of the time in his autobiography, shared his firm belief that the Momyer incident "had come within inches of destroying the future of black pilots forever."

Mission by mission, Davis and his men were proving the naysayers wrong and gaining on the Double V. But there was no time to luxuriate in the successes. Awaiting Davis was another challenge: command of the newly-constituted 332nd Fighter Group, with its three freshly-minted, all-black squadrons.

Meanwhile, amidst the cotton fields of southeast Alabama on the outskirts of the small town of Tuskegee, a town whose public square was decorated by a monument honoring Confederate troops, Harry Stewart and his fellow cadets, unaware of the potentially fatal machinations swirling around the black flying program, were preoccupied with winning their own battles. The program on which the fulfillment of Harry's dream of silver wings depended had come within a hair's breadth of being snuffed out as he trained at Tuskegee starting in the spring of 1943. Because of the reprieve that Davis succeeded in winning for the Tuskegee flyers, there would be no stopping Harry now.

Chapter Five

TRAINS BEFORE PLANES

*No horizon is so far that you cannot get above it
or beyond it.*
—Beryl Markham, *West with the Night*

Before Harry arrived at the flying fields of Tuskegee, Alabama, he had to go through basic training at Keesler Field in Biloxi, Mississippi, beginning in late April 1943. His journey started with a ride on the Long Island Rail Road from Camp Upton, New York. Harry was traveling with a detachment of Army inductees headed to different destinations down south, and the first transfer occurred at Manhattan's Penn Station. A sergeant was gathering the men on the arrival platform with the intent to escort them to their southbound train when a woman's voice pierced through the clatter of the station.

"Jujybewks! Jujybewks!" the woman in chichi dress and flowered hat kept shouting in the direction of the detachment. The sergeant looked quizzically at the woman, clearly mystified by her nonsensical callout and probably wondering if she needed to be sedated. Approaching the sergeant with a broad smile, the woman identified herself as Harry's aunt, pointing to her blushing nephew.

Margaret Bright, the sister of Harry's mother, was anything but shy. She had no problem with loudly calling Harry by the nickname she had used for him since he was a baby. Whether it was by coincidence or premeditation that she happened to be on the platform just as Harry was transferring will never be known, but either way Harry was embarrassed. Margaret told the sergeant she wanted five minutes with Harry to say her goodbyes.

The sergeant responded that her nephew was in the Army now and subject to orders and discipline, but Margaret wouldn't take no for an answer and got her private face time with Harry, who by then was cringing inside. Harry remembers his Aunt Margaret wishing him safe travels in her inimitable way. He grinned at her but, before the five minutes were up, broke away and hurriedly rejoined the detachment on the train for points south.

Growing up, Harry had never traveled far from home, so the train ride was especially exciting. He sat with three friends from the neighborhood, two of whom were also high school dropouts. The friends were taking in the scenery and yukking it up.

As the train screeched to a scheduled stop in Philadelphia, one of the three friends, Vincent Dean, keeled over with what turned out to be appendicitis. He was taken off the train for medical treatment and eventually got to Tuskegee. The next stop for Harry and his two remaining friends was Union Station in the nation's capital.

At that point everything changed. As the train prepared to roll out for southern cities, the conductor appeared and, hunched over Harry, told him to move to "the colored car" and pointed in the direction of the locomotive up front. Harry's remaining friends, who were white, objected. Harry remembers one, Anthony "Red" Lanese, arguing with the conductor.

The exchange got heated, but the conductor was adamant. Harry's friends offered to go to the segregated car with him, but he didn't want to make a scene. He calmed his friends and said he would go alone.

It was an awakening of sorts for the teenager from Queens. The racial harmony that he had known growing up in his multiethnic neighborhood was now a memory. Harry was encountering the stark reality of a world in which a person of color was consigned to the permanent indignity of second-class citizenship. Harry's parents—especially his mother Florence, the family censor—had shielded their children from the racial prejudice outside the bubble they had created.

So many years after Harry's father had extricated himself and his family from the purgatory of Jim Crow, Harry was back in it. How ironic that someone embarked on a quest to defend liberty against Hitler's racist tyranny should be subjected to race-based discrimination.

The feeling of being an exile in his own country was accentuated when Harry decided to use his government voucher for dinner. He was ushered into the dining car and seated at the table nearest the busboy station. Next thing he knew, a green curtain was unfurled around him, forming a screen on all four sides—to remove him from the sight of the whites seated in the dining car. It was a surreal measure used by the railroads to enforce segregation. Harry considered getting up and walking out, but, no, it would be wiser to sit and eat.

He was in the South now and would have to adjust. Harry chowed down his dinner as fast as possible. Then, not waiting for the curtain to be slid to the side, he stepped out from behind it and made his way back to his seat in the segregated car.

By the end of the day, as the train pulled into the terminal in Atlanta, his uniform was filthy from the locomotive's smoke and soot, as a consequence of the segregated cars being closest behind the loco-motive—a standard operating practice of the railroads. There was nothing Harry could do but clean the grime off his uniform that night.

The trip continued the next morning, and Harry recognized a passenger sitting several rows behind him. Lemuel Custis was an imposing figure, not least because he was attired in the uniform of an

Army Air Forces officer, the silver bar of a first lieutenant visible on his collar. Harry had seen photos of the black pilot and read about his background: a 1938 graduate of Howard University, the first African American police officer in Hartford, Connecticut, and a member of the first class of five cadets to complete fighter pilot training at Tuskegee.

Custis had been in the initial overseas deployment of the 99th Pursuit Squadron (and would return overseas for a second tour in 1944, when he would shoot down a Focke-Wulf in one of his ninety-two combat missions, receiving the Distinguished Flying Cross). He was one of Harry's heroes, a role model the young man wanted to emulate. Being shy, Harry had to summon up his confidence to introduce himself. He ran through several possible opening lines in his head before he dared to approach the seasoned black pilot.

Custis was polite but distant, leaving Harry to wonder if the loss of friends in war had made the officer reluctant to warm up to others in uniform or if, as a patriot subjected to contemptuous treatment back home, Custis had become indifferent or maybe even cynical. Then again, maybe he was just having a bad day. Custis got off at the next stop, presumably to transfer to Tuskegee. And Harry's mind drifted to thoughts about what he would be like if he, too, earned his wings and survived war in the air.

■　■　■

On the last leg of the train ride to Biloxi, Harry had to use the lavatory. But the onboard facilities for black passengers were utterly deplorable. The toilet had overflowed, causing the floor to turn into what could only be described as a putrid mess.

Harry decided to delay relieving himself until the train pulled into the station. But the truck from the base had a driver waiting to take

Harry and the other arriving men right away. Harry had no choice but to defer nature's call and climb into the truck.

By the time the truck stopped to unload at the processing center, Harry's urgency to go was excruciating. As he filed with the other men into the building where their physical exams were to take place, he spotted a lavatory in the distance. With no time to spare, he made a beeline for it.

A sergeant yelled at him in a rising voice not to go in there. "Stop! Stop! Stop!" Focused on addressing nature's call, Harry kept running.

Afterwards, when Harry exited the lavatory, he learned that he had run into the one reserved for white officers. Fortunately, the senior enlisted men on duty were understanding of the extenuating circumstances and they recognized that Harry was new to the base and therefore did not know his way around. Harry had dodged disaster, but there were other challenges soon to follow.

Dozens of young men from around the country were in line for physical exams. Harry could see up ahead that the assembly-line exams included the patellar reflex test in which the doctor taps a mallet on the tendon just below the knee. Because Harry's right leg was devoid of reflex from his bout with polio as a child, he feared that he would fail the exam and be relegated to the infantry before ever getting to see an airplane, let alone fly one.

But when Harry's turn came, he was prepared. Just as the doctor swung the mallet and hit his tendon, Harry faked a reflex with a kick that nearly knocked the mallet out of the doctor's hand. It was a masterful performance; the doctor checked off the test. And Harry concealed the atrophied muscle in his right calf by shifting his weight from his right side to his left side when rising to stand, as he had done since his early days recovering from the effects of polio.

The other condition that threatened to nix his flying career in the Army Air Forces before it could even begin was his systolic heart murmur. If the doctor detected an irregularity, Harry knew he would be cut from the program. Alarmingly, when the doctor put his stethoscope on Harry's chest, he frowned and then listened again. Harry knew he was in trouble.

The doctor asked an older doctor performing exams in an adjoining line to take a listen. After hurrying over to do so, he slapped his stethoscope against Harry's chest and told Harry to take a deep breath. Before Harry finished inhaling, the doctor looked over at his younger colleague and waved off any concern, muttering a few unintelligible words before turning around to get back to the men in his line. Harry could have jumped for joy, but he was careful to hide his euphoria.

The weeks at Keesler were a combination of boot camp and military indoctrination. The Army was acclimating its recruits, getting them used to taking orders in austere surroundings. For Harry and most of the other prospective cadets awaiting the chance to prove themselves at Tuskegee, for whom the rigors of the Great Depression had been a daily reality, Keesler's regimen was no big deal. The one exception was the base's segregated setup, in which white recruits trained separately from blacks. Regrettably, it would be the military's standard arrangement throughout the rest of the war and for several years beyond.

Chapter Six

THE QUEST FOR SILVER WINGS

They shall mount up with wings like eagles . . .
—Isaiah 40:31

W hen Harry arrived at the Tuskegee Institute, the "experiment" to create black squadrons in the Army Air Forces had blossomed into a full-fledged flight training operation with supportive infrastructure. At the institution of higher learning that had been led to national prominence before the turn of the century by Booker T. Washington, the campus was enlivened by the presence of uniformed trainees attending classes and poring over books in study halls in their quest to fly—palpably debunking the service's long-standing and offensive dogma that blacks had neither the mental capacity nor the mechanical aptitude to be military pilots.

As the war intensified and the need for pilots grew, the Army Air Forces relaxed the requirement for some college. By this stage the service would accept pilot candidates with only a high school diploma or, as in Harry's case, no diploma at all—as long as they passed the written test and the physical and mental exams. The College Training Detachment (CTD) program was initiated for recruits like Harry, to compensate for their lack of college credits.

In the short time they had, they would be brought up not to the level of a college graduate but to the level of a college student.

The CTD curriculum included mathematics, physics, geography, history, and English. Considerable time was also spent on military and physical training. The focus was on providing the underpinnings for the aviation-centric instruction to come, and there was not much specifically on flight. The exception was a short course in Civil Air Regulations.

Harry was housed with other trainees, officially known as aviation students, in one of the four two-story brick buildings known as the Emery Dormitories, reserved for those in the CTD program. The dorms were clustered together near a "drill field," which got extensive use. The aviation students took their studies seriously because once they completed the program in four to six months, depending on how much of an educational gap needed to be filled, they would go from being aviation students to aviation cadets and get to fly military training aircraft.

Until then, the only flying was ten hours of instruction in a Piper J-3 Cub, a light high-wing, two-seat civilian type used in the Civilian Pilot Training Program (CPTP), which had morphed into the War Training Service (WTS) after America's entry into the war. This introductory flying course occurred over twenty-eight days and included the fundamentals of airmanship, engine operation, traffic patterns, and flight safety. This flying occurred at Field No. 1, more often referred to as Kennedy Field, a small grass field on Union Springs Highway about five miles south of the campus.

This was the field where Eleanor Roosevelt had gone up in a Cub for a half-hour scenic flight on March 29, 1941. The pilot was Charles Alfred "Chief" Anderson, the pioneering African American pilot who had been hired as Tuskegee's chief primary flight instructor. It was the first time a presidential family member flew with a black pilot at the controls, and it generated lots of publicity, in large part because Mrs. Roosevelt was photographed smiling contentedly in the aft seat of the Cub's cockpit with Chief Anderson in the forward seat. The gesture endeared Mrs. Roosevelt to the Tuskegee Airmen, so much so that many would refer to it late in their lives as the breakout moment for blacks in aviation.

The First Lady had been in town to attend a meeting of the Julius Rosenwald Fund, the charitable foundation established by the late chairman of Sears, Roebuck. As a trustee of the fund, she used the occasion to urge the board to advance monies to the Tuskegee Institute to enable it to build a larger airport, a necessary move if Tuskegee Institute was going to be the home to the Army's black flight-training program. By September, Field No. 2 was in operation four miles north of campus, accommodating Army primary trainers, mostly Boeing PT-13 Stearman biplanes and later Fairchild PT-19 monoplanes. It was named Moton Field after Robert Russa Moton, who had served as Tuskegee Institute's second president.

Harry recalls his maiden ascent in September 1943 as being drastically different from what he had imagined it would be. Instead of a silky-smooth excursion, it was a decidedly bouncy affair. He found himself holding on to balance his inner butterflies as the heated air over the fertile Alabama farmland jostled the tiny Cub.

Beginner's logic suggested that from altitude everything is laid out in the same familiar pattern one is used to on the ground. But from the vantage point of the Cub's cramped cockpit, landmarks seemed confusingly askew and Harry quickly lost reference to his origination point. In the air, nothing below appeared the way he had envisaged it.

The flight instructor, Archie Smith of New York, like the other flight instructors in the WTS program at Tuskegee, was a black civilian under contract. He called for his aviation student to take the controls. For Harry, trying to hold the Cub straight and level required intense concentration.

When the command came to turn the plane, Harry handled the stick as he might the wheel of his go-cart. But the Cub didn't respond in kind. Harry discovered that control inputs are different in the air. Smith started cursing profusely at the confused novice. The worse Harry's handling, the nastier Smith's insults.

"You're never gonna become a cadet!" Smith shouted over the din of the engine. "You don't have what it takes!"

Harry, flustered and humiliated, began to cry. Unmoved, Smith kept up his assault on Harry's pride. "Oh, now you're crying! Are you a baby or are you a pilot?" the instructor asked rhetorically.

Angling to final approach, Smith put Harry down with the ultimate affront. "When we get back, I'm personally going to make sure you wash out!"

On the ground, Harry stood next to the Cub, head in his hands, sobbing inconsolably. Alice Dungey Gray, the wife of another of the contract flight instructors who worked in the parachute rigging shop, happened to be on the flight line and took pity on the new arrival standing alone and crying his heart out. She called out to Smith, "Archie, what did you do to this boy?"

Smith said that he was just trying to toughen up the aviation student, who had seemed to be too much of a softie. How would this young man from Queens ever make it past the military check rides if he didn't show a little more strength, Smith wanted to know. Mrs. Gray, her finger wagging, retorted, "You went too far this time, Archie!"

Mrs. Gray put a sympathetic arm around Harry. Soothing his hurt, she whispered, "It'll be all right." Harry's anguish had been assuaged, and in the days ahead he would look to the sky again.

During the rest of his time aloft in the Cub, Harry got accustomed to the stick-and-rudder coordination at the heart of flying. The diminutive plane, powered by a 65-horsepower engine, was quite docile, especially when compared to the aircraft that were in store for the aviation students if they managed to complete CTD. Three trainer types awaited them, each more complex than the one before.

After the full six months of CTD, Harry made the transition to aviation cadet. It was a major milestone, marked by his being authorized to wear a small propeller symbol pinned to his hat. He took up residence in the barracks at Tuskegee Army Airfield, the large air base built ten miles northwest of the campus expressly to train the black cadets to Army standards.

The more senior aviation cadets greeted him and the other rookies as upperclassmen in a fraternity house would: when the younger aviation cadets unloaded from the trucks that had brought them, they were called "dummies" and told to watch themselves. It was human nature in action, but also a way to nip dangerous overconfidence in the bud.

One of the upperclassmen was Joseph Gordon, Harry's boyhood friend. After the hazing, when they met one-on-one, Joseph warmly welcomed Harry. Because they were in different classes and because the training regimen kept them so busy, the two friends barely got to see each other. When they did, the topic always reverted to their cowboy-and-Indian "shootout" and the unlikely coincidence that they would both have entered the Army flying program with their paths crossing at Tuskegee. They promised to stay in touch.

Harry was in class 44-F, the number reflecting the year of graduation, 1944, and the letter reflecting the month of graduation, June. For the next ten weeks he was in preflight training, with the term split into two parts of five weeks, known as lower preflight and upper preflight. Classes covered aerodynamics, navigation, and meteorology.

Being near the basic and advanced trainers and seeing them taxi out, take off, and bound over the base in smart formations got his heart pounding. Soon, he thought, he would be up there, one of the pilots in formation. Each of the three phases of flight training—primary, basic, and advanced—would, like preflight training, be divided into ten-week periods, with those periods subdivided into so-called lower and upper halves.

When the time finally came for Harry to start flying in earnest, he was transferred back to quarters on the Tuskegee Institute's campus. At this stage, aviation cadets were housed in Sage Hall, a pristine dormitory with only two men sharing each room. They were bussed to Moton Field for primary flight instruction. As in the WTS program, the primary flight instructors increasingly were black civilians employed by the Tuskegee Institute. But the planes at the primary school were the Army's, decked out in the colorful trainer paint scheme of blue fuselage and yellow wings.

In contrast to Tuskegee's earlier primary flight classes, Harry's class would not fly the rotund Stearman biplane. This trainer had a high center of gravity, closely-coupled main landing gear, and poor forward visibility in the landing position that made ground handling difficult, especially during landing rollouts. There had been many ground-looping accidents, and though the cadets had generally escaped unscathed, repair of the damaged planes was time-consuming and costly. So the Army Air Forces decided to replace the biplanes with what was presumed to be a less problematic trainer.

That's where the PT-19 entered the picture. It was also a two-seat open-cockpit trainer, but it had a single low cantilevered wing and main landing gear with a wide stance. Because of an inline engine rather than a radial engine, forward visibility was enhanced. With this airplane, the officers overseeing training believed that landing accidents would become much less common.

While the PT 19 definitely offered improved ground handling, the wings in the early models assigned to Moton Field made use of plywood sections, and their exposure to the hot and humid conditions in Alabama (and other southern training locations) caused rot to set in. For all their advantages, these models were not a long-term solution. But maintenance crews did their best to keep the Fairchilds in the air.

On December 8 Harry got his chance to fly open-cockpit, like the military pilots and barnstormers of the pulp magazines and the silver screen. Yes, he thought, there really is glamour to it! His white silk scarf was wrapped around his neck, puffed up under his chin, with the ends tucked into his sheepskin-lined leather flight jacket. He wore a sheepskin-lined leather helmet, too, with goggles to slide down over his eyes when he was ready to launch.

Harry's instructor added power, and they rolled across Moton Field's sod until they traded the emerald green of the ground for the azure blue of the air. The Fairchild climbed slowly as its 175-horsepower six-cylinder inline Franklin air-cooled engine struggled to overcome gravity, but they were airborne. Harry breathed in the fragrance of the rich soil below and felt the wind nuzzling his face.

It was nothing short of exhilarating—simply magical! These were the invigorating sensations that Spencer and White had known, the sensations of a certain kind of freedom they wanted the next generation of African Americans to assimilate in the bigger, more powerful, and faster planes that only the Army possessed. Harry was their quasi-descendant, in love with this kind of flying and determined to spring even higher.

At the same time, Harry recalled that he was the familial descendant of Preston James Stewart, who had been born into slavery in Alabama during the Civil War. Somewhere on the landscape below, in the very state which Harry was flying over as a cadet preparing to fight to protect the freedom of his countrymen, his grandfather had been born into a world closed off to any semblance of freedom. In the skies above Tuskegee, things were changing in ways Grandpa Preston never would have thought possible!

Harry recorded his flights, making entries representing his progress through climbs and glides, stalls and steep turns, side slips and crosswind landings in a personal logbook that was separate from his military Form 5. About seven hours into this scarf-and-goggle flying, his instructor, Jack Johnson, told him to taxi over to the wind tee. Once the plane stopped, Johnson unbuckled his harness as the propeller loped over with the throttle set at idle. Harry knew what that meant, and his heart began to race.

Johnson leaned over the cockpit coaming and declared, "You're doing fine." Looking trustingly into Harry's eyes, he added, "Now take it around the pattern and do one full-stop landing. Then, bring it back here to the wind tee."

Harry had been waiting for this moment. He felt the great weight of responsibility, and at the same time he felt enormous pride. In giving him the green light to solo, his flight instructor had given him the opportunity of a lifetime.

Pointing the Fairchild's nose into the wind and easing the throttle forward, Harry was ecstatic, for he was consummating the act of flight on his own. As the plane gained momentum and the controls lightened up, he realized that he could do this—it was really happening! He drew the stick back, and the wood-and-fabric wonder lifted skyward!

The Fairchild was all his. Upwind leg, climb to five hundred feet, and then bank left into the crosswind turn. Keep the turn coming to downwind. Level off at eight hundred feet, with the airstrip sited parallel to the port wingtip. Take a breath, enjoy wings level, but watch for pattern traffic. Abeam the touchdown point, chop the power. Crank the wing to the left again onto base leg, and at five hundred feet set up for final approach.

The machine responded to his every move just as it was supposed to. Harry was the master of his fate, carving out his direction in the three dimensions of the sky, watching the ground below scooch lazily backwards. He was on top of the world!

When he taxied back to the wind tee, Jack Johnson was waiting with a smile. "Take it around again," he said in a loud voice over the idling engine, as he made a circular motion with his arm.

Altogether Harry made three takeoffs and landings as pilot-in-command that memorable day. His sway over the ship was affirming. In the weeks to come there would be figure eights, lazy eights, aerobatics—and Harry nailed them all, as if he had been meant to fly.

Ground training for instrument flight was part of the program and included time in the Link trainer, a booth-like device with an operator who sat at a nearby control panel. He would start by asking for turns and then complicate the exercise, calling for a flight plan to be flown by radio beacons. Invariably he would plug in adverse conditions and spin the cadet around, trying to disorient him.

On more than one occasion Harry stepped out of the boxy trainer with beads of sweat pouring down his face. The strain of the training was exacerbated by the Alabama heat in the non-air-conditioned simulator building. But he was getting through it, and his skills were being honed.

Some cadets were not so lucky. One day Harry returned to his room to find his roommate, Kenneth Kildare, distraught with reddened eyes. He had been crying because he had failed his check ride. He had fallen victim to the dreaded washout.

Harry's next roommate, Wilberforce Clark, experienced the same awful fate. Washing out was devastating. It usually happened in the primary phase because of difficulty landing the taildraggers.

Harry's roommates' washouts were a reminder of the ominous lecture on the first day of flight training. The cadets stood line abreast in a long row facing one of the flight instructors. "Get a good look at the cadet to your right," the instructor barked. "Do the same with the cadet to your left …" Then, without missing a beat, he dropped the bombshell: "because at the end of this program they won't be there."

Some of the cadets who washed out turned bitter and blamed their rejection on white instructors and check pilots. Certainly prejudice was afoot, but overall Harry considered the staff to be fair. He believed that with enough time almost anyone could be taught to fly, but he understood that in the middle of a war the military could pass only the cadets who got the hang of it in the allotted time frame.

Harry offered this explanation as solace to friends who had suffered the ignominy of being washed out, but it did little to alleviate the sting of rejection. Much later in life, he saw that some who washed out exhibited lasting psychological effects. It was sad, but washing out was an inescapable fact of life at training bases everywhere. Tuskegee's class 44-F started with seventy-five cadets, and by the end only twenty-six remained.

For those fortunate enough to make the cut in primary, the two subsequent phases of the training took place at Tuskegee Army Airfield, the separate and larger facility where the instruction wasn't contracted out but done by the Army itself. The cadets lived in the barracks. They ate, studied, and flew at what was, in every sense of the word, a military post. Except for its racial composition, the operations at the base were like those at any other in the Army's flight training system.

Harry and his friends, fellow aviation cadets like Yenwith K. Whitney of New York, Rupert C. Johnson of Los Angeles, and Charles A. Hill Jr. of Detroit, were drawn to the base's airplanes. In the cool morning, scores of big-barreled, all-metal trainers with powerful radial engines and raised all-glass canopies were arrayed wingtip to wingtip. During the day the planes would range into the temperate winter sky like a swarm of oversized bumblebees, giving off a raspy rhythm that reverberated across the landscape.

For young men seeking to fly, the place was intoxicating. The aroma of burnt fuel permeated the air, and whenever you looked up there were silvery ships roaring overhead. The four wide runways, each nearly a mile long, practically backed up to your living quarters.

And the glue that held it all together was the camaraderie, the brotherhood between you and your fellow cadets united in common purpose—waking to reveille, marching to orders, and saluting officers who saluted you back. For most of the day, the sky above was occupied by a fleet of impressive planes with the Army Air Forces star-in-circle insignia painted on their wings, which made you think that you were part of something big, something magnificent. You weren't just learning to fly; you were serving your country and you were going to fight. There would be an opportunity to prove yourself in a way that had never been possible until this program started.

The program's importance to the black community could hardly be overstated. It was demonstrated by the visits of many black celebrities to the base. Before Harry had arrived, heavyweight champion Joe Louis dropped by. One day while Harry was there, Lena Horne toured the flight line and sat in the cockpit of an AT-6. In the evening she mingled with the cadets, even Lindy Hop dancing with some of them at a party on base. Though Harry was too shy to cut in, many cadets did, and the popular singer seemed to enjoy it.

Yet for all the attention the base garnered from famous figures in civil rights, sports, and entertainment, the town of Tuskegee was anything but welcoming to the cadets. There had been stories of cadets going downtown to check out the stores or just to have a look around—frequently ending with the cadets being either verbally or physically attacked by white residents. Harry simply avoided venturing into town. In his judgment there was no reason to tempt fate. Graduating from the flight program was enough of a challenge.

Because Harry confined himself to the campus and the base during his entire time in training, which lasted more than a year, he looked to on-site extracurricular activities to occupy his time when he wasn't studying or flying. Intramural sports were a big thing on base. Disregarding his bad right leg, he played football.

Harry held his own in the games until, in the foolery of youthful competition, he pivoted wildly to make a catch. The twisting of his torso while his stunted leg remained firmly planted on the ground threw out his back. He was diagnosed with sciatica and landed in the base hospital.

Worried that his infirmity would lead to his being ejected from the program, he spent his first days in bed in agony from both the physical pain and the psychic stress. Luckily the nurse on his ward was unfailingly upbeat. Lieutenant Irma Cameron Dryden, a very pretty young lady recently married to fighter pilot Charles W. Dryden, came into the ward early every morning and gently wiggled Harry's toe to wake him up. Her compassionate care helped him while away the hours until time healed the inflamed nerve.

On February 11, 1944, Harry clambered into the cockpit of a Vultee BT-13 Valiant. The intermediate phase in his flight training had begun. The basic trainer featured a greenhouse canopy, giving the cadet protection from the elements while ensuring excellent visibility in all directions. It was a step-up in sophistication, but only to a point. Like the Fairchild, this plane had fixed landing gear.

The BT-13 was designed to ease the cadet from a slow-moving primary trainer to a faster and more complex aircraft. Those who flew the 450-horsepower trainer remember it for the extremely loud thumping thrown off by the fast-twirling propeller blade tips. They called it the Vibrator, not so much because of the ear-splitting noise but because the aircraft was known to shake briskly when stalled.

Proficiency in the fundamentals of flight was now largely a given, and the new trainer was intended to infuse proficiency in the mission. Cadets were taught how to, in a manner of speaking, spread their wings. Harry charted out and flew cross-country flights to places like Union Springs, Columbus, Clanton, and Greenville. The syllabus included formation flight and night operations.

On March 16, little over a month after Harry began flying the Vibrator, he was introduced to the North American Aviation AT-6 Texan, powered by Pratt & Whitney's R-1340 Wasp 650-horsepower nine-cylinder air-cooled engine. The advanced trainer took flight to a wholly different level; taming the Texan meant that you had crossed a threshold. The instructors told you it was an honest airplane, but it moved faster and had more controls to manipulate and instruments to monitor. There were also certain characteristics peculiar to its "personality," so that if your attention wavered, the airplane could come back to bite you. With some justification, they called it the Pilot Maker.

The Texan came from the same company that was, at that very moment, churning out the war's premier piston fighter, the P-51 Mustang. Both planes were handsome, sporting clean lines and an aesthetic that made them incredibly alluring. They bore out the old adage that if an aircraft looks right, it'll fly right.

For the next month and a half, Harry alternated between flying the BT-13 and the AT-6. He was feeling increasingly comfortable in both planes. On May 2 he soloed in the advanced trainer, making eight landings and memorializing the occasion with the logbook notation "happy do—soloed today."

But as cadets knew all too well, their status and the course of their careers in the Army Air Forces was subject to change without notice; a washout could come at any time. Harry's elation turned to concern the next day when he was slated for a check ride at the twenty-hour interval: his check pilot was an especially hard-nosed white lieutenant with suspect views on race.

Because the flight was an instrument check ride, Harry pulled the AT-6's collapsible fabric hood over his head once established in level flight at altitude. Now Harry was totally reliant on his instruments as the check pilot fed him coordinates over the intercom. The headings were being held pretty well in Harry's mind, but the officer had other thoughts.

Without warning, the control stick slammed to the forward stop, jerking Harry's arm. Just then, Harry heard a sneering sound over his earphones. Clearly, the check pilot was dissatisfied.

Harry complied with each command, turning to the designated heading and climbing or descending to the designated altitude, but the control stick kept getting thrown sharply from front to back and from side to side. The check pilot's voice wasn't just critical, it was spiteful. The harangue built up until the agitation spilled over into the utterance of a vile racial epithet.

Harry felt trapped. All of his efforts could be for naught because of this one check pilot. After landing, Harry was so angry that in a cathartic fit he blurted out an account of what had happened to the first person he came across in the ground support squadron, an administrative clerk. By coincidence, the black clerk was friendly with one of the base's top white instructors.

Though no one ever told Harry what happened after he had vented his frustration, the check pilot did not resort to epithets in any future contact he had with Harry, including another check ride. Harry theorized that the check pilot got a talking-to from his superior. Whatever intervention may have occurred, or whatever change of heart may have taken hold, Harry was grateful that the verbal abuse did not recur and that he was still on the path to graduation. That was the only time he had encountered overt racism in the flight training program.

Harry had good relations with all the other white pilots, who he believed were upright and equitable. According to Harry, the white flight instructors at Tuskegee could be split about evenly into three categories: those who sought to avoid going to war, others who just wanted to be close to their families, and the remainder who were driven by altruism.

In a nutshell, Harry described the white flight instructors as "tough but fair." His point was illustrated when he went up for a check ride in an AT-6 with Major Donald G. McPherson, the second-ranking flying officer on base and the director of flight training. Knowing he could be eliminated from the program at any time if his flying was rated deficient, Harry always went on check rides with a degree of anxiety. Each successive check ride required a higher skill level, and McPherson's call for Harry to execute a 2¼-turn spin to the right raised the stakes.

Pulling out exactly at the end of the last quarter turn would require exacting technique. Harry aligned the trainer's nose with the groove of a section line in order to have a ground reference. Then, pulling the stick back into his lap, he stalled the wing and induced the spin with full right rudder.

The plane flipped over on its back and started rotating to starboard. As the two-ton trainer corkscrewed through the air, Harry scrupulously counted each quarter turn. Anticipating the recovery point, Harry applied left rudder in advance to arrest the rotation and then relaxed back pressure on the stick to roll out on the final quarter-turn. He was right on the money! And McPherson acknowledged it!

This kind of precision was expected by the check pilots. Anything less put you in jeopardy. Until the plane was shut down and parked you were under scrutiny, and any weakness in procedure, any foible in performance could be grounds for the feared washout. In Harry's opinion, high standards could be mistaken for racial bias and, while race could be a determinant, it usually wasn't.

In their history of the Tuskegee Airmen, *Tuskegee's Heroes*, Charlie and Ann Cooper explain that the white flight instructors at Tuskegee Army Airfield "were extremely demanding and often very vocal." In general, they were anxious "to make sure that the cadets were trained in just the same ways and just as well as their white counterparts."

The Coopers implicitly make the point that white cadets complained about their flight instructors too, especially when a washout occurred. In their balanced view, Tuskegee's three most senior white flight instructors "worked especially hard in the early days" of the "experiment" and, like flight instructors at white training bases, they were not "fully appreciated until actual combat flying proved the wisdom of their instruction and their method of imparting it."

Near the end of May, Harry was part of a twelve-ship formation in a flight that evoked Harry's sense of the pilots' brotherhood and that presaged the thousand-plane formations in his future. At Tuskegee, formations were flown multiple times and followed by three-hour day and night cross-country flights. This was real flying, Army flying. Harry savored the last hours aloft in the program, for it was then that he could tell he had mastered the art of flying.

On June 20, Harry completed the flight training program with 212.3 hours of flight time. The accomplishment was duly noted in his logbook: "Finished Advanced! Happy Day."

In anticipation of his graduation, about a week earlier he received a $250 allotment to buy custom-fitted officer uniforms so he would have one to wear at his graduation. It was another affirmation of his dream to become an Army aviator. On June 27, 1944, in a ceremony appropriate for the occasion, Colonel Noel F. Parrish, the commander of Tuskegee Army Airfield, delivered the commencement address in the base's chapel.

Colonel Parrish was revered by the cadets both for his insistence on high standards and for his evenhandedness. Without him at the helm, the program might have failed. Of the blacks under his command, he said, "[I]t took an extra amount of dedication and idealism to really stick to it."

The graduating cadets were called to the front individually and presented with the Army's coveted silver wings and a scroll acknowledging their new rank. When his name was called, Harry stepped forward as a member of Tuskegee's class 44-F. With a handshake and a salute, he

Harry at the end of advanced flight training at Tuskegee Army Airfield, awaiting graduation in June 1944. Soon Harry would receive the Army Air Forces' coveted silver wings and a commission as a second lieutenant. *U.S. Air Force via Harry Stewart Jr.*

was commissioned a second lieutenant in the Army Air Forces. He was still only nineteen years old and not yet licensed to drive a car!

Years later, when asked what it was like to be one of the relative handful of cadets to break the Army Air Forces' color barrier, Harry would say in his self-effacing way that he was too busy enjoying the flying to know that he had made history. He was one of 992 African Americans instated into the Army's flying officer corps during World War II. The skies would never be the same again!

Outside the chapel, the newly graduated Army pilots were surrounded by family members who delighted in pinning the silver wings on their loved one's uniform. Harry, though, was by himself because his parents and siblings were not able to make the trip. Seeing him

Before they left Tuskegee, each graduate of class 44-F received ten flight hours of fighter lead-in training in hand-me-down P-40s. This photo shows graduates mainly from the New York area, clustered together for targeted publicity. White newspapers tended to disregard these items, but black newspapers featured them prominently. Harry is seated in the cockpit. *U.S. Air Force via Harry Stewart Jr.*

all alone, classmate Frank N. Wright and his fiancée Anita Harris walked over and asked if anyone was coming to celebrate with him. Harry shook his head.

With a bright smile, Anita volunteered to pin Harry's hard-earned silver wings on his uniform. She got them on straight and then gave Harry a kiss on the cheek. It buttressed Harry's feeling of belonging; his passage from cadet to officer was complete.

■ ■ ■

In mid-July 1944, before Harry left Tuskegee, he and the pilots from his class received ten flight hours of fighter lead-in training in hand-me-down P-40 Warhawks. These were weary and otherwise obsolete planes, but with performance superior to that of any of the trainers. Because air combat was a certainty for the recent graduates, they welcomed any flight time in real combat platforms, even if lackluster compared to the war's more modern fighters.

Later in July, all the graduates got extended leave. Harry went home to visit his family. His younger brother Donald, who had been drafted into the infantry, was home on leave too.

While he was in Corona, Harry visited his junior high school, P.S. 16. He wanted to see his teachers and thank them for their encouragement, especially Mrs. McLaughlin, his history teacher and guidance counselor. The school was in summer session and much quieter than Harry remembered it.

He had come in his uniform, replete with silver wings. When his teachers saw him, they stood and embraced him. Mrs. McLaughlin hugged him hard and wouldn't let go.

Of course, the greatest test for Harry lay ahead. He and his eighteen classmates assigned to fighters would set out from Tuskegee bonded by their love of flight and their sense of duty to the nation. The way in which these pertinacious young men acquitted themselves in the unforgiving crucible of hostile skies would win them reputations as outstanding flyers and etch their names as brave patriots in the honor roll of history.

Chapter Seven

"YOUR FRIENDS OF THE 332nd FIGHTER GROUP"

As the sun makes ice melt, kindness causes
misunderstanding, mistrust, and hostility to evaporate.
—Albert Schweitzer

War makes strange bedfellows. On December 29, 1944, just a matter of days before Harry arrived at the 332nd Fighter Group's base of operations in Italy, bad weather caused many Fifteenth Air Force bombers returning from missions to divert to alternate airfields. Eighteen B-24 Liberators landed at Ramitelli Airfield, the home of the 332nd.

All but one of these Liberators belonged to the 485th Bombardment Group, based at Venosa, about seventy-five miles southeast of Ramitelli. During their mission against the rail yards at Verona, heavy snow shut down their home base, which resulted in vectors to Ramitelli. The fighter base there was never intended to accommodate large aircraft; because the taxiways were too narrow for the bombers to maneuver, they had to park at the end of the runway.

For five days, including New Year's, the 170 white bomber crewmen of the 485th were snowed in at Ramitelli, leaving them no choice but to eat, drink, and sleep with the 332nd's black personnel, in what is believed to be the only such occurrence during

93

the war. The 332nd seized this unique opportunity and pulled out all the stops to be welcoming. It only made sense for the men of the fighter group to get to know their accidental guests. After all, the fighter group's pilots had been risking their lives to protect these bomber crews.

For their part, the bomber crews had no idea what to expect. Most were pleasantly surprised at the warm reception they received. According to a story handed down through word of mouth, even one obstinate Southerner, who at first slept in one of the bombers and refused to fraternize with the base's black servicemen, eventually came into a heated tent to escape the cold and found his hosts to be obliging.

Colonel Davis described breaking out a case of Johnnie Walker for the New Year's Eve party. "We drank, ate cheese, crackers, and nuts, sang the New Year in, and played poker." He referred to the stranded bomber crews as "our bomber friends" and said they "took communion with us at the Sunday service." Of these visitors, who had landed out of necessity, Davis wrote, "They enjoyed their stay and learned that, in matters of humanity, we were not any different from them."

The preponderant feeling among the bomber crews was captured in the January 7 edition of the 485th's newsletter, *Bombs Away*. The article was titled "Crews Feted by 332nd!" and subtitled "Receive 'Wonderful Treatment' During 5-Day Visit with All-Negro Fighter Group!" It reported "hospitality far beyond expectation" and quoted Lieutenant Leland Larsen, one of the bomber crewmen who had landed at Ramitelli. According to Larsen, "We were treated like kings. Every one of the men was wonderful to us, and the Q[uarter] M[aster] immediately sent out to another field for food and five blankets apiece for us. We remained in the private tents with the men and sleeping quarters were ideal. They insisted on serving us our breakfast in bed, and provided us with beer, PX rations (their own), Cokes, writing paper, and whiskey; and the New Year's Day dinner they served us was out of this world."

Clearing weather on January 3 enabled the bombers of the 485th to fly back to Venosa. Each departing crew member found a letter typed out in caps waiting for him in the planes. It had been placed by the 332nd's public relations officer, Captain Eugene D. Weaver. The letter conveyed the sentiments of the unit's personnel towards their visitors:

> TO THE VISITING PILOTS AND CREWS:
> YOU HAVE BEEN THE GUESTS OF THE 332ND ALL NEGRO FIGHTER GROUP. WE HOPE THAT OUR FACILITIES, SUCH AS THEY ARE, WERE SUIT-ABLE AND ADEQUATE ENOUGH TO HAVE MADE YOUR STAY HERE A PLEASANT ONE. ON BEHALF OF COLONEL DAVIS AND THE COMMAND, I EXTEND TO YOU OUR HEARTY WISHES FOR A HAPPY NEW YEAR AND MANY HAPPIER LAND-INGS. YOU ARE WELCOME TO RETURN HERE AT ANY TIME AND I AM SURE THAT WE CAN MAKE YOUR STAY AN ENJOYABLE ONE. THE PILOTS OF THIS COMMAND HAVE EXPRESSED THEIR DESIRES TO HAVE IT MADE CLEAR THAT IT IS A PLEASURE TO BE ABLE TO PROTECT YOU AND LOOK AFTER YOUR WELL-BEING BOTH IN THE AIR AND ON THE GROUND. REMEMBER, WHEN YOU ARE UP THERE AND SEE THE RED TAILED MUSTANGS IN THE SKY, THEY ARE YOUR FRIENDS OF THE 332ND FIGHTER GROUP. HERE IS HOPING FOR A QUICK ENDING OF THE WAR AND A BETTER AND MORE PEACEFUL WORLD.

MANY HAPPY LANDINGS,
/s/ Eugene D. Weaver
EUGENE D. WEAVER
Capt., Air Corps,
Public Relations O.

On January 6, the 485th's commanding officer, Colonel John P. "Jack" Tomhave, replied with a letter of appreciation to Major E. D. Jones Jr., commander of the Tuskegee Airmen's 366th Air Service Squadron:

Dear Major Jones,
On behalf of the Officers and Enlisted Men of the 485th Bombardment Group, I want to personally thank you for the courtesy and assistance which you and the personnel of the 366th Air Service Squadron so splendidly offered to our crews which landed at your base on 29 December 1944. I fully realize what an inconvenience this forced landing must have made on your facilities, and the remarkable manner in which you people of the 15th Fighter Command rose to the situation is all the more commendable.
The very able assistance which your Service Squadron has given to the 332nd Fighter Group is well known, and now you have proven yourselves just as capable in servicing our heavy bombers.
Sincerely yours,
/s/ Jack P. Tomhave
Jack P. Tomhave,
Colonel, Air Corps,
Commanding

Sadly, as proof of the abrupt and cruel nature of war, Colonel Tomhave, an enlightened officer who had earlier earned the Distinguished Flying Cross leading a mission over the Ploesti oil fields and who, as a West Point graduate, had a promising career ahead of him, was killed the next month. On February 16 his plane was disabled by flak when he was returning from a raid over Villach, Austria, which prompted him to bail out. Two days later he was captured, and on February 22, while being transported to a prisoner-of-war camp via train, he was mortally wounded by the strafing of Allied fighters.

Against the war's misery and iniquity, the unplanned hookup of Colonel Tomhave's and Lieutenant Larsen's bomb group with Colonel Davis's and Captain Weaver's fighter group stood out as a bright spot. The consensus among the men of the 332nd was that most of the white bomber crews enjoyed their interlude at Ramitelli. In fact, the novel encounter that briefly brought blacks and whites together was, as Colonel Davis suggested, a reminder of their shared humanity. Shortly after the bombers left for Venosa, one of the Tuskegee Airmen sagely commented, "There's no such thing as segregation when you're fighting side by side."

Within days, Harry would report for duty as a replacement pilot at Ramitelli and join these young men whose vestigial idealism was evidenced by gestures of kindheartedness—against the backdrop of brutish battles for control of the air and for dignity on the ground.

■ ■ ■

In mid-August 1944, several days after Harry finished his P-40 training at Tuskegee and as he awaited transport to his advanced gunnery training base elsewhere in the South, he got sad news. Joseph Gordon, the childhood friend from Corona who had played cowboys and Indians with him and whose training at Tuskegee had overlapped with his, had gone down on a strafing mission near Toulon, France. Members of the 332nd had taken a lot of punishment from antiair-craft fire as they dove on German radar stations and other targets in support of Operation Dragoon, the impending Allied invasion of southern France. A flak burst had turned Gordon's fighter into a fireball, killing him instantly.

The news stopped Harry in his tracks; idealized notions of being a fighter pilot did not correspond to the reality that was hitting him now. Soon he would be flying the same kind of missions as his friend, and fate might be as callous to him. Harry still wanted to go, but visions of chivalry and glamour quickly ebbed. Only twenty years old, Harry was maturing rapidly.

Harry's final prepping before deployment overseas occurred at Walterboro, South Carolina. From late September through mid-November 1944 he accumulated an additional eighty flight hours in the P-47D and G, identical Thunderbolt models built by Republic in Farmingdale and under license by Curtiss in Buffalo, respectively. He was flying real frontline fighters and getting the kind of air combat maneuvering experience that would prove invaluable overseas.

Some of his best training came unexpectedly when he was performing aerobatics alone in the base's practice airspace. Another Thunderbolt appeared from out of nowhere. Being a fighter pilot, Harry engaged the presumed tenderfoot. Before he knew it he was in a knock-down, drag-out dogfight to see who could get on whose tail.

Harry employed every maneuver he had been taught, rolling and twisting to get behind the other fighter, but the other pilot kept gyrating to avoid becoming prey. The exercise went on for what seemed an eternity, with the other pilot eventually gaining the advantage. At that point, the two planes broke off their joust and landed. From a distance, Harry craned his neck to see his competitor step out of the other P-47. He wanted to get a glimpse of the skilled aviator.

The pilot stood on the wing and when the helmet was pulled off, a full head of long, red hair flowed out. "I'll be damned," Harry said to himself. The pilot who had given him a run for his money was one of the female flyers in the groundbreaking Women's Airforce Service Pilots (WASP) program.

Apparently, the WASP pilot had been ferrying a new fighter to Walterboro when the aerial encounter happened. It was a reminder that flying talent is not bound by such irrelevant characteristics as gender or race. Equally as important, the mock combat's lessons would help to save Harry's life when he was maneuvering in actual combat in the not too distant future.

With the Thunderbolt training behind him, Harry transferred to Camp Patrick Henry in Virginia, near Newport News, for shipping out. At last he would be joining the 332nd Fighter Group at war. But before his ship was ready to sail, he had a few days of leave, and he intended to make the rounds of his parents' former hometown, his birthplace.

Harry connected with his parents' schoolmates and friends in the city. They told him about a big football game scheduled at Huntington High School, his father's alma mater. Thinking it would be a great way to see where his father had gone to school, he hopped on a trolley shortly before game time and sat down near the attendant up front. An elderly black man sidled up to Harry and, apparently thinking he was doing the out-of-towner a favor, leaned over and whispered in his ear that he would be wise to get up and move to the rear before being ordered to do so by the attendant.

The fact that Harry was in uniform did not make a difference. This was the South, and its customs were ingrained even if African Americans were in the military and about to ship out to a combat zone to fight and possibly die for the country. In shades of the movement that was to emerge when Rosa Parks refused to give up her seat on a municipal bus in Montgomery, Alabama, eleven years later, Harry had too much pride to comply with the local restriction. Yet he did not want to do anything that could jeopardize his flight status. He jumped off at the next stop and walked the rest of the way.

Not everything during his short stay was negative. When his parents' schoolmates and friends visited at the base, the guard on duty, who was white, gave Harry a crisp salute and referred to him, a second lieutenant, as "sir." The visitors, who were black, started elbowing each other with approving nods. Maybe the South would change after all.

In early December the Liberty ship SS *Nathan Hale* launched from Hampton Roads carrying Harry and another fourteen or so replacement pilots on a slow-motion voyage across the Atlantic. With cargo filling most of the ship, the only other passengers were about fifty black soldiers in a service unit who had no idea that there were black pilots in the U.S. armed forces. During the trip the aviators cultivated a rapport with the soldiers and even helped them compose letters back home to family and sweethearts.

Harry and his fellow flyers also developed an interest in a singing sparrow that hitched a ride on the ship's stern. The little bird sustained itself by swooping down to pick at the leftovers thrown overboard every day by the mess hands.

One day, about midway across the Atlantic, a terrible storm enveloped the ship and a strong headwind swept across the deck. The poor sparrow dipped down to the ocean's surface to catch its daily nutrients on the normal schedule, but the unusually potent wind held it back from catching up with the ship. The pilots watched in horror as their unofficial mascot, to which they had become attached, fluttered back to the ocean and drowned. It was sad, and a harbinger of losses even more profound to come.

Nineteen days after leaving Virginia, the ship pulled into the French port of Marseille. It was two days before Christmas, and the

Battle of the Bulge was unfolding. The Allies had been caught by surprise as Hitler's forces attempted to change the battlefield's dynamic in a desperate final push. Harry heard that Allied commanders were so distressed that they would take every able-bodied serviceman, even sailors and airmen, and put them into the land forces holding on at the frontlines.

Terrified that all they had worked for would go down the drain, Harry and the other pilots with him wanted to get going as soon as possible on the final voyage to the 332nd. As things turned out, the threatened redeployment did not happen.

Instead, the travelers celebrated a boisterous New Year's in Marseille. At midnight the locals fired their guns into the air, and Harry and the other pilots pulled their Colt .45-caliber service pistols out of their shoulder holsters and joined in the festivities, firing off rounds into the air until the guns were empty.

A few days later, the French luxury liner *Ville d'Oran*, which had been converted into a troop transport operated by Cunard after the fall of France, was ready to sail. Harry laughs when relating this leg of his wartime travels.

The ship's tables were covered with fine linen cloth, and the dining utensils looked like pure sterling silver. Harry and the other pilots were waited on at tea by deferential British stewards immaculately attired in white jackets and versed in the King's English, intent on bending over backwards to satisfy their guests. It was wondrous and more than a little odd to have a caricature of the stereotypical English butler bowing to your every whim as you sailed to a war zone where you were to be thrust into life-or-death combat.

Upon reaching the southern Italian port of Taranto, conditions changed dramatically—from opulent to decrepit. The pilots were led to dirty, malodorous boxcars destined for Naples, in a reminder of their humble rank and of the age-old exigencies of war. From there

British trucks carried them to their final destination, the air base at Ramitelli near the Adriatic coast. It was early January 1945, and Harry had arrived—anxious to fly and fight.

Chapter Eight

"A SIGHT TO BEHOLD!"

We few, we happy few, we band of brothers;
For he today that sheds his blood with me
Shall be my brother.
—William Shakespeare, *Henry V*

Ramitelli had become the operational nerve center for the 332nd Fighter Group and its four fighter squadrons by July 1944. At that time, the 99th Fighter Squadron had already been in action for a little over a year; whereas the three other squadrons had experienced their baptism of fire in February 1944. Some members of the 99th reportedly bemoaned their squadron's linkup with the relative greenhorns of the 332nd. And the reservations of the battle-hardened trailblazers were said to be reciprocated by some of the newcomers, who feared that the experienced pilots would crowd them out of plum assignments.

The 99th's greater disappointment was that this consolidating of the all-black fighter squadrons into a single group precluded the once hoped-for synthesis with white outfits. As the Tuskegee Airmen's initial in-theater combat squadron, the 99th had previously been attached to white fighter groups. From this perspective the consolidation was a setback. The fact that the 332nd Fighter Group had four squadrons, when a fighter group normally had three,

showed the lengths to which the Army's hierarchy would go to preserve the institution of segregation.

But the reservations in the fighter group about the conjoining of
the new squadrons with the old soon faded. Starting in May 1944,
the 332nd had been assigned to the Bari, Italy-based Fifteenth Air
Force. In sync with the Eighth Air Force operating out of a multitude
of bases in England, it pressed the bombing campaign to the enemy's
home territory.

The shift in focus from tactical missions, such as ground attack
under Twelfth Air Force, to mainly strategic missions, such as long-
range bomber escort under Fifteenth Air Force, meant a different kind
of flying. The new missions would give the Tuskegee Airmen more of
an opportunity to make a name for themselves. In July, the 332nd
started flying missions with the P-51 Mustang, the most effective
fighter that the group had yet operated.

Thankfully for Harry, the pilots of the 302nd Fighter Squadron
who were already there took him under their wing. They mentored
him as only grizzled combat flyers could, filling in the gaps in his
stateside flight training, so that when his time came to face fighter
pilots of the vaunted Luftwaffe in eyeball-to-eyeball encounters, he
would be ready.

As things turned out, Harry's affiliation with the 302nd was
short-lived. On March 6, the squadron was inactivated to normalize
the group's structure so that it would have three squadrons like the
other six fighter groups of Fifteenth Air Force. The 302nd's personnel
were disbursed among the 99th, 100th, and 301st Fighter Squadrons;
Harry ended up in the 301st, where the mentoring continued.

During a panel discussion in 2012, when he was asked who his
heroes were, Harry turned to the other Tuskegee Airmen on the panel
who were a few years his senior and, with a knightly motion of his arm
in the direction of those seated around him, said in his quiet voice,

"These gentlemen up here with me now. They were there for me; they are my heroes."

Harry's first day at the base was less than auspicious. He remembers that "it was raining and cold … not a good first impression at all." In the late-night darkness, he and his fellow replacement pilots were issued tent poles, canvas, cots, and so forth, and then told to set it all up on a designated spot. "It was about dawn before we had everything ready and finally laid down for some sleep."

When Harry walked the flight line, he noticed that all the

One of the few photos of Harry while deployed in Italy with the 332nd Fighter Group in 1945. *Harry Stewart Jr.*

Mustangs on the field had their tail sections and spinners painted a solid red. The markings had been adopted when the 332nd was transferred to Fifteenth Air Force. At that time, the Fifteenth Air Force commander, Major General Nathan B. Twining, ordered the group to adopt the solid red scheme as its identifying mark.

Decorating combat aircraft in assigned colors was in keeping with Army Air Forces protocol, whereby a group's aircraft were made easily identifiable. Just by looking at the nose or tail markings, pilots could tell which group was in the air flying alongside them. Because the 332nd's markings were not striped or checkerboard, and because they were a bright color, they were generally regarded as the most distinctive among fighter groups within Fifteenth Air Force. Not surprisingly, the group's flyers became known as the Red Tails.

Color coding didn't end there. Each squadron had its own identifying color. The 99th's was blue, the 100th's black, the 301st's white, and the 302nd's yellow. The squadron color was applied to the rudder and elevator trim tabs—the point being not merely quick recognition in flight but esprit de corps among the squadron's pilots.

As part of Fifteenth Air Force, the 332nd soon established a reputation for success in protecting bombers on escort missions. Colonel Davis would write, "We took deep pride in our mission performance. Our pilots had become experts in bomber escort, and they knew it."

He was especially happy with the compliments from bomber crews that came by teletype or telephone. "They appreciated our practice of sticking with them through the roughest spots...." When the 332nd was increasingly solicited for escort by the bomber crews, Colonel Davis famously changed his fighter's nose art. Painted across the nose were the words: "By Request."

Despite January's wintry weather and the muddy conditions around the runway built of pierced steel planking, Harry was excited to be a part of a winning organization. The morning after his arrival, he and the other new replacement pilots were shown their airplanes and introduced to their crew chiefs. Harry wasn't sure how to start the conversation with his crew chief, Sergeant James Shipley.

Harry explained, "I didn't want to ask 'Is this my aircraft?' because he might retort with 'No, this is my aircraft!'" That first tentative interaction led to a lifelong friendship. Both men have continued to stay in touch, talking by phone every once in a while.

"The safety and preparation of the plane was entirely in the hands of Jim," Harry was quoted as saying in Jim Shipley's biography, by Jeremy Paul Amick. Keeping the fighter airworthy was a team effort, with Jim as the point man empowered to declare the airplane ready for flight or in need of grounding. Harry knew that his success—and his survival—in the air would depend upon Jim's talents and work on the ground. "It was," Harry says, "definitely a pilot–crew chief relationship."

One day when Harry was not on the mission roster, he strolled down to where his aircraft was parked and found Jim performing heavy maintenance on the engine. It was freezing, but Jim wasn't able to wear gloves because the task required the kind of meticulous tactility that was possible only with bare fingers. Jim compensated for the cold by blowing on his hands, trying as best he could to keep them warm. Observing such dedication reinforced Harry's feeling that he had a great crew chief.

The bond between the two only grew over the next several months. In his biography, Jim is quoted as saying that Harry was such a zealous strafing pilot that on a couple of occasions the plane returned to base with "a bunch of gravel" in the coolant air intake, the conspicuous scoop on the Mustang's belly. Jim would humorously scold Harry not to fly so low.

The day Harry met Jim, he was handed an instruction manual on his P-51 Mustang. Reading the manual and asking questions would be Harry's only preparation for transitioning to the unfamiliar fighter. Before he was given the green light, Captain Dudley Watson, the 302nd's operations officer, insisted he had to pass a "blindfold check" in which he was required to identify cockpit levers, switches, dials, etc. by touch only.

On January 20, Harry flew a Mustang for the first time, though not his own. Harry's regular plane was a hand-me-down P-51C with the words "Miss Jackson III" emblazoned on its nose, because it had been the fighter of Melvin "Red" Jackson, the former commander of the 302nd. But if the pilot's primary aircraft, the one tended to by his crew chief, wasn't ready, another would be substituted. Before the end of the month, Harry made six orientation flights of from one to two hours each in all three Mustang models, the P-51B, the C, and the D.

Harry was pleased with his new fighter. It was smooth-handling and responsive to control inputs. In February, he started to fly escort missions, and because of their extended duration—in some cases, as long as six hours—he rapidly amassed flight time (more than seventy-five hours in that month alone) and became increasingly comfortable in the cockpit of the Mustang.

■ ■ ■

The Mustang was born out of Britain's need for more first-rate fighters in a hurry when the resources of the Royal Air Force were stretched dangerously thin in defense of the empire in 1940. A British delegation came to America on a buying spree and in May of that year ordered a new fighter from North American Aviation that, on paper, promised to outperform what could be bought off the shelf. It was a leap of faith for the Brits; some might even say it was an act of impetuosity, since the contracted company had never built a fighter.

North American Aviation's senior operating executives, James H. "Dutch" Kindelberger and John Leland "Lee" Atwood, had a strong personal interest in the project but turned to chief engineer Raymond H. Rice for engineering oversight and to inhouse design impresario Edgar Schmued for leadership of the design team. In a poetic irony, Schmued had been born in Germany and immigrated to America only ten years earlier. His central role in crafting the fighter that would contribute so much to the defeat of the Third Reich spoke volumes about the disparities in culture between the warring countries and the inherent advantages of America versus the Axis powers.

Despite serious racial and ethnic biases embedded in American society, the diversity of the U.S. population was represented in the

When Fifteenth Air Force's white bomber units began calling on the 332nd Fighter Group for bomber escort, Benjamin O. Davis Jr. changed the nose art on his fighter to "By Request." *Air Force Historical Research Agency*

war effort, with members of each group contributing their zeal and expertise. Hitler's exclusionary model, in contrast, extirpated many of the Fatherland's most capable citizens. The cause of freedom, though promoted unevenly by the U.S. at the time, was a rousing and unifying force even for shunned or ostracized communities. It was eminently fitting that the Tuskegee Airmen were among the pilots who flew Edgar Schmued's extraordinary fighter to victory.

A mostly self-taught aeronautical engineer, Schmued had been fascinated by airplanes for almost all of his thirty-nine years. As Ray Wagner describes in his biography of Schmued, the journey from Germany to the U.S. with a detour in Brazil was not easy, but the up-and-coming designer's passion for aviation sustained him. After a career spent perfecting transports and trainers, the fighter assignment was nothing short of a dream job.

In fact, in the years leading up to this moment, Schmued had conceived of key fighter subassemblies in his spare time. Now he had his chance to pull his existing concepts together with state-of-the-art technologies in a clean-sheet configuration to maximize speed, maneuverability, lethality, and ease of construction. Fortunately, there was a wealth of talent within the company from which he could draw.

Among his team's major innovations was the cultivation of a laminar-flow airfoil based on research conducted by the National Advisory Committee for Aeronautics, the government agency that eventually morphed into NASA. The wing shape, as viewed in cross-section, has a symmetrical top and bottom with the thickest point much farther aft than in a conventional airfoil. With this atypical configuration, boundary-layer air sticks to the wing for a comparatively longer time, resulting in lower drag and thus greater endurance and higher speeds.

Schmued's team also adopted an interesting feature employed in a competitor's design. The failed Curtiss XP-46 had a radiator scoop located in the lower aft fuselage, enabling the smoothing out of the fighter's forward section. At North American Aviation the concept was refined with the water-cooling radiator, oil cooler, and aftercooler squeezed into the scoop. As the air passed through, it became heated and was then exhausted out a narrowed duct, actually producing thrust to partially offset the scoop's unavoidable drag. This phenomenon, known as the Meredith effect, was named after the British engineer whose experiments in the mid-1930s discovered the secret for drag mitigation.

The Mustang's design gave the pilot as many advantages as engineering considerations would permit. The main landing gear legs, for example, were set substantially outboard under the wings, giving the inwardly-folding gear an impressive spread of almost twelve feet when extended. This wide stance dramatically improved handling at take-off and landing, in comparison to many earlier fighters with closely-coupled main landing gear.

One of the things Schmued insisted on was clean lines throughout the airframe. He told a colleague, "I want smooth surfaces." So it was no coincidence that the Mustang had compound curves and flush skin joints.

The British had been promised a flying prototype in 120 days. Schmued set a more ambitious working group aim of 100 days. After laboring nonstop and generating an amazing 41,880 engineering man-hours and 2,800 drawings, the first completed airframe was rolled out between the internal and external deadlines.

But the Allison engine was not ready. The engine builder's executives had not believed that the prime contractor could possibly develop an airframe from scratch in such short order. A rush was made to get the engine, and the first flight occurred on October 26, 1940. By the following August, Mustangs were being shipped to the Royal Air Force.

As anticipated, the new fighter was faster, with double the range of the latest Spitfire model in use by the British. But the Mustang's climb rate and high-altitude performance left something to be desired. The answer to transforming the aircraft from a middling fighter to a superb fighter was blending its streamlined airframe with the incomparable Rolls-Royce Merlin engine.

The non-supercharged Allison was replaced by the 12-cylinder liquid-cooled Merlin 61, and the rest is history. Updates and modifications ensued, and the Mustang grew into a legend, widely regarded as the best all-around propeller-driven fighter of World War II. Its combination of an aesthetic profile with a superlative combat record has made it the epitome of warplanes.

The P-51B and P-51C were substantively identical, the only real difference being their construction sites. The former was built in Inglewood, California, and the latter in Dallas, Texas. The ultimate wartime model was the P-51D, which incorporated improvements that added to combat efficacy. These included a Plexiglas bubble canopy to enable 360-degree visibility; six wing-mounted .50-caliber machine guns compared to the prior models' four machine guns; a dorsal fin faring to enhance stability; and the 1,400-horsepower Merlin V-1650-3 or -7.

The aircraft arrived none too soon as a long-range escort fighter. By early 1944, the fighters could be equipped with two externally mounted and detachable fuel tanks—75-gallon drop tanks and later, two 108-gallon drop tanks—that extended their range, so that heavy bombers could be protected on the longest missions.

■ ■ ■

Colonel Davis often led his pilots on the escort missions, which he preceded with memorable briefings in which he was always fully in charge; no whispering on the side. His stare was magnetic. You dared not look away.

Those who were there, sitting at close quarters in the briefing hut, say more than seven decades later that their leader stood with his trademark erectness, glaring at the flying officers assembled before him. And everybody could count on him coming out with his trademark stentorian exhortation, which the fighter group's pilots knew they had to uphold at all costs. "Gentlemen," he would exclaim with a messianic fervor, "stay with the bombers!"

Colonel Davis held his men to an unwaveringly high standard. It was as though he willed his fighter group to success in the long-range heavy bomber escort missions. His forceful personality had an almost

Colonel Benjamin O. Davis Jr., commander of the 332nd Fighter Group, in the top row on the left, with crew chiefs of the 301st Fighter Squadron in front of a red-tailed P-51D at Ramitelli, early 1945. The colonel's facial expression says it all—victory is the only option! Note the pierced steel planking used to facilitate flight operations. *U.S. Air Force via Harry Stewart Jr.*

hypnotic power that contributed incalculably to the remarkable record of minimal losses from enemy interceptors on the 179 such missions flown by the Red Tails.

When a maximum effort was called for on a big bomber mission, the 332nd's four squadrons would each put up sixteen fighters and two spares, for a total of seventy-two Mustangs. Because Ramitelli had only one runway, the aircraft of two squadrons took off in one direction while the aircraft of the other two squadrons took off in the opposite direction. So much for aligning your plane with the wind!

The mass takeoffs were an amazing feat of both organizational coordination and pilot skill. Harry admitted years later that the first time he participated in one of these extravaganzas, he didn't have a clue what was going on. He just followed the plane ahead of him.

A green flare was fired and the first plane started to roll down the runway. In what Harry calls "an intricate ballet," the fighters that followed into the sky would form up on the leader, who would be maneuvering in gently ascending circles. Once everybody was airborne and gathering in the beginnings of squadron formations, the leader turned to a heading calculated to intercept the bombers on their way to the designated target.

The missions regularly involved hundreds of heavy bombers, the Boeing B-17 Flying Fortresses and the Consolidated B-24 Liberators, each carrying a crew of ten, with strategic targets preselected in cities with war-related industries. The aircraft were layered in massive formations that stretched for miles from front to end, the likes of which were never to be seen again. Condensation trails would sometimes flow from the exhaust of the Mustangs, on the climb to cover them.

Harry's squadron would stream the white lines in a magnificently symmetrical latticework that crossed with the trails of the other escort squadrons to form a colossal if temporary reticulation, an ostentatious show of men occupying different sections of the sky but united in a common purpose. Climbing higher than the bombers, typically at altitudes between twenty and thirty thousand feet, the escort squadrons were stacked one thousand feet above each other, starting at one thousand feet on top of the bombers. The escort squadrons flew an "S"-shaped pattern so as not to outrun the slower heavies underneath. Each of the four-engine bombers emitted an equal number of contrails, adding to the effect of a giant filigree superimposed against an endless blue slate.

The white plumes, splayed across cerulean skies for as far as the eye could see, evinced America's unprecedented mobilization as well as the fantastic discipline, skill, and courage of the flight crews. From his aerie, riding shotgun well above the flying armadas of bombers,

Harry was stirred by the sheer magnitude of the assemblage, especially on missions where he, as a junior member of his squadron, flew
as Tail End Charlie. Harry, his eyes beaming, recollects that these
spellbinding formations were "a sight to behold!"

The first sign that these missions were not a game but deadly
serious came when flak began to punctuate the sky. Black puffs of
smoke with flashes of red in the center appeared everywhere. When
the bursts were close, you felt your P-51 shudder.

Worse, some of the bombers cruising below, caught in the field
of fire, could be seen falling out of formation and sinking awkwardly
earthward like toys made of papier-mâché. These mighty ships—
metal molded into aerodynamic shapes and filled with fuel, bombs,
and young men—were transformed in an instant into clunky dead-
weights whose fate belonged to gravity. The antiaircraft artillery
shells came in salvos, seeming to damage bombers at random, as if a
blindfolded contestant at a county fair were shooting rapid-fire at a
row of rubber ducks and intermittently scoring hits.

Strapped tightly in his seat, encased under his Plexiglas canopy,
and breathing heavily into his oxygen mask, Harry was overcome
with a sense of helplessness as the scene played out. At escort altitude
he felt closer to God, closed his eyes, and prayed for the poor souls
peculiarly suspended in the sky below after having taken hits. Perhaps
the flight crews could regain control and dead-stick their crippled
planes to a pasture—or maybe the men aboard the tumbling giants
could jump and they'd get lucky, floating down on their billowed
parachutes into the welcoming arms of partisans in the Resistance.

Harry never really knew the fate of the bombers that were hit
going in; though it seemed to last a lifetime, the drama passed quickly,
and the mission always pressed on. Coming out of the target area,
the escort fighters did everything they could to help their big friends
in trouble. Colonel Davis prided himself on always ordering a couple

In February and most of March 1945, Harry flew combat missions—primarily long-range bomber escorts lasting up to six hours each—virtually every other day. In late March, he was sent to the 332nd's rest camp near Naples, where he commissioned a street artist to create this caricature portrait of himself. *Harry Stewart Jr.*

fighters in the group's formation to latch onto straggling bombers, affording them protection when they were most vulnerable to interceptors as they limped back in the direction of their home bases.

Arguably, the 332nd's most famous mission occurred on March 24, 1945. The group put up fifty-nine Mustangs to escort the 5th Bombardment Wing's B-17s all the way to Berlin to hit the Daimler-Benz tank assembly plant. At sixteen hundred miles round-trip, it would be the longest mission flown by Fifteenth Air Force.

Harry was not on the mission because he had flown missions an average of every other day since being checked out in the P-51. He was at the 332nd's rest camp near Naples, where a local artist was drawing his caricature portrait. Meanwhile, back at Ramitelli, his airplane had been borrowed for the mission by his squadron commander, Captain Armour G. McDaniel. As things unfolded, Colonel Davis had to drop out due to excessive engine vibration in his Mustang, and Captain McDaniel assumed the lead in *Miss Jackson III.*

The American bomber and fighter formations ran smack-dab against the Luftwaffe's revolutionary jet fighter, the Messerschmitt Me 262. Dogfights broke out, and the Tuskegee Airmen shot down three of them. But the German jets inflicted their share of damage, too. According to one account, an Me 262 blew off the wing of Harry's plane, causing Captain McDaniel to bail out. He survived and spent the remainder of the war as a prisoner at Stalag Luft VIIA.

When the group lost its frontline leaders, Colonel Davis replaced them quickly to avoid any lapse in the chain of command. Captain Walter M. "Mo" Downs was tapped to fill the vacancy left by McDaniel. A man of few words, Downs projected an aura of determination and was universally respected by the men of the 301st.

Upon Harry's return to Ramitelli from the rest camp, he was informed of what had happened and was sent to Foggia to pick up a brand-new P-51D, the most advanced version of the Mustang. The shiny fighter had only five hours on the engine. It was so pretty and clean, Harry thought it would be a shame to fly it in combat—though he knew his fantasy was unrealistic.

When Harry's crew chief Jim Shipley asked what artwork he wanted on the nose of his new Mustang, Harry had his answer at the ready. He was without a steady girlfriend at the time, so he chose the title of his favorite song, "Little Coquette," a lively and popular ditty played by such notable bands as Duke Ellington's and Guy Lombardo's. It was that simple: the young pilot would plunge into his next round of escort missions in a dangerous machine decorated with the gaudy name of a big band tune.

Chapter Nine

SHOWDOWN AT FIVE THOUSAND FEET

If one has not given everything, one has given nothing.
—Georges Guynemer

Of Harry's forty-three combat missions in 1945, none clings to his memory as vividly as the one he flew on Easter Sunday, which also happened to be April Fool's Day. The briefing called for his element of eight Mustangs to fly cover for a formation of Liberators of the 47th Bomb Wing over the railway-marshalling yards at St. Polten, Austria. Once the bombers had completed their runs over the target area and were headed back to their bases, Harry and his squadron mates received permission to veer west in the area of the Danube and a Luftwaffe base near the town of Wels, where they could look for targets of opportunity.

One of the planes in the element had mechanical problems and had to drop out. Then, at five thousand feet, one of the seven remaining pilots spotted four German fighters below, not far from the air base. The Tuskegee fighter pilots easily outnumbered the Germans—until the latter sprang their trap. The men of the 301st Fighter Squadron had been lured into an ambush—and Harry suddenly found himself in his first real dogfight.

As his survival instincts—and his training—kicked in, Harry sped to within firing range of the two German fighters nearest to his own plane. They were Focke-Wulf Fw 190D-9s, the best piston-powered fighter planes the Nazis had. Harry pulled the trigger, firing his plane's .50-caliber machine guns at the closer of the two German planes.

As it went down in smoke and flames, Harry shadowed the second Luftwaffe plane ahead of him. The German pilot, realizing his deadly peril, resorted to high-G maneuvering in a desperate attempt to throw Harry off his tail. But to no avail; the young American fighter pilot stayed with the Fw 190 through the excruciating hard-right turn and made use of his first opportunity for a good shot. And the second German plane went down in smoke and flame.

It was at this point that Harry suddenly went from the pursuer to pursued. As tracer rounds whizzed past him, it was Harry's turn to try every evasive maneuver in his bag of tricks. Now, roles reversed, he dove to the deck and made another extreme right turn. With the enemy following his every move, the Fw 190 was right on the tail of the Mustang.

And then, just as suddenly, Harry was free!

In the corner of his eye, as he craned his neck to get a look behind him, he spotted the Focke-Wulf cartwheeling across the ground, curling up, and then exploding in a ball of fire. Somehow, in the heat of the chase, the German fighter had gone from feared predator to smoldering cinders—all in the blink of an eye! Unlikely outcomes like these were in the matrix of air combat possibilities. It was not the first time that a combatant holding on for dear life escaped death's clutches while the beast ready to pounce suffered an ignominious demise.

Afterwards Harry and his fellow 301st pilots speculated that the enemy fighter had inadvertently stalled and snap-rolled in the high-stress, low-to-the-ground maneuvering. Perhaps the unlucky pilot became fixated on Harry's Mustang and failed to pull up over the undulating terrain as the dogfighting planes skimmed fast and low. Then, too, it was possible that with banking at exaggerated angles in unusually steep turns an outboard section of the Fw 190's wing had nicked a tree.

Youth and lack of seasoning on the part of the Luftwaffe fighter pilot could also have been a factor. By this late in the war, the Germans had experienced horrendous attrition in the ranks of their pilots. Unlike the 332nd's pilots, who generally flew seventy combat missions and then rotated home, the German pilots operated under a regime summed up as "You fly until you die."

Harry was credited with three aerial victories for the day: for purposes of calculating the tally, it didn't matter exactly how the third enemy ship went down, just that it had crashed as a result of Harry's flying. Harry assiduously avoided asking for the third Focke-Wulf to be added to his score, but with fellow 301st pilot Carl Carey vouching for the downing (in the absence of gun camera footage), Harry's bosses chalked it up to his performance in the engagement.

When Percy Sutton, the squadron's intel officer (later to gain prominence in New York City as the Manhattan borough president), debriefed Harry after the mission, he recognized that what Harry had done would qualify for the Distinguished Flying Cross and put in the recommendation.

The public relations value of Harry's three kills in a day was recognized by the higher-ups at group and command headquarters. The next day Harry was posed in the cockpit of *Little Coquette* with three fingers raised, signifying his air-to-air victories. Behind him, standing on the P-51's wing, was his trusted crew chief Jim Shipley.

Photos and press releases went out to the black press in hopes of favorable coverage that might give the war effort a shot in the arm. The *New York Amsterdam News* ran a laudatory article under the

Recognizing the public relations value of Harry's downing of three long-nosed Focke-Wulf Fw 190s in a single day (April 1, 1945), the Army Air Forces posed him in his P-51D *Little Coquette* the next day holding up three fingers to signify his victories. Looking on is Harry's loyal crew chief Jim Shipley. *U.S. Air Force via Harry Stewart Jr.*

headline "Corona Flyer Shoots Down Three Planes." The newspaper described the air battle as a "wild and vicious dogfight" and quoted Harry's abbreviated description of the action. "'It was a heck of a fight. It seemed as if Jerry was all over the sky that day.'" The "modest young flyer," as the article called Harry, said "'I guess I was just lucky.'"

Nine other victories were credited to the 301st in the same melee. But the day's triumphs did not come without a price. One of Harry's squadron mates, William P. Armstrong, was killed during the intense air battle and a second, James H. Fischer, bailed out but survived. A third, Walter P. Manning, was shot down after scoring a kill, but what happened next would remain a mystery for decades.

301st Fighter Squadron pilots at Ramitelli in April 1945. Their somber expressions reflect the toll of war. The squadron had recently suffered the loss of William P. Armstrong, and the fate of Walter P. Manning was unknown at the time. Standing, left to right, Robert J. Friend (Harry's future brother-in-law), Walter M. "Mo" Downs (the new squadron commander), Samuel L. Washington, and Harry. In the foreground, Harold M. Morris. *Harry Stewart Jr.*

It wasn't until more than seventy years later that Harry learned Walter Manning's fate. Manning survived the disabling of his plane by parachuting to a safe landing at Kematen. But enraged civilians who had witnessed the aerial combat and resented the Allied bombings surrounded Manning, some wanting to shoot him on the spot. Two Wehrmacht officers showed up on the scene, and an argument broke out on whether to kill the American pilot then and there, or hold him as a prisoner of war.

Before the issue was settled, German airmen from the Linz-Horsching Air Base arrived and took Manning back to the base in their custody. But the public anger grew as word of Manning's capture spread. The Nazi propaganda machine had ginned up racial hatred against blacks, whom Hitler's *Mein Kampf* included among what it called inferior races. The Ku Klux Klan existed in America for a reason, the Nazi hatemongers said.

As researchers Georg Hoffmann and Nicole-Melanie Goll would eventually discover, Lieutenant Manning was released to a couple of German air officers at about 3:00 a.m. on April 4. He was then tied up and dragged outside the base, where he was roughed up by members of a local vigilante group known as Werewolf. Reveling in their orgy of violence, the gang of haters strung Manning up the nearest telegraph pole, where he hanged by the neck until dead.

To avoid repercussions the lynch mob buried Manning's body under trees on the grounds of the base. But the grave was shallow, and the body was discovered by U.S. authorities soon after the war. There was not enough evidence to bring charges against anyone, and the lynching was forgotten for many decades, lost among the countless atrocities in one of history's darkest hours. Manning's remains were reburied at the Lorraine American Cemetery in St. Avold, France.

But Hoffmann and Goll's new research prompted Austrian officials to face up to the past injustice. On April 3, 2018, the Austrian Ministry of Defense dedicated a memorial to Lieutenant Manning on the grounds of the base where his body had been buried in an attempt to cover up the war crime. Senior Austrian and American military leaders, including the commanders of the Austrian Air Force and land forces as well as the deputy commanding general of the U.S. Army Europe, were present for the dedication.

Also present was Harry, the sole surviving pilot from that aerial confrontation seventy-three years before. When the memorial plaque was unveiled in the main courtyard of the base, Harry approached it solemnly, but with a sense of relief at the closure that the recognition of his friend brought. Memories of his friend of long ago unwound in his mind—swimming together in a lifeguard-training class at Tuskegee, watching Walter and his fiancée Dicey Thomas dance at the cadet soiree, sharing rations, flying on each other's wing, and giving each other a thumbs-up as if tomorrow would always come. Flanked by the Austrian military commanders, Harry came to attention and, facing the plaque that features a likeness of Lieutenant Manning, he saluted his fallen comrade. A wreath was laid, and taps was played. Then a flyover paid tribute.

■　■　■

In general orders issued May 29, 1945, Fifteenth Air Force headquarters listed Harry and nineteen other officers from various fighter groups and one bomber group in connection with the award of the Distinguished Flying Cross. The general orders covered the officers' individual actions spanning a nine-month period, including the April 1 dogfights. The citation read, in part:

> [T]hese men have gallantly engaged, fought and defeated
> the enemy without regard for their own personal safety and
> against great odds. Their conspicuous and extraordinary
> achievements throughout these many missions against the
> enemy have been of inestimable value to successful combat
> operations and have reflected great credit upon themselves
> and the Armed Forces of the United States of America.

It was high praise from a service that a few years earlier had come unnervingly close to ending Harry's career before he had even earned his wings.

Harry's logbook entry on the day of the mission is perhaps the most authentic and eloquent statement of the events and emotions the young pilot experienced in the ferocious clash: "3 Fw 190s Long Nose shot down over Wels Airdrome, between 20–30 Fw's + Me's. Two of us got shot down, Manning & Armstrong. I was most scared. They lost 12. A terrific battle. Thank God, I'm alive."

■ ■ ■

Harry's air-to-air victories brought his flying skill to the attention of the 332nd's executive officer, whose duties included scheduling the pilots who would fly the group commander's wing. Harry was tapped for that honor several times before war's end. His impression of Colonel Davis had been shaped in their first encounter, back when he first reported to Ramitelli in January 1945. Harry readily remembers that moment, for he was "awestruck, intimidated."

At the 332nd's headquarters, Colonel Davis never let up his imposing military bearing. Ramrod straight, he projected his ethos, the military ethos, even before you heard him utter a word. He looked and sounded like exactly what he was: the archetype of a curt, no-nonsense officer committed to the service above all else, a believer in formality and protocol, an unforgiving disciplinarian who led by example, from the front. Like all good air commanders, he often flew on combat missions.

And in the air Colonel Davis was the same man—which wasn't necessarily for the better. Harry did not like flying as his commander's wingman. Asked why not, he answered that Colonel Davis was "too by the book." Harry explained further, "Davis flew rigid, like a West Pointer." Rather than swiveling his head, for example—a precautionary technique for self-preservation common among fighter pilots—Davis tended to look straight ahead.

Be that as it may, Colonel Davis was aggressive, a true warrior, when encountering Luftwaffe fighters. On June 9, 1944, the bomber formation his group was escorting through German airspace found itself swarmed by more than a hundred interceptors. Davis led a flight against a large contingent of those interceptors and dispersed it, thereby saving vulnerable bombers. Ten months later, on April 15, 1945, he led his group on a strafing mission in which thirty-five locomotives and many other units of German rolling stock were destroyed despite withering enemy fire. For these victories Davis received the Distinguished Flying Cross and the Silver Star, respectively.

Shortly after V-E Day, Colonel Davis's superior at Fifteenth Air Force, Brigadier General Dean Strother, was moved to say that Colonel Davis "is a fine soldier and has done wonders with the 332nd. I am positive that no other man in our Air Corps could have handled this job in the manner he has." The praise from his frontline commander at the end of the European air war was a sharp contrast with the hostile commentary that had been directed at him and his fellow black flyers when they had initially entered combat.

A review of operational statistics by Daniel L. Haulman of the Air Force Historical Research Agency has revealed that while the Red Tails did not score as many aerial victories as the six other fighter groups of Fifteenth Air Force, they lost only twenty-seven bombers to enemy interceptors while providing air cover. This compared to the average loss of forty-six bombers for the other fighter groups. The Tuskegee Airmen had laid down an enduring mark.

When Colonel Davis bade his men farewell in a letter from the group's headquarters, he quoted Strother: "The 332nd has been a credit to itself and to the Army Air Forces." In concluding, Davis wrote, "All of us who have been connected with the 332nd know this to be a fact. I am proud to have been associated with you.... I wish all of you Godspeed, and may all of us carry on in the future as nobly as we have in the past."

Harry's last flight before returning stateside occurred on August 31, 1945. He was ordered to deliver *Little Coquette* to Foggia, where he had picked it up as a factory-fresh product only five months earlier. At Foggia he rolled out on landing and, following the hand signals of a lineman, parked the fighter on a dirt section of the airfield.

A man came over and said that he would handle things from that point. Then, to Harry's astonishment, the man raised a blowtorch and set its flame to the P-51's tail. As Harry stood and watched in disbelief, his beloved airplane, the machine that had given everything the specs had promised and then a little more, was dismembered, the severed tail falling off the fuselage.

Harry's heart sank. Years later, recalling the episode, he shook his head. Almost sobbing as he plucked the memory from the rich tapestry of his distant past, he said, "It was an injustice. Why did they have to do it?" After a pause, in a voice that tapered off with sadness more than anger, he added, "It was such a beautiful airplane...."

The Tuskegee Airmen had done their job and done it well. It was time to go home. Setting foot back on American soil should have been a jubilant moment, but for too many of the combat-hardened flyers the experience was an unforgettable nightmare.

Harry's friend Alexander Jefferson, who had been liberated from Stalag Luft VIIA near the Dachau concentration camp, steamed into New York Harbor on June 7 aboard the USS *Lejeune*. With his spirits soaring as the Statue of Liberty came into view, everything seemed to be picture-perfect. But then, as Jefferson described in his memoir, upon disembarking, "a short, smug, white buck private shouted, 'Whites to the right, niggers to the left.'"

The experience abroad had been transformative for the Tuskegee Airmen. They had risked their lives, and some of them had made the ultimate sacrifice, to save the lives of white bomber crews. Harry and the men of the 332nd had every reason to believe they would be greeted as heroes, like their white counterparts. But America's population as a whole was transforming at a much slower pace than the American military, leaving the returning black servicemen to face a still unfriendly and unappreciative society—much as had the returning black troops of World War I.

In December 1945, Harry would be back at Tuskegee Army Airfield as a decorated air combat veteran and flight instructor. There he saw Anita Harris again. She worked in one of the offices and had been waiting for the love of her life, Frank Wright, to return so they could get married. But nine months earlier, in late March, shortly before the European war ended, Frank had died when his fighter went down in pursuit of an enemy plane near Landshut, Germany.

The happy girl with the bright smile Harry remembered from the day he got his wings was now overcome with grief. Heartbroken himself, Harry looked with sadness into Anita's eyes. He saw only sadness reflected back. There was nothing for either to say.

Harry's salvation was in the flying and the camaraderie of the men with whom he had served on the frontlines of the air war. He and his

Harry, a newly-designated flight instructor immediately after the war, in the front seat of an advanced trainer leading a three-ship formation over Tuskegee Army Airfield, 1946. *U.S. Air Force via Harry Stewart Jr.*

comrades-in-arms, his fellow Tuskegee Airmen, did not yet know how profound a contribution they had made in changing the country for the better; that would not become apparent until much later. For now, Harry looked to where he could be free—up to the sky.

Chapter Ten

AT THE MERCY OF THE WINDS OF FATE

Here the essential seems to have been merely a smile.
—Antoine de Saint-Exupery

The years immediately after the war saw big changes in Harry's life—both personally and professionally. On January 21, 1947, at the Church of the Master in Harlem, he married Delphine Friend, the twenty-year-old sister of a squadron mate. The young lady, a shy New Yorker, was notable for her wholesome manner and simple elegance. From the moment Harry's flying buddy Bob Friend brought Harry home to Harlem on leave upon their return to the States after the war, Harry was head over heels for Delphine. Their marriage was the

Harry and Delphine on their wedding day, January 31, 1947, at the Church of the Master in Harlem. The joyous union lasted nearly seven decades! *Harry Stewart Jr.*

consummation of a whirlwind courtship. Delphine would be Harry's loving and devoted partner for the next sixty-eight years.

On September 18 of the same year, with the Truman administration's postwar reorganization of the military, the War Department was transformed into the Defense Department and the Air Force became an independent service. What didn't change was the camaraderie Harry enjoyed with his fellow pilots and the thrill-a-minute flying in captivating fighters. Also not changing—and it wouldn't for nearly the next two years—was the Air Force's continuing to operate under the rubric of segregation.

The initial reception the Tuskegee Airmen received in the community where they were stationed sadly manifested the prejudice that they had experienced all too often during the war. The 332nd Fighter Group settled in at Lockbourne Air Force Base outside of Columbus, Ohio. Colonel Davis considered this a milestone because it represented the first time blacks had administered an air base in the continental United States without the immediate supervision of white officers. In fact, the mostly white civilian workers at the base had to adjust to the new command structure, and after a break-in period they got along just fine: Davis would praise their commitment, writing that "they joined us in a spirit of mission accomplishment."

But in an echo of the howls of protest that had greeted the first black airfields around Tuskegee, a central Ohio newspaper editorialized against locating the all-black unit at the base, stating that "this is still a white man's country." The group's pilots were accustomed to such hostility and though they did not like it, they went about their flying as they always did—with diligence and eagerness, in case the order came to spring into action. Top elected officials from the state and city as well as leading citizens from the community toured the base and "ultimately came to view Lockbourne as their base . . . More slowly, Lockbourne became understood as a major asset in the minds of all Columbus' residents."

Lockbourne made a mark in other ways too. The group hosted track and field events that featured Staff Sergeant Mal Whitfield, a 1948 Olympic Gold medalist assigned to the 100th Fighter Squadron. A special services officer in the group—who had to overcome initial skepticism on Davis's part—organized a traveling entertainment ensemble under the name Operation Enjoyment, subsequently called Operation Happiness. The performances were a hit at Air Force installations around the globe and featured Daniel "Chappie" James Jr., later to become the first four-star African American general in the U.S. military.

The group was part of Tactical Air Command (TAC), and its mission was focused largely on protecting ground forces through close air support. TAC's commander, General Elwood R. "Pete" Quesada, was a notable proponent of air-land cooperation who had developed successful air-to-ground doctrine during World War II. The 332nd worked to keep up its proficiency in peacetime through training missions that involved short stints at other bases around the country.

On March 20, 1948, Harry and four of his colleagues were at Greenville Air Force Base in South Carolina and anxious to get back to Lockbourne. The flight of five had been on an armed reconnaissance training mission in coordination with Army ground forces that was supposed to be a one-day exercise, but maintenance issues and foul weather had delayed them. Having completed the mission two days earlier, they were ready to go home.

The morning's weather forecast called for some thunderstorms en route, with multiple layers of clouds. Facing these less than ideal conditions, the flight leader, First Lieutenant Charles V. Brantley, filed an instrument flight plan with a cruising altitude of eighteen thousand feet, where he hoped the formation could skirt the worst of the weather and stay in clear skies to preserve the formation's integrity. In any case, the pilots were qualified on instruments and had flown through inclement weather before. They considered the coming flight as nothing out of the ordinary, just a routine hop. But the "milk run" would prove to be one of the most terrifying flights of Harry's Air Force career.

Shortly after takeoff, he and his fellow pilots joined up in a five-ship V formation with the flight leader up front and Harry trailing to starboard. In a few minutes the pilots reached the planned altitude, where they seemed to find their sweet spot between cloud decks. They trekked on a northwest plot.

■ ■ ■

They were flying late-model World War II holdovers, Republic P-47N fighters. The "N" model was the final production variant of the famed Thunderbolt, which in the earlier "D" configuration had distinguished itself in the war's European theater as both an effective dogfighter and a tough ground-attack platform. The aircraft had an unusual genesis. Its seedling was the brainchild of Alexander de Seversky, a Russian engineer and naval fighter-bomber pilot in World War I who lost a leg on his first combat mission but reentered the fray with an artificial limb, ending his service as a thirteen-victory ace.

Tsar Nicholas II personally awarded de Seversky Russia's highest military decoration. In 1917, when the Bolshevik Revolution toppled the Romanovs, the heroic pilot fled his homeland. He immigrated to the United States, where his remarkable flying record and his charisma, charm, inventive genius, and entrepreneurialism combined to open up new opportunities.

In his adopted country, de Seversky's aeronautical innovations included an inflight refueling system and a complex mechanical bomb-sight to improve bombing accuracy. He became a much sought-after dinner party guest on the New York social circuit, where he mingled with prominent figures. His new circle of friends included Brigadier General William Mitchell, the doyen of American air power.

In the mid-1930s the enterprising émigré's conceptualization of a modern fighter ripened into the P-35, a proposed replacement for the Air Corps' antiquated P-26 Peashooter. De Seversky's low-wing monoplane featured a big-barreled profile with enclosed cockpit and retractable landing gear. In one of its iterations, the fighter gained a measure of fame as Jacqueline Cochran's winning mount in the 1938 cross-country Bendix Trophy Race. But government-mandated refinements and production delays hobbled the promising fighter program, which caused Seversky Aircraft Company to incur heavy losses and sink perilously into debt.

By the end of the 1930s, disgruntled investors ousted the founder from his Farmingdale, New York, start-up, which was soon renamed Republic Aviation Corporation. Disappointed but no less ambitious, de Seversky channeled his expertise into a new life as an outspoken advocate for air power in the mold of his friend General Mitchell. De Seversky authored the prophetic *Victory Through Air Power*, published in 1942, and was featured in a wartime Walt Disney film advancing his theory of aerial bombardment.

Alexander Kartveli, a fellow Russian émigré who had served as de Seversky's vice president of engineering, stayed with the reorganized firm, applying his considerable talents to improve the P-35's basic form. Under his guidance the fighter evolved further into the P-43 Lancer, which proved to be only a transitional design. Additional enhancements were part of the ongoing improvement effort, which resulted in the illustrious P-47 Thunderbolt.

Harry, who had cut his teeth on the P-47D/G during pre-deploy
ment fighter lead-in training at Walterboro in the fall of 1944, considered the "N" model to be the best fighter he had ever flown—even
surpassing the highly regarded P-51 Mustang. Although the P-47N
did not match the Mustang's roll-rate, it had greater endurance
because it had been designed for ultra-long-range bomber escort missions over Pacific waters. Indeed, the wings had been elongated and
strengthened to accommodate extra fuel.

The "N" model was powered by an uprated Pratt & Whitney
R-2800 Double Wasp engine. The cockpit was spacious and ergo-
nomic by the standards of the day. To top things off, the last of the
Thunderbolt breed had an autopilot, an augmentation that was notable for easing pilot workload on long missions. Taken together, these
elements produced a regal effect for the pilot.

The type held great promise in its planned role. But once the
P-47N reached Pacific squadrons in 1945 it saw minimal action
escorting B-29 Superfortresses. The war against Japan ended abruptly
with the dropping of atomic bombs on Hiroshima and Nagasaki in
early August. In the immediate postwar years, the Air Force kept
some of the planes in active units as a bridge to the next generation
of fighters, which were practically all jets.

About forty-five minutes into the flight, heavy clouds loomed
straight ahead, causing the formation to push nose down and reestablish level flight at twelve thousand feet, where there appeared to
be a clearing. But it turned out that the bright light in the distance
below was a reflection of sunlight off an array of clouds. Flight lead
had shifted to Captain Carol S. Woods, who directed the formation
to enter a gradual ascending 180-degree turn to the left, in search of
a piece of open sky.

But it was like looking for a vineyard in the desert. Visibility
rapidly dissipated until the formation was swallowed completely by

clouds. Harry's inability to see even his next closest wingman made formation flying untenable. Concerned he might collide with another fighter, Harry veered sharply to the right. Suddenly, as if living out an intensifying nightmare, his Thunderbolt's engine began to sputter. It was the kind of crisis that can cause a pilot to panic—especially since, based on navigational calculations, Harry's plane was at that moment over the jagged highlands of eastern Kentucky.

On the outbound flight to Greenville two days earlier, the plane's fuel transfer system had malfunctioned, necessitating the replacement of the fuel transfer switch. But the engine on a plane like the Thunderbolt wasn't supposed to cut out. Unofficially called the "Jug"— short for "juggernaut"—the P-47N was seen as a rugged mud fighter, the antithesis of the kind of plagued aircraft that pilots scornfully referred to as a "widow maker" or a "flying coffin."

During World War II, the P-47 usually brought its pilots back from strafing missions—even when the engine had a whole cylinder completely blown off by antiaircraft fire. Depending on dates of deployment, some of the Tuskegee Airmen had flown the "D" model in combat and could attest to its sturdiness and durability in the most violent missions. Harry, having arrived in-theater after P-51s had replaced the 332nd's P-47s, had heard the old hands heap praise on the planes. Thunderbolts, they said, had delivered them in circumstances that would have been catastrophic in any other plane.

Following the war, when the 332nd switched back to the P-47— albeit the newer "N" model—Harry took solace in the stories he remembered about how Thunderbolts had brought his friends back from the dead. Shot up, mangled ships would be nursed back to base only to have the mechanics swarm around them and marvel at their indestructibility. They counted the bullet holes in the fuselages and gaped at the disfigured engines, shaking their heads in wonderment that such severely ravaged equipment could fly at all, let alone return their occupants to base unscathed.

Pratt & Whitney produced more than 125,000 of the powerful twin-row, 18-cylinder R-2800 engines in one form or another for a variety of warplanes and civil airliners. It was precisely because these radial engines were so reliable that they were used in such enormous quantity. De Seversky had insisted from the outset on an air-cooled engine, Pratt & Whitney's 1,050-horsepower R-1830, for his P-35.

It could be argued that the radial's blunt frontal cross-section precluded the dramatic streamlining seen in the competing fighter designs under consideration by the Army Air Corps in the 1930s. But in the view of de Seversky and his lead engineer Kartveli, the power of the radial engine more than compensated for its higher drag. More important, the radial engine's air cooling offered unmatched simplicity and reliability—obviating the vulnerability inherent in the liquid-cooled alternative. With a radiator system, a single bullet hole is all it takes to create a leak that can cause the whole engine to seize up and stop.

Unlike the Thunderbolt, the Army's other main wartime fighters—the Mustang, Lightning, and Warhawk—were powered by liquid-cooled engines. The service had made the conscious decision to prioritize streamlining over system simplicity. The Navy, whose planes would have to fly over water for extended durations, took the diametrically opposite approach: all of its major wartime fighters—notably the Wildcat, Hellcat, and Corsair—had air-cooled radial engines. Not coincidentally, the latter two fighter planes were powered by the R-2800, just like the Thunderbolt.

Despite Harry's confidence in the aircraft and its power plant, things quickly went from bad to worse. The moment dreaded by single-engine pilots, the kind that induces a sickening feeling in the pit of the stomach, occurred when the Pratt's thousands of finely-crafted moving parts stopped firing altogether. The heart-palpitating standstill precipitated an eerie silence.

Compounding the loss of power, the gyroscopic instruments began to fail. Still in the clouds and without a reference to the horizon, Harry was literally flying blind. Soon the plane stalled and fell off into uncontrolled flight like a whale flailing in a riptide, having lost its sense of balance.

But Harry had known crisis in the cockpit before. He drew on his wartime experience, knowing that the key to making it out alive was keeping cool. The first order of business, as training manuals directed and as Harry knew firsthand, was "flying the airplane." Ensconced in a powerless, out-of-control plane and trapped in clouds without working gyros, Harry tried unavailingly to regain customary flight attitude using the plane's needle-and-ball in conjunction with its airspeed indicator. It was as if the plane had gone rogue and wouldn't allow the pilot to wrestle it back to normalcy.

As Harry's mind raced through memorized emergency procedures, he attempted to revive the 2,000 horses under the cowling. There was a sequence to make that happen, and he would gladly settle for a fraction of the rated power output: beggars can't be choosers. His inability to reestablish equilibrium or any sense of controlled flight made the challenge of a midair engine restart that much more difficult.

Harry kept trying, but no matter what he did in his desperation to restore his plane's muscle, the engine simply wouldn't crank over. No combination of frantic adjustments to the engine quadrant levers could get the fighter's slumberous horses to wake up. The instruments that tell you your engine has a heartbeat—the tachometer, the manifold pressure gauge, the oil pressure readout—remained lifeless, their needles limp.

Lacking its brawn, Harry's hefty platform was like a sack of potatoes or—as pilots describe a plane without power—a lead balloon. In a cruel instant Harry had gone from the embodiment of the bold fighter pilot to a beleaguered waif struggling just to make it out alive.

Without engine thrust, he could attempt to sail down glider-like on the stricken fighter's wings and pancake the inanimate husk onto a flat stretch of land in a valley between foothills. If he could ride the plane all the way to a wheels-up belly flop, he wouldn't have to fling himself into the uncertainty of the dark, roiling sky. And he could also spare an expensive piece of government equipment, a feat certain to be much appreciated by the honchos back at Ninth Air Force headquarters.

But with neither power nor control Harry was slipping further into the clouds during his forced descent, and they were thick, turbulent, and spewing heavy precipitation. As he struggled furiously with his unresponsive ship, trying in vain to right it, he fell ever deeper into the abyss. The opacity seemed bottomless, but Harry knew that the sky was not. One instrument on the panel kept working, revealing a worsening predicament. The altimeter continued to unwind: Harry's plane was losing altitude at a frightening pace. Torrents of rain pelted the big bubble canopy in a drumbeat that escalated the tension and sense of urgency. Totally consumed, he did not have the precious time to make a radio call to alert the others in the formation of his plight— not that they could do anything anyway except give search crews on the ground a general idea of where to look for the smashup.

Now down to six thousand feet, Harry reckoned it was too risky to cling to some vague hope that the aircraft-turned-deadweight would redeem itself. Charts showed elevated terrain below and, for all he knew, the blanket of "pudding" he was falling through might retain its gelatinous consistency all the way to the ground. And even if by some fluke he popped out of the cloudbank's underside with the ability to take back control of his roguish fighter while he was still on the way down, there was no way of knowing whether a valley suitable for landing would even be within coasting distance. It was time to jump!

As he jettisoned the canopy, the drenching downpour flooded the cockpit and the winds howled tauntingly. It was a contest not of man against man, like his dogfights with enemy combatants, but a contest of a higher order: here a mere mortal faced the imposing forces of nature. With adrenaline pumping at the max, Harry unstrapped. He tried to fling himself into the unforgiving air, prepared to yank on his parachute's D-ring the moment he cleared his ungovernable ten-ton mechanical shell—but his left shoe got stuck in the cockpit's framework.

Harry kept tugging until his foot slid free from the shoe. In a heartbeat the wind sucked him from the cockpit. Everything was out of kilter, upside-down, contrary to normal orientation, and happening so fast. Harry felt a pulverizing thump against a lower extremity and then a jolt surge through his whole body. The slip-stream had caught him like a piece of driftwood in a wild vortex and slammed his left leg against the doomed plane's fin, fracturing the bone in two places.

The wallop dazed him. "When I came to, I was in the clouds and I could hear flapping," he would say, describing how he reflexively pulled the D-ring and heard the parachute's fabric unfurling in the wind. "I thought it was the angels and I said 'I'm ready.'"

Looking down, he noticed what appeared to be a red sock on his left foot and a brown sock on his right, in what would have been an uncharacteristic mix-up for a fastidious fighter pilot like himself. Suspended in his harness, Harry was temporarily bemused, wondering what other surprises were in store for him on this ill-starred day. But his stupefaction soon ended when he observed the left sock dripping blobs of red; he realized it was blood seeping from where his leg had been hit.

He eventually broke out of the clouds with only an estimated seven to eight hundred feet left to go until reaching the dim and moistened ground. The hilly contour of the land and the low cloud ceiling reinforced Harry's belief that he had opted to do the right thing—though he hated to lose an otherwise perfectly good fighter.

Training for pilots of Harry's generation did not include a parachute jump, the theory being that if the occasion ever arose the pilot's survival instincts would kick in and save him. Instruction involved little more than some verbal tips in a show-and-tell: keep your feet together, don't try to land standing up, fall to one side.

Harry tugged on his risers in an effort to pivot away from the craggy terrain punctuated with thickets that was directly beneath him, in hopes of landing in a better spot. But he had never done this before, and the more he exerted himself, the more his chute deflated. Rather than risk undoing the fully-deployed dome that was his salvation, he let go, allowing the wind to blow him in whatever direction it decreed. Harry's mindset had changed: now, with his arms folded across his chest as a safety measure, he wasn't fighting nature but flowing with it.

He drifted precariously into a stand of pine trees and, closing his eyes, raised his arms to cover his face. His chute got snarled in the high boughs of a dead tree, leaving him dangling a couple feet off the ground. Luckily, the tree's withered branches gave way, so that he did not sustain so much as a scratch in his final plunge to earth, alongside the rotted bark. Quick-release snaps permitted an easy drop to the surface, but the pain in his left leg was nearly paralyzing.

Because the spring shower continued unabated, he staggered to the underside of a rocky escarpment which provided shelter. Harry began to assess the injury on his left leg. There was a deep laceration above the ankle and a less serious cut about five inches long higher up on his leg. He improvised a tourniquet with his belt to stanch the bleeding and protected the wounds by tying his aviator's silk scarf over the affected area.

Meanwhile the vacated Thunderbolt streaked across the cloud-laden sky in a shallow arc. It hurtled like an out-of-control missile over a family's private burial ground and unceremoniously rammed into the ground, exploding upon impact in sight of where Harry had come to rest. The plane's .50-caliber machine gun rounds, which festooned the ammo belts within the wings, popped like firecrackers in the ensuing inferno. It was a good thing that the five-hundred-pound bombs and napalm canisters used in the training flights out of Greenville had not been loaded for Harry's flight that day.

Interestingly, before the government could excavate the crash site, local residents scavenged the charred wreckage, picking it clean for souvenirs. The main chunks were reportedly sold to a local scrapyard for sixty dollars.

The other Thunderbolt pilots flew on through the dense clouds, unaware that one fifth of their formation had been lost. It was not until they reached Lockbourne that it became apparent Harry had gone missing. Soon efforts to pinpoint Harry's whereabouts got underway.

Meanwhile, Harry's left leg was an excruciating bloody mess, and of course his right leg had been compromised years earlier in his bout with polio. Hurting and stranded in a remote location, Harry worried that his impairments might prevent him from ever moving beyond his immediate surroundings and that, if he wasn't found, his untreated wounds would turn gangrenous. And if he was found, how would the inhabitants of this far-off backwater react to an uninvited black man who had literally dropped into their insular environs?

This was unvarnished Appalachia, the Daniels Creek area of Johnson County near the communities of Odds, Van Lear, and Butcher Hollow. The latter was destined to become famous as "Butcher Holler" in a country ballad sung by an as yet undiscovered local songstress, a coal miner's daughter named Loretta Lynn. Coun try music related the hardships of rural life and lauded the values of close-knit families, but Tuskegee Airmen of the 477th Bombardment Group had been stationed at Godman Army Airfield about thirty miles southwest of Louisville during the latter part of the war, and their reception had not exactly been hospitable. Fairly or not, border state "hillbillies" were not considered high up on the list of racially tolerant citizens.

Harry didn't know it at the time of his awkward ingress into the rough-hewn landscape of alternating hillocks and canyons, but a nine-year-old girl named Callie Daniel, sitting in her family's cabin, had observed the parachute glide into the hillside pines like a "big white eagle." Her dad Lafe and brother Joshua set out across the scabrous countryside with a mule to find the flyer gone astray. It did not take them long.

In the area bracketed by his alert daughter, Lafe repeatedly shouted an owlish "Halloooo!" hoping to make contact. Hearing the call, Harry responded in kind. As Harry described the encounter to *Aviation History* contributing editor Stephan Wilkinson in 2012, the parties took in a deep breath when they first laid eyes on each other.

Those initial glances turned into disbelieving stares. Lafe was shocked to see a black man bedecked in an Air Force flight suit; Joshua had never seen a black man before. Harry, for his part, didn't know quite what to make of the two mountain-dwellers. Momentarily each side sized up the other. To Harry's eternal relief, Lafe and Joshua gently assisted him in mounting the mule they had brought along just in case.

The rain had stopped by the time they got to the Daniels' cabin. Lafe's wife Mary was doing laundry with a washboard in her front yard. As soon as she glimpsed Harry, she dropped the clothes and rushed inside, emerging a moment later with a clean bed sheet, which she ripped into pieces for bandages to replace the tourniquet Harry had improvised from his belt. The only color relevant to her was the red oozing out of the deep gash in Harry's leg, which she cleaned thoroughly before covering the wound with her homemade dressings.

Harry was helped into the cabin, where he sat to relieve the pressure on his leg. But the pain did not dissipate. Wanting mightily to alleviate his guest's suffering, Lafe resorted to the most potent remedy he could think to employ: he handed Harry a glass whose contents looked like water. But the aroma left little doubt that it was a home brew of natural spirits—moonshine.

At first Harry was reluctant to swallow, because this was the run-up to Easter and he was observing Lent in deference to the teachings of his Episcopal faith. A stern expression animated Lafe's face, a sign of his insistence that his guest take the "medicine." Harry shuddered to think what might happen to the cordiality that had prevailed so far in the hill country of eastern Kentucky if he didn't comply.

Holding his breath, he chugged back the whole drink in a giant gulp. When he was asked about it later, he said that the analgesic effect was "unbeatable!" Harry added that no medicinal treatment could have done any better in taking him out of his misery.

Harry was transported closer to town by horseback. On the way, he was taken to the home of McKinley Collins, who cleaned the wounds again and put new dressings on them. Meantime the Collinses' fourteen-year-old daughter Lois took Harry's scarf to the creek to wash the blood out. Before she could return with it, a truck came to take the injured guest into Van Lear.

The local Army recruiter, Sergeant Victor Minich, was advised of the situation. He accompanied Harry to the nearby Paintsville Clinic. Eyeing the wounds, the doctor injected Harry with a dose of morphine. Years later Harry would joke that the combination of

Lafe's do-it-yourself blend and the narcotic gave him a "high" unlike anything he ever had before or since.

While the downed flyer was resting in an exam room, officials from the area—including a mayor, police chief, and sheriff—filed in to meet the surprise visitor and to extend their greetings. And three of the townspeople who had scavenged the crash site brought Harry his missing shoe. Harry's unorthodox entrance into the sleepy hinterland had made him a local celebrity, notwithstanding the dissimilarity between him and his hosts.

It was a good thing the whole incident turned out so well, considering that in the hours before the bailout and rescue were understood, a cockamamie rumor had spread throughout the area that a renegade black pilot intent on instigating an insurrection had hijacked a bomber and been stopped only when interceptor jets shot it from the sky. Harry spent a restful night in the clinic. The next morning an Air Force staff car from Lockbourne arrived to take him back to base.

Soon after he got to his quarters, Harry sent a letter of thanks to his rescuers. But the letter, addressed to Odds, was returned unopened. The post office in that town had closed a few years earlier, and no forwarding address was provided.

The cause of the Thunderbolt's engine failure was never conclusively determined. A defective part, improper maintenance, fuel blockage, or any number of other possibilities could have been the culprit. The engine's inflight stoppage served as a reminder that any mechanical device is subject to a failure rate of some proportion, for nothing that bears the human imprint is infallible.

Over time, the unlikely episode, in its real and imagined versions, wended its way into the fabric of local folklore. Harry's short stay in Van Lear had a bigger impact on the area than he could have imagined. Eventually, stories that had been handed down through word of mouth for more than half a century made Danny Blevins, president

In 2005, Danny K. Blevins, president of the Van Lear Historical Society, invited Harry back to the town in rural Kentucky whose citizens had rescued him when he bailed out fifty-seven years earlier. Here, Blevins and his seven-year-old son Daniel Trevor escort Harry during the twentieth annual Van Lear Town Celebration parade, August 6, 2005. Harry served as grand marshal of the parade on what the county proclaimed as "Harry T. Stewart Jr. Appreciation Day." *Harry Stewart Jr.*

of the local historical society, curious enough to research the bailout and the community's compassionate response. He recognized the experience as something the whole town could take pride in.

In 2005, Harry accepted an invitation from Blevins to come back and serve as the grand marshal of the twentieth annual Van Lear Town Celebration parade on August 6, a day the county proclaimed "Harry T. Stewart Jr. Appreciation Day." It would be Harry's chance to thank those still living who had helped him in his hour of crisis. His high-profile return prompted retellings of the story as it had actually happened, clarifying details for local audiences and bringing a long overdue end to lingering nonsense about a hijacked warplane.

Harry made an appearance at the Johnson County Alternative School, where he encouraged the students "to strive to achieve your goals." The message was well received. Harry's VIP treatment also included a private tour of Loretta Lynn's birthplace given by members of her family.

In the biggest surprise during Harry's visit to Van Lear in 2005, the girl who had cleaned the blood from his silk aviator's scarf, Lois Collins, now grown up, came to the festivities with a gift. She had kept the scarf as a memento of the exciting day when the injured Air Force pilot had entered her life. At last, the unwitting bestowal that she had safeguarded for most of her life could be returned, as she had intended more than a generation ago—before Harry was abruptly whisked away for further medical care.

Harry, who had presented the Daniel and Collins families with a glass-encased model of a P-47N as a token of his gratitude, welled up with tears. With a nod to the residents assembled to reminisce about what had happened on March 20, 1948, he wrapped his old scarf around his neck and then tied it ascot-style, as if once again he were going up in his fighter. In the emotion of the moment, it seemed his friends in Van Lear would have unreservedly followed him into the sky.

Harry felt flattered at every stage of his latter-day visit to this alien land, with its humble citizens into whose warm and friendly embrace the winds of fate had carried him fifty-seven years earlier. As a wayfarer in distress, he had experienced the helpfulness of strangers—as Chauncey Spencer and Dale White had on their flight to Washington in the previous decade, and as the crews of the 485th Bombardment Group had on their return from a mission during the war. By sheer happenstance, the itinerants had landed in pockets populated by Samaritans who assisted them at the most critical juncture in their journeys, making the difference between success or failure, relief or calamity.

Each case was a small miracle in which people brushed aside vile and divisive preconceptions and, without compensation or recognition, offered a hand to somebody in need, simply because it was the right thing to do. The experience of falling into a welcoming oasis where one might reasonably have expected antipathy reinforced Harry's faith in humanity—a faith he would need to draw upon in the years ahead. Meanwhile, his left leg healed, and his flying status resumed.

Chapter Eleven

THE BEST OF
THE BEST

Success is to be measured not so much by the
position one has reached in life
as by the obstacles which he has overcome.
—Booker T. Washington

On June 19, 1948, the Soviet Union began to shut down road, rail, and canal access to West Berlin in what would develop into a full-fledged blockade later in the month. By cutting off the sectors of the city controlled by the Western powers, the Soviets were hoping to starve those sectors into submission and force the Allies out. West Berlin's supplies of food and coal were estimated to be enough to last only thirty-six and forty-five days, respectively.

This was the first major crisis of the Cold War. Military action to address the provocation was ruled out as impractical. The United States, Britain, and France did not want to risk sparking another world war. At the same time, maintaining the Allied occupation was seen as essential to preserving the prestige of America and its partners.

So the Western powers agreed to resupply their sectors of the city through an enormous airlift. Because of West Berlin's time-critical needs, resources were mobilized quickly. The resupply flights began four days before the end of June. The frequency of flights was eventually ramped up to an incredible rate of one every thirty seconds, with a total of eight thousand tons of supplies delivered daily.

The Berlin Airlift, referred to as the Air Bridge by West Berliners, ran well into 1949. It ended up shattering Soviet designs on the whole of the German city. But it demonstrated the need to be ready should the rivalry between superpowers turn hot.

The U.S. Air Force took the Soviet threat seriously. With the airlift in full swing, the hard-charging, cigar-chomping Curtis LeMay took over as the head of Strategic Air Command. He immediately went about revitalizing the service's intercontinental bomber force to be prepared to devastate the nation's nemesis with a massive nuclear strike. War planners knew that nuclear war would be catastrophic for both sides—an understanding that would later be formalized as "mutually assured destruction," or MAD, the guiding principle behind a strategy of deterrence.

If rational minds prevailed, any war between the superpowers would be conventional—requiring highly skilled airmen capable of reliably shooting down enemy aircraft and putting conventional bombs on a wide range of ground targets. The Air Force was taking steps to prepare for this kind of a confrontation. Harry and fellow Lockbourne pilots would play a key role.

A first post–World War II, Air Force–wide fighter gunnery meet was scheduled at Las Vegas Air Force Base (later renamed Nellis Air Force Base) from May 2 through May 12, 1949. As the official program of events stated, "Lessons learned in tactical weapons competition will pay huge dividends for all of us should the need arise to engage another aggressor. We must develop these skills to survive in modern combat."

Air Force leaders recognized that it is not uncommon for fighting skills to atrophy between wars. The answer to the problem would be to test and improve those skills. Indeed, the program of events pointed to "a return to basics" as the most important aspect of the competition and the way "to achieve professional excellence."

With this first in a planned series of annual competitions, the Air Force was determined to up the game of every tactical fighter unit. The gunnery meet's participants would return to their home stations and "transmit to the rest of the tactical air forces" the "improved techniques and tactics."

The 1949 gunnery contests on the desert ranges sixty miles northwest of Las Vegas, in the area known as Frenchman Flat, validated the need for such exercises and proved to be a solid foundation for future competitions. Virtually all tactical fighter groups based in the continental United States were represented at the maiden event by their best pilots and maintenance crews. The meet was divided into two broad classes: jets and conventional (propeller-driven) aircraft. The contestants would be graded and ranked in five categories: dive-bombing, skip bombing, rocketry, panel gunnery, and aerial gunnery at both twelve and twenty thousand feet.

Selection was highly competitive. Colonel Davis decided to choose the team members that would represent the 332nd based on scores achieved at the last gunnery training mission, which had occurred at the auxiliary fields of Eglin Air Force Base in Florida's panhandle during the preceding three weeks. For the pilots of the 332nd, scoring in these training missions was taken very seriously; they knew the results would be scrutinized by their superiors, including Davis himself.

Harry well remembers arguments breaking out among his squadron mates in the aftermath of a day's gunnery practice over whose bullets had pierced a towed target sleeve. The tips of the .50-caliber bullets were dyed different colors to identify which pilot had hit the target, but sometimes the dye colors were not easily distinguishable—leading to the disputed interpretations.

A review of the rankings from the Eglin maneuvers showed that the three highest-scoring pilots were Captain Alva N. Temple of the 301st Fighter Squadron, who would serve as team leader due to his superior rank; First Lieutenant James H. Harvey III of the 99th Fighter Squadron; and First Lieutenant Harry T. Stewart Jr. of the 100th Fighter Squadron (having earlier been transferred from the 301st Fighter Squadron). The next in line, First Lieutenant Halbert L. Alexander of the 99th, was selected as an alternate. By a happy coincidence, all three of the 332nd's squadrons would be represented on the team.

But the team's enthusiasm about the upcoming meet was tempered by the fact that the U.S. armed forces had yet to implement President Truman's forward-leaning desegregation order of the year before. The meet was to be another case—indeed, the last time—when a contingent of Tuskegee Airmen would fly in a large exercise with mostly white pilots, but still under the old modality of segregation. Harry would call it "the Last Hurrah."

Just before the team departed Lockbourne for the Nevada air base, Davis gathered the four pilots who would be representing their fighter group at the gunnery meet. In a rare flash of humor, the steely commander sardonically stated, "I just want to say if you don't win, don't come back." After the nervous laughter died down, he added on a more serious note, "Gentlemen, you know we are all behind you, wishing you all the best."

With that energizing sendoff, the team's three primary pilots and one alternate climbed into their late-model Thunderbolts for the trip west. Reminiscing, Harry describes the experience as an adventure—not just the gunnery meet itself, but concomitant events, including the cross-country traverse to the competition's venue.

The outbound route included refueling stops at air bases in Oklahoma and New Mexico. The trip's final leg was a straight shot from

Albuquerque to Las Vegas. The four fighters flew in loose echelon formation across a mostly brilliant blue sky, as the scarred landscape of the high desert passed below.

Harry marveled at the sight of nature's scraggy carpet, interrupted by ridged peaks, the variations in elevation distinguishable by the tincture of the terrain, the highest blanketed in snow. Along the course line, the San Mateo Range burst above the surface in ginger and russet, a sign that the Continental Divide lay ahead. Later the Painted Desert, with its oatmeal complexion bordered by caramel-glazed plateaus, came into view.

Near the destination, a rise in the surface was noticeable to the northwest. Off the flight's starboard wings stood a mottled piece of ancient geological artifice with a peak topping out at over nine thousand feet. From a distance it was a mass of auburn accented by cinnamon-tinged ridges. The Kaibab Plateau was a defining feature, a checkpoint, on the tawny desert floor. The chart folded on Harry's lap showed the Grand Canyon wrapped around the mighty plateau's southern edge and extending westward in a squiggly serpentine form.

As Harry and his fellow pilots closed in on the landmark, mischievous thoughts quickly germinated; the daredevil in the team leader took over. Alva Temple angled straight for the mile-deep chasm and his teammates stayed with him, faithful to the bond between element lead and wingman. In twin two-ship tactical formations abreast of each other they held steady for the top of the canyon.

The pilots powered up their big-barreled ships to run like speedsters parallel to the rough-textured edge of the natural wonder. Man, machine, and nature blended together unrehearsed. The roar of the engines reverberated across the crusty landscape while the cascading rapids of the Colorado River continued to etch their ragged imprint into the canyon's steep sidewalls below.

The sensation of the storied canyon surging underneath was as high a rush as pilots can get in peacetime flying. To one side Harry saw tourists lined up at eye level behind overlook railings. They were waving to him and the other pilots in a surreal blur as they blew past at breakneck speed.

Describing his feelings about the unique flyby, Harry said, "It was a sight that will never return." For him the only flights comparable were his escort missions in the war, when cobalt skies were blazoned with countless strands of white contrails emanating from the prodigious heavy bomber formations.

This stunt en route to the gunnery meet contravened regulations. In fact, it was an offense punishable by grounding or possibly even court-martial. But the team members' delicate admixture of self-confidence and audacity was typical of the fighter pilot milieu. The flat-hatting, hotdogging—whatever you call it—was arguably, up to a point, an expression of the attitude that naturally animated those flyers who aimed to prove themselves the best shooters in the whole Air Force. Tuskegee group commander Benjamin Davis was a stiff disciplinarian, but he knew the qualities required of fighter pilots and left them enough latitude so as not to squelch the aggressor impulse in the best of them. He chose his team well.

This first postwar service–wide fighter competition, known as the Continental Air Gunnery Meet, pitted the best pilots and crews of twelve fighter groups from across the continent against each other. The meet subsequently evolved into two much-ballyhooed biennial events known as the Gunsmoke air-to-ground competition at the same sprawling base in Nevada and the William Tell air-to-air competition at Tyndall Air Force Base in Florida. Gunsmoke was discontinued after the 1995 competition, but it resumed at Nellis in 2018. As an outgrowth of Gunsmoke, a biennial competition expressly for A-10 Warthog close air support aircraft known as

Hawgsmoke started at a training range in Alpena, Michigan, in 2000.

Because of Las Vegas's proximity to the open desert, the locale was ideal not only for gunnery competition but also gunnery instruction. The dry climate, superb visibility, and vast stretches of barren land spreading out from the city's northern edge made air combat training activities common there in the years to come. These included the Vietnam-inspired Red Flag exercises to hone flight crews' skills through intense air-to-air maneuvering and ground

The 332nd Fighter Group's team on the flight line at Las Vegas Air Force Base (later Nellis Air Force Base) for the first postwar Air Force–wide gunnery meet, May 1949. Segregation was still in effect. Team members, from left to right: Captain Alva N. Temple, Harry, First Lieutenant James H. Harvey III, and the alternate First Lieutenant Halbert L. Alexander. *U.S. Air Force via Harry Stewart Jr.*

attack simulations. The Navy's well-known Topgun program at the Miramar Naval Air Station in southern California had started as a reaction to poor kill-loss ratios early in the Vietnam War, and it was eventually relocated to northern Nevada where it was combined with strike and sensor training to prepare carrier air wings for operational deployments.

Nellis became the headquarters of the Air Force Fighter Weapons School and the home of the Thunderbirds air demonstration squadron. Indeed, the base became known as the "Home of the Fighter Pilot." Over time, auxiliary facilities within its vast reservation were dedicated to the top-secret flight-testing of Soviet MiGs, the standup of the first operational squadron of stealth fighters, and the hub of today's tactical unmanned combat air vehicles.

On April 24, 1949, Harry and his pilot teammates landed at the desert outpost. Their efficiency and esprit de corps would help set the standard that has become the base's hallmark.

Invigorated by their escapade at the Grand Canyon, the Tuskegee fighters were determined to prove that they were the best of the best in the Air Force.

The 332nd's maintenance crews had arrived a day earlier via a C-47 transport. Their senior officer, Captain James T. Wiley, met with the event's planning group, which included base officials. He had looked forward to these planning sessions, but he received belittling treatment. The higher-ups acted as though the "Negroes" had no chance of winning, and thus they did not take the 332nd's team seriously.

As an original member of the 99th Pursuit Squadron, the first all-black flying combat unit, Wiley wasn't going to take that snub lightly. He turned all his energies to motivating his armorers, communication specialists, mechanics, and crew chiefs to do their utmost. A short time later, Harry and his fellow team pilots conferred with base liaison personnel, experiencing a reception similar to Captain Wiley's. But as with their maintenance chief, the cold shoulder only strengthened the pilots' resolve to win.

For a week the teams familiarized themselves with the gunnery ranges and readied themselves for going game-on. The pilots and maintainers who had come from across the nation to prove their skills could sense the competitive spirit in the air. The 332nd's team members buoyed each other as the May 2 start date neared; any butterflies in the pits of their stomachs were banished by cool self-assurance. Harry, for his part, was raring to get on with the competition, eager to show what he and the other Tuskegee Airmen could do.

■ ■ ■

Because Nevada's scorching midday temperatures cause the air to roil in waves of convective heating, all competition flights commenced at the crack of dawn. The early start time meant that maintenance crews had no option but to labor through the night to prepare the planes for the demanding sorties. Even today, seven decades later, Harry can hardly find words to express the gratitude for his team's maintainers.

According to Harry and the team's other pilots, the enlisted personnel who traveled from Lockbourne to service the aircraft were the unsung heroes of the competition. The 332nd's ground crews, like champion pit crews in motor racing, swarmed around the machines under their charge when they returned to the ramp at mid-morning. Diagnostics ensued, and the mechanics used the cool evenings to fine-tune the planes, continuing their work almost nonstop until flying resumed the next morning at sunrise.

The competition's jet class included venerable F-80 Shooting Stars and newer F-84 Thunderjets. Jets were clearly the cutting edge, but the Air Force's fleet recapitalization was taking time. Thus many units still flew conventional fighters, some that were even war surplus. The Tuskegee Airmen's F-47 Thunderbolts were set to face F-51 Mustangs and F-82 Twin Mustangs. (In Air Force nomenclature, the "P" for pursuit had changed to "F" for fighter.)

To even the playing field, the F-47s, each with eight wing-mounted guns, had two guns disabled, leaving six in operation. This matched the six guns of the other propeller-driven fighters in the meet.

On May 2, the event formally got underway with the aerial gunnery contest, in which participants fired at twenty-by-six-foot wire-
mesh sleeves towed behind medium bombers. As everyone had hoped,
the sky remained clear for the duration of the meet. Because the 332nd
was assigned to Ninth Air Force at the time and because that parent
organization was tasked with tactical missions such as ground attack
in support of infantry and had overseen meticulous training of its
constituent fighter groups, it was to be expected that Harry and his
teammates would score high in the parts of the competition that
involved surface targets.

Conversely, it was expected that teams from other units would
dominate the competition's air-to-air component. Yet in the aerial
gunnery category, one of Harry's colleagues, Captain Temple, got the
highest score. It was a terrific omen!

■   ■   ■

Early in the competition, the 332nd's team was patched into a call
from an all-black elementary school in the area. The segregated student
body and faculty reflected the racial division of the public education
system of the time. The school's principal, who had heard that a contingent from the Air Force's black flying unit was in town for the meet,
requested that "one of the colored pilots" come to speak at the school.

Harry gladly accepted the invitation. The afternoon appearance
would temporarily take his mind off the consuming challenge in the
skies over Frenchman Flat and act as a tension-reliever. The memory
of the principal ushering him into a packed gymnasium remains fresh.
The children were spellbound by a black fighter pilot in flight suit
with rank, insignia, and wings.

Here was the real thing, a living legend—one of the Tuskegee
Airmen—gracing the school with an in-person visit. The principal

introduced Harry by reading from a one-page resume that had been handed to him, announcing that the school's guest had flown forty-three fighter combat missions and scored three air-to-air victories against the most formidable version of the Luftwaffe's Focke-Wulf Fw 190, for which he had received the Distinguished Flying Cross. Now, the principal explained, Harry was taking a break from flying a high-performance fighter in a competition with Air Force pilots from around the country at the air base north of town.

The students greeted their guest warmly. They sat in silence, hanging on Harry's every word. It occurred to Harry that he was a kind of Bessie Coleman spreading the "gospel" of aviation in the jet age.

Scanning the faces of the students arrayed before him, Harry wanted with all his heart to make a positive impression and to plant the seeds of an aviation future. In his soft-spoken style, he offered insight into his wartime experience and the Air Force flying life. He talked about the planes he flew and the teamwork that made it all possible.

None of it came easily, he told the students; one had to work at making it come true. But there were rewards—camaraderie, a sense of self-worth, and the knowledge of serving a cause greater than any one person. The gist of his message was that the same opportunity he had experienced could be theirs as well.

The audience of youngsters expressed their regard with an avalanche of applause. Harry wrapped up his presentation by inviting the classes to the air show scheduled at the conclusion of the gunnery meet. The principal stepped close to Harry and said, loudly enough for the students to hear, "We'll be there!"

The outpouring of support touched Harry's heart. He gained new strength from the visit and mused that it might have done as much if not more for him as it had done for the students who heard his talk. Immensely thankful for the time with the students, he was soon on his way back to the base to rejoin his teammates in the competition.

The next day the focus turned to ground targets, where it would remain for the rest of the meet and where Harry's team expected to excel. In the panel gunnery contest pilots swooped in low over the sagebrush, aiming their machine-gun fire at the bull's-eye painted in the middle of a square ten-by-ten-foot easel-mounted target. Despite the early morning start, the air was already unsettled at the lower altitudes.

Harry and his teammates were rocked by the turbulence, but they thought the F-47N gave them the advantage because it had been designed to be such a dependably stable gun platform. In fact, trying to hold their fighters steady during the runs at the target in the bedeviling air proved to be a chore for the Thunderbolt team. Given the rough air, the 332nd's pilots put in a credible performance. Harry felt especially good, since his score topped those of his teammates.

But when all the competing panel gunnery scores were posted, Harry and his colleagues were stunned to find that the team from the 82nd Fighter Group, flying F-51s, had outshined everyone else, with remarkably high scores achieved by two of its three pilots. Harry realized that if any of the other teams was going to pull ahead, it was likely to be the talented one from the 82nd. For the moment, though, the 332nd's team held a slight lead in the overall competition, so Harry and his teammates were still feeling good about their prospects.

Then, at a time when cautious optimism was percolating throughout the team, tragedy struck. As Harry remembers it, one of the 332nd's maintenance members, Staff Sergeant Kenneth Austin, had yearned to ride in a fighter during the dive-bombing contest. The only type that could accommodate him was the Twin Mustang because of its second cockpit. The unusual aircraft, allowing two pilots to share the workload during long flights, had been introduced shortly after World War II. (In time the right cockpit would be changed into a radar observer's position.)

During the meet, the right cockpit was usually left vacant, but Staff Sergeant Buford Johnson of the 332nd had already been treated to a dive-bombing run in one of the dual-cockpit fighters. So Sergeant Austin was also approved for a ride in an F-82's right cockpit, with the pilot to fly from the left cockpit.

First Lieutenant Ralph M. Tibbetts of the 27th Fighter Group took off with Sergeant Austin as his passenger and headed to the range. The details of what happened next are remembered differently by different observers who were there, but in any case the outcome was tragic. According to Harry, "On its first dive, the F-82 smashed into the ground," killing the two men on board instantly.

It was later determined by the official accident inquiry that the pilot had misjudged his altitude. The F-82, pitched at a thirty-degree angle, kept bearing down on the target laid out neatly on the desert floor. When finally, at only 150 feet from the ground, the aircraft began to pull up, it was too late to break the downward inertia. The plane's twin fuselages mushed into the desert surface, igniting into a fireball.

The decision was made to carry on with the meet. The participants who had combat experience, like Harry, had known the feeling of having to proceed when friends were lost. Still, the loss suffered by the 332nd's team was a hard burden to bear. They had come so far and now this—the death of a team member. The incident dampened the team's spirit, and the scores tallied for the dive-bombing contest, which was underway, reflected that reality. Each member hit only half the targets in their passes—a mediocre performance. Harry and the others would have to do better in the remaining contests if they hoped to salvage any chance of winning the overall competition in their class.

Meanwhile Captain Wiley—the head of the 332nd's maintenance support team whose only response to the racial prejudice he had initially encountered on base had been to squeeze extra performance out of his men—sought a release, both from the stresses of working on the Thunderbolts without a day off during the competition and from his grief for his colleague. One night Wiley and a few of his enlisted men strolled into the casino of the Flamingo Hotel wearing their uniforms.

But the 332nd's ground support team members didn't get far before hotel security guards stopped them and told them to leave. Insult was added to injury when a racial taunt was hurled at them. As they were making their way to the door, one of the guards blurted out, "Keep moving!" The experience was humiliating, but the servicemen had run into such ridicule at other times in their lives. As the unwelcome visitors exited they held their heads high, refusing to be deprived of their personal dignity.

Air Force personnel knew that the service's old system of segregation would soon be ended because of the pending implementation of President Truman's Executive Order 9981. Harry was anxious to see the new day arrive. As he and his fellow Tuskegee Airmen could attest, prejudice still reared its ugly head in all too familiar ways both inside and outside the fence.

The 332nd's team shook off the ill effects of their experiences both on the range and in town, for they had work to do. Skip bombing was next, and it happened to be the forte of Harry and his colleagues. Proficiency in this specialty required intensive practice—which the team members had had during exercises in the recent past at other air bases like Eglin.

The pilots of the 332nd's team didn't huddle together the way football teams do before a play, but they were unanimously committed to honoring the memory of their fallen teammate Kenneth Austin by pulling out all the stops to score high in the remaining contests. They were all feeling the "win one for the Gipper" sentiment—from the classic words of the dying George Gipp to Notre Dame football coach Knute Rockne in 1920, reenacted in the 1940 film of Rockne's life starring Ronald Reagan as

Gipp. The football analogy was in keeping with Harry's way of casting the 332nd's team as the underdog: as he said, it was like Grambling going up against the Big Ten.

When the skip bombing scores were tallied for the day, the 332nd's team had registered an extraordinary six hundred points, a perfect score across the board. That meant the team's three pilots had hit the targets with each one of their eighteen bombs. It was a performance unmatched by any of the other teams in the skip bombing contest—or any other contest during the entire meet!

It was an exceptional showing, and it boosted the team's confidence going into the air-to-ground rocketry, the sole remaining contest. In that contest, the 332nd's team beat all the others, though with a combined score that fell slightly short of a clean sweep. Temple was eight for eight while Stewart and Harvey each hit seven out of eight.

It appeared that Temple was poised to finish in first place among the pilots in the conventional class. But, according to one account, First Lieutenant William W. Crawford of the 82nd Fighter Group was allowed to repeat runs on the course due to equipment failure that had plagued his F-51 during the original runs. The makeups were said to have allowed Crawford to edge ahead of Temple, giving Crawford the top ranking among all pilots in individual scoring for the conventional class and relegating Temple to second place.

The "redo" reportedly caused members of the 332nd's team to grumble that any equipment failure on board an aircraft was a maintenance issue that did not justify second chances. Could the dispensation granted to the 82nd's star performer have been driven by an ulterior motive? Was the Air Force simply unwilling to countenance a black pilot outperforming his white peers?

Harry has no recollection of Crawford benefiting from a second chance because of extenuating circumstances. In Harry's version of events, Crawford came from behind in a flying performance that was "absolutely fantastic." Rather than finding fault with the scoring, Harry believes that Crawford won the individual first-place honor fair and square, in a hard-fought contest that came down to the wire.

The controversy aside, Harry and his colleagues had eked out the winning team score in the propeller class with 536.588 points, having retained a narrow margin over their competitors from the 82nd Fighter Group, who came in second with 515.010 points, followed by the 27th Fighter Group's team, the third-place finisher with 475.325 points. The Tuskegee Airmen, the underdogs, had come out ahead!

Harry and his teammates were ecstatic. It was further validation that black pilots and ground crewmen could perform as well as or better than their white counterparts.

In the jet class, the 4th Fighter Group's team in F-80s commandingly outperformed the other six jet teams. Individual honors for first and second place went to 4th Fighter Group pilots First Lieutenant Calvin Ellis and Captain Vermont Garrison respectively. Harry was not surprised, because the 4th Fighter Group belonged to Ninth Air Force. Indeed, the 332nd and the 4th had sharpened their tactical air-fighting skills by training together at Eglin's auxiliary fields in Florida. As Harry opined at the time and continues to believe, those days spent in intensive practice down in Florida's panhandle explained why teams from the two fighter groups performed so well at the big meet in Nevada.

As a reflection of the dawning of the new era in race relations, some white pilots from the 4th Fighter Group invited Harry to come with them to the Flamingo Hotel's casino. Probably because he was in their company, Harry had no problem roaming the hotel's lobby and casino that night. Harry and the other pilots enjoyed the evening partying together for, as fellow aviators who jockeyed fiercely in the skies over Frenchman Flat, they had much more in common than not.

Before the fighter groups departed for home, the base hosted the air show, which was open to the public. The transient pilots, relieved of the pressures of the competition, could strut their stuff for the local residents who came out to see the exhibition. Harry's team, like the others, was slated to perform a formation flyover.

While taxiing to the runway as part of a ceremonial procession, Harry caught sight of the classes from the elementary school where he had talked days earlier. They sat in the grandstands, excited to be watching the variety of Air Force planes parading in front of them.

Harry slipped off his helmet so that his newfound friends could recognize him. He waved, which drew their attention. The students rose to their feet with the principal and returned the wave enthusiastically. It was a testimonial to the esteem in which he was held by those to whom he had reached out. Harry relished the moment.

Within minutes, he and his teammates were airborne. When their turn came, they closed in on each other's wings and dipped to the preassigned altitude to give the crowd an obliging look at their formation. With their radial engines synched, the power of their combined strength funneled back through the pilots' grip on the control columns. Their formation flight was machinelike, scrupulous, precise.

As he flew over the desert base for the last time, it hit Harry viscerally: he and his teammates had been adjudged premier fighter pilots, the Air Force's top guns, as it were. The consciousness of having achieved what a few short years ago would have been inconceivable imbued Harry with an extra measure of pride. It was like his first solo flight. He and his colleagues up in the air were riding on top of the world.

■   ■   ■

The meet's official doings culminated at an awards banquet back at the Flamingo. Colonel Davis had flown in for the presentation. He would not be present to greet his men upon their return to Lockbourne because of a pending assignment at the Air War College at

Maxwell Air Force Base in Alabama. So this was his way to say thanks and, on a more subdued note, to show support in the wake of the loss of one of the team's members. Davis and the other black officers filtered into the hotel among clusters of white officers.

Each team sat at its assigned tables, and Davis joined his men at the head of one of the 332nd's. The jet class was recognized first. The 4th Fighter Group's pilots were called to the front to be pictured with their awards amid a round of clapping.

The main team prize was a three-foot-tall amphora-like trophy that would be shared by the winners of both the jet class and the conventional class. The pewter device was mounted on a solid block of teak wood with a bronze plaque on the front awaiting the inscription of the names of the winning teams and their pilots. The trophy was crowned by a silvery figurine with arms raised skyward.

Winners in the propeller class of the 1949 gunnery meet celebrate with their trophies at the banquet in Las Vegas's Flamingo Hotel. From left to right: alternate First Lieutenant Halbert L. Alexander, First Lieutenant James H. Harvey III, Captain Alva N. Temple, and Harry. *U.S. Air Force via Harry Stewart Jr.*

The words engraved on the body of the trophy were sparse, in the military tradition, but it was a case where less meant more: "United States Air Force—Fighter Gunnery Award." A second, smaller trophy of a foot in height but bearing a similar design was also presented to each of the winning teams. The large trophy was to be safeguarded at the Pentagon, where subsequent winners would have their names added to plaques on the wooden base. The smaller trophy was to go to the home base of the winning team.

Next, as winners of the conventional class, the pilots of the 332nd's team stepped to the front for their turn to be recognized with the trophies. The ballroom erupted into another round of clapping. The four Tuskegee Airmen, in the presence of their commander, received perhaps their highest honor—the admiration and respect of their peers.

■ ■ ■

On May 13, during the return flight to Lockbourne, the adrenaline finally started to drain. But when the air base came into sight, the team

The winners' welcome home! On the team's return to Lockbourne Air Force Base after their triumphant performance at the gunnery meet, the 332nd's leadership made sure the returning pilots would know how much their success was appreciated. Note the honor guard cordon and the band on the tarmac as service personnel and family members watch from the edge of the parking apron, May 13, 1949. *U.S. Air Force via Harry Stewart Jr.*

Delphine and Harry together again on the ramp at Lockbourne, May 13, 1949, evincing an infectious ebullience and imparting a sense that goodness can win out, that hope is not an illusion, and that dreams can come true. *U.S. Air Force via Harry Stewart Jr.*

members perked up. They swept in fast and low, almost as if they were strafing their own field. Glancing at the rows of airmen below who had been assembled to welcome them home, the pilots waited until they reached the airfield's midpoint and then pulled up and over into separate victory rolls!

Buzzing Lockbourne was technically a no-no. Colonel Davis ordinarily insisted on strict adherence to the regulations and frowned on stunting. But this was one of the rare times when, even after Davis heard what happened, the pilots who had indulged their fancy enjoyed impunity.

On the ramp, the team's pilots were treated like royalty. The 332nd's band blared out lively music as each of the returning pilots marched through the saluting honor guard cordon. Harry and his flying teammates received a welcome worthy of heroes. They had done more than simply uphold the stature of the Tuskegee Airmen. By carving another notch in their unit's string of achievements, they had added to its already awe-inspiring reputation.

Harry felt joy, for he had not let the members of his unit down; he had done them proud. And he had another reason to be joyful. When the returning F-47s had announced their arrival at Lockbourne with aerobatic maneuvers, Delphine was on the tarmac waiting to greet Harry. The couple posed for photographs. Harry, grinning smartly in his flight suit, and Delphine, mirroring her husband's elation, together emitted an infectious ebullience that imparted a sense that goodness can win out, that hope is not an illusion, and that dreams can come true.

Chapter Twelve

HARRY TRUMAN KEEPS HIS PROMISE

Your values become your destiny.
—Mohandas Gandhi

Before the summer of 1949 was over, the Air Force inactivated the 332nd and began to disperse its people to numerous units in far-flung locations as part of the Truman directive to integrate the military. There had been little in Truman's early years to suggest that he would emerge as a staunch civil rights advocate. His grandparents had been slave owners, he was a direct descendant of two Confederate soldiers, and he grew up in Missouri, a border state where slavery was not outlawed until 1864.

Truman's mother, Martha Ellen Truman, known to her family as Mamma, reviled Abraham Lincoln from her days as a child during the Civil War when marauding Union troops burned the family farm as she watched. In fact, when Mamma's son ascended to the presidency and invited her to overnight at the White House, she adamantly refused to sleep in the bedroom named after the Great Emancipator. Truman himself had used racial epithets in correspondence and conversation.

But there were also competing influences in his life. For one thing, Truman was a voracious reader. He most enjoyed the works of Charles Dickens and Mark Twain. Great literature is likely to have softened his view on race, for in his years as a senator and even more as president, he espoused the idea, incorporated in some of the classics he digested, that hatred is a wasteful and destructive force.

Truman's outlook was broadened when in 1917, at the age of thirty-three, he left the confinement of the family farm near Grandview, Missouri. It was then, upon America's entry into World War I, that he rejoined the Missouri National Guard. He was shipped overseas and, having risen to the rank of captain, commanded Battery D of the 129th Field Artillery, 60th Brigade, 35th Division in the bloody Meuse-Argonne Offensive. During his wartime assignment, Truman was a tough taskmaster, but he had an abiding empathy for the enlisted men.

Following the Armistice, Truman dined at Maxim's, attended the Paris Opera, and toured the French countryside. When the order came for his unit to pack up for the voyage home, he knew that he would not be returning to the drudgery of the farm. Something else awaited him, perhaps a career in politics where, he imagined, he could stand up for the veterans, the citizen-soldiers, the men who took the orders from the higher-ups.

More than a quarter-century later, on April 12, 1945, Truman stepped into the enormous vacuum created by the death of Franklin Roosevelt. There were many issues pressing on the unheralded Missourian who had been thrust suddenly into the presidency, not the least of which was whether to use the atomic bomb. But despite many opportunities to fall back on convenient alibis when it came to addressing the touchy matter of race relations, Truman faced it squarely on December 5, 1946, by establishing a multiracial Committee on Civil Rights through Executive Order 9808.

The next summer, Truman became the first president to address the National Association for the Advancement of Colored People (NAACP). Standing on the steps of the Lincoln Memorial on June 29, 1947, the president gave a speech presaging the famous "I Have a Dream" speech that Martin Luther King would give from the same spot during the March on Washington sixteen years later. Where King would proclaim, with poetic resonance, his dream of the day when his four children would not be judged by the color of their skin but by the content of their character, Truman told three thousand people gathered along the Reflecting Pool, "The only limit to an American's achievement should be his ability, his industry and his character."

Days before he delivered his address to the NAACP, Truman wrote to his sister Mary Jane describing how he felt about it. The letter speaks to the evolution of his beliefs on the matter of race. "Mamma won't like what I say because I wind up by quoting old Abe. But I believe what I say and I'm hopeful we may implement it."

On October 29, 1947, Truman's Committee on Civil Rights issued its report, titled *To Secure These Rights*. It detailed the discriminatory practices, inequality of opportunity, and vicious racism which still ran rampant across the land. And the committee laid the groundwork for racial progress with thirty-five recommendations, some of which were sweeping—including the one urging passage of legislation to end discrimination in the armed forces.

Truman wasted no time. In his State of the Union address on January 7, 1948, he spoke solemnly of an America where "We believe in the dignity of man." The president stressed five priorities for the country, with civil rights topping the list. "Our first goal is to secure fully the essential human rights of our citizens." He promised to forward a comprehensive civil rights program to Congress.

Less than a month later, Truman sent a ten-point civil rights program up to Capitol Hill. Predictably, Southern Democrats opposed the initiatives fiercely, employing the coarse instrument of the filibuster to block them. Meanwhile, pressure from civil rights advocates to desegregate the armed forces was accelerating.

A month after the report's release, A. Philip Randolph and Grant Reynolds, who had been an Army chaplain during the war, formed the Committee Against Jim Crow in Military Service and Training. On March 27, 1948, a group of the country's leading African American organizations, representing more than six million members, met in New York. Under the aegis of the NAACP, the group issued the *Declaration of Negro Voters*, which endorsed the recommendations of the Committee on Civil Rights and also called for the passage of pending civil rights bills. In April, sixteen African American leaders conferred privately with Secretary of Defense James V. Forrestal to demand integration of the military.

Less than two months later, Randolph announced the formation of the League for Nonviolent Civil Disobedience Against Military Segregation and followed up with a letter to Truman with Reynolds as a cosignatory. The two men were disappointed that nondiscrimination protections had not been included in the recent Selective Service Act and asked for a meeting to discuss an executive order that would abolish segregation in the military. Their letter stopped short of an ultimatum, but it explained that without such a presidential directive, "Negro youth will have no alternative but to resist" the draft.

By the time of the Democratic Party Convention that summer in Philadelphia, the fracture within the party was about to boil over. The adoption of an unequivocal civil rights plank in the party's platform championed by Minnesota liberal Hubert Humphrey only infuriated Southern delegates that much more. On July 15, after long and wearisome proceedings, Truman accepted his nomination as the party's presidential candidate.

Although Truman gave a rousing acceptance speech that was greeted with wild enthusiasm by most of the delegates, the party's Southern wing split off. In two days, the disaffected Democrats nominated an alternative presidential candidate under the Dixiecrat banner. South Carolina governor and avowed segregationist Strom Thurmond picked up the mantle.

In the heat of the Washington summer and in the middle of an increasingly tenuous reelection campaign, Truman did the unthinkable. Despite the division within his party and a Gallup poll in March indicating that a whopping 82 percent of the public opposed his civil rights program, he acted unilaterally to advance his formidable civil rights agenda. On July 26, 1948, Truman issued Executive Order 9981, which mandated "equality of treatment and opportunity for all persons in the armed services without regard to race, color, religion or national origin."

The once little-known border-state senator who had pledged to champion the cause of the two *Old Faithful* pilots a decade before had delivered on his promise. With a stroke of the pen, the dream that had been carried to Washington on the Lincoln-Page's fragile wood-and-fabric wings was close to realization. Of course, there would be obstacles along the way in the implementation of Executive Order 9981, but at least the formal governmental edict was in place for the integration of military aviation and the rest of the armed forces.

The Army chief of staff voiced his reservations about the new directive, but the Air Force, which had become an independent service the preceding autumn, embraced Executive Order 9981. The service's first secretary was Stuart Symington, a friend of the president and a dynamic defense industry executive from St. Louis who would later, like Truman before him, represent Missouri in the

Senate. In recognizing the immorality of discrimination as well as its inefficiencies, Symington was ahead of the times.

Symington had had an enlightened view on race as a young man and as a successful businessman. In fact, he had instituted fair employment practices at his defense plants in 1938, before such practices had become mandatory. According to historian Michael R. Gardner, Symington, acting as secretary of the Air Force, called his senior staff together soon after Executive Order 9981 was issued and told them, "We're going to integrate the air force now—okay, let's go do it."

As Dr. Haulman of the Air Force Historical Research Agency has pointed out, even prior to the issuance of the Executive Order the Air Force "was already moving toward racial integration." With Symington setting the tone, the Air Force's uniformed leader sent a letter to the *Pittsburgh Courier* on April 5, 1948, expressing the view that it was the service's goal "to eliminate segregation among its personnel." Carl Spaatz, who had signed his name to the infamous Momyer assessment in 1943, signed his name to the letter endorsing the service's plan for integration only five years later as the first chief of staff of the Air Force.

Economic factors also played a role in fostering integration. Lieutenant General Idwal H. Edwards, an air commander in the European and Mediterranean theaters during World War II and the deputy chief of staff for personnel in the late 1940s, recognized the efficiencies to be achieved through the elimination of separate facilities for black airmen. Benjamin Davis went so far as to state in his autobiography that by 1949 "the Air Force was anxious to inaugurate desegregation for budgetary reasons."

The Committee on Equality of Treatment and Opportunity in the Armed Services established by Truman's Executive Order 9981 was unquestionably a major catalyst for progress. This seven-member panel, which came to be known as the Fahy Committee after its chairman, former U.S. Solicitor General Charles Fahy, explored ways to achieve the presidential mandate by working with the services. On May 22, 1950, the committee submitted a report titled *Freedom to Serve*. Interestingly, one of the committee's members was John H. Sengstacke, who had replaced his late uncle Robert Abbott as the editor at the *Chicago Defender*, the newspaper that had so vigorously supported the Spencer-White Goodwill Flight under Abbott's leadership.

What motivated Truman to issue the landmark desegregation decree is a matter of historical debate. Looming large were Truman's humble beginnings, which made him a champion for the underdog throughout his life. Some argue that political self-interest contributed to the decision. In this view, the issuance of the executive order was shrewdly calculated by Truman and his political advisers to attract African American voters after several Southern states were perceived as lost, when the Dixiecrats rose to support Thurmond.

Others claim the exact opposite, pointing to the moral conviction best exemplified in a letter Truman sent to an old chum during the 1948 presidential campaign. The letter was not discovered until well after Truman's presidential term had concluded—a provenance that lends credence to the view that Truman's motivation was rooted at least in part in altruism.

Shortly after the announcement of the historic executive order, one of Truman's friends from Kansas City by the name of Ernest W. Roberts hurriedly typed out a letter to dissuade the president from pressing the civil rights issue. In his simple, down-home appeal, Roberts referred to Truman's lineage, suggesting that he would share the typical Southern white's view on race. Truman's friend warned him of certain electoral defeat unless the whole business of desegregation was dropped. Reflecting the prejudiced mindset not uncommon for the time, Roberts summed up his feelings crudely: "[L]et the South take care of the Niggers...."

In mid-August Truman wrote back. The president's letter makes it clear that as a proud veteran he was outraged that some of his fellow veterans who happened to be black—and even some currently serving black members of the armed forces—had been harassed, maimed, and brutally murdered solely because of the color of their skin. In a highly publicized case in 1946, black veteran George Dorsey, his wife, and two of their friends were cut down in rural Georgia when a racially motivated mob riddled their bodies with more than sixty bullets. The subsequent investigation failed to result in a single indictment.

This and similar injustices were intolerable to Truman. He had been an officer in the field artillery, and he had commanded soldiers in combat. To him, the color of the uniform transcended the different pigmentations inside the battle dress. The flinty old captain of Battery D felt so strongly on the issue that all other considerations were subordinated.

Truman exhibited no animus. He headed his letter "Dear Ernie," reflecting his long and continuing friendship; he channeled his deep difference of opinion into a heartfelt argument. Truman stated that he would send a copy of the report prepared by his Committee on Civil Rights and that he hoped this would change his friend's anachronistic views on race.

Truman explained, "The main difficulty with the South is that they are living eighty years behind the times and the sooner they come out of it the better it will be for the country and themselves.... I am asking for equality of opportunity for all human beings and, as long as I stay here, I am going to continue that fight. When the mob gangs can take four people out and shoot them in the back, and everybody in the country is acquainted with who did the shooting and nothing is done about it, that country is in a pretty bad fix...."

Near the letter's end, Truman described another example of abusive treatment of blacks. Then he wrote, "I am going to try to remedy it and if that ends up in my failure to be reelected, that failure will be in a good cause."

Clearly, Truman's revulsion at the Dorsey incident and others like it accounted for much of his drive to rectify the state of race relations. Of course, there were other influences working to sway him, too, such as his meetings with civil rights leaders like the NAACP's Walter White. Most assuredly, the successful performance of black servicemen over the years, starting with Crispus Attucks's sacrifice in the 1770 Boston Massacre and including the Buffalo Soldiers on patrol in the Southwest and Great Plains after the Civil War, as well as the black drivers of the "Red Ball Express" in World War II—the Tuskegee Airmen were among the latest in the long list—must also have played a role.

It is pure speculation whether Truman's airport visit with Chauncey Spencer and Dale White in May 1939 contributed to his decision to satisfy the flyers' ultimate aim of an integrated Air Force. The major histories do not reference the encounter or offer it as a reason for the executive order. Like the 1949 gunnery trophy, the meeting faded from the historical record, kept alive only by word of mouth and occasional articles.

But if it is true, as biographer David McCullough asserts, that Truman "had an unusually retentive mind," then it is only logical to think that he would have remembered rendezvousing with a couple of African American pilots and chatting with them on the wing of their airplane. That occurrence would have stood out distinctly from his workaday appointments on the Hill. And the meeting had ended with Truman committing himself to follow through, not something that the can-do politician took lightly.

Whether or not Truman remembered the two black flyers from Chicago, Chauncey and Dale had symbolically handed off the baton to the younger generation of aspiring black flyers, men like Harry Stewart who distinguished themselves in service to the country. Because of the one breakthrough, those who followed proved themselves and contributed to another breakthrough—a leap of historic proportions. Harry was anxious to participate in the new integrated military that he and his fellow Tuskegee Airmen had helped to foster. But the Air Force had other plans.

Chapter Thirteen

A DREAM
DEFERRED

When it is dark enough, you can see the stars.
—Ralph Waldo Emerson

On July 1, 1949, the Air Force formally entered a new era in the treatment of its African American personnel. The long-awaited end of the service's officially sanctioned racial segregation meant that the 332nd would be inactivated. It was little more than a month after members of the unit had achieved "top gun" status, and the all-black flying unit would go out on a high note.

Harry gave credit to the service for its welcome, if overdue, transition to a desegregated model. He noted, "The Air Force senior leadership insisted on implementing integration." What the Tuskegee Airmen and their predecessors had always wanted had finally come to fruition.

Before desegregation went into effect, Harry had decided, with the blessing of Colonel Davis, to accept an opening in the "weather school" at Chanute Air Force Base in Illinois for an advanced course in meteorology, reasoning that it would make him a better pilot.

Loving the flying and the sense of high purpose, Harry had bonded not just with the men of his tight-knit unit but with the

Harry at Lockbourne Air Force Base near Columbus, Ohio, in the late 1940s, standing under the .50-caliber machine gun barrels of his F-47N Thunderbolt. *U.S. Air Force via Harry Stewart Jr.*

institution of the Air Force. He was grateful to it for having given him wings and the chance to serve the country, and he was intent on staying in and making the most of it.

Yet not all of Harry's comrades shared his positive outlook about their future in the reconstituted Air Force. They worried how they would fit in when transferred to otherwise all-white units. With integration coming soon, the black pilots would be dispersed throughout the service, depriving them of the built-in support network they had known from the day they first arrived at the Tuskegee Institute.

For Harry, such concerns would prove moot because the Air Force, which had been scaling back since peaking in World War II, continued its drawdown. The latest round of draconian budget cuts imposed by the Truman administration ripped deeply into the pilot ranks. Colonel Davis broke the heartbreaking news to Harry that he would be among those separated from active-duty service.

The extreme reduction in force structure was a shortsighted decision that would be reversed soon enough because of the outbreak of hostilities on the Korean Peninsula. The up-and-down rollercoaster repeated the familiar pattern of ill-preparedness followed by a rapid buildup followed by yet another deleterious downsizing to start the cycle all over again. Colonel Davis told Harry in regretful tones that there was nothing he could do to save his spot.

In early January 1950, only weeks into his meteorological classes at Chanute, Harry left the active-duty Air Force. He was dejected yet proud: he had earned the Distinguished Flying Cross and the Air Medal with six Oak Leaf Clusters. He could also lay claim to a piece of the gunnery meet trophy. And, as he stared into the uncertainty of life "outside the wire," he was at least able to retain a commission in the reserves (eventually retiring at the rank of lieutenant colonel).

Harry and Delphine moved in with her mother, who had recently divorced. Using the Harlem apartment as a base of operations, Delphine went to work as a business machine operator at the headquarters of a retailing company in the Empire State Building, and Harry quickly contacted an employment counselor at the local Veterans Administration office.

The VA counselor, aware from a standard questionnaire that Harry lacked a high school diploma, started the conversation with the query, "Tell me what you can do." At twenty-five years of age, Harry was enthusiastic about the presumed opportunities that lay ahead. He theorized that since he had developed the skill of flying high-performance airplanes there would be something available in commercial aviation, and so he rattled off all of his accomplishments as a first-rate fighter pilot—the forty-three combat missions, the dogfighting near Wels, the gunnery meet trophy. The counselor seemed unmoved, as though Harry's story of mastering the complexities of flight and of valor in combat were unremarkable. And in fact it was one of hundreds of thousands of other, sometimes similarly compelling, stories being recounted by job-hunting veterans in VA offices around the country.

Harry was allowed to finish without interruption. Then, after an abnormally long pause to be sure Harry had nothing more to say, the counselor impassively restated his initial interrogatory. "So, now tell me what you can do." Crestfallen, Harry realized that what he had revealed to this stranger, the pouring out of the details of his flying life, mattered not at all.

In the flash of an eye, Harry's balloon of high expectations was burst. As an inveterate optimist, he had hoped the VA office would be a launchpad to his old dream of occupying a seat on the flight deck of the big propliners. But he wouldn't be carrying travelers to exotic capitals around the globe. His vision would have to shrink to more earthly pursuits.

Despite having helped to make the world free of domination by the Axis powers, in important ways Harry was back to where his life had stood before the war. He had a flashback of Mrs. McLaughlin, the teacher at his junior high school, tearfully advising him that his dream of piloting airliners was a nonstarter. Now someone else, a dispassionate government bureaucrat, was making the same point without actually speaking the words. It was simply a given in 1950, as it had been in 1939 to all but young, starry-eyed dreamers, that flying jobs with the airlines were out of the question for African Americans.

The counselor wasn't impolite, but he had a caseload and Harry had already taken up more than the usual amount of time. With hardly another word spoken, the counselor handed Harry a scrap of paper with a midtown Manhattan address scribbled on it. It's manual labor, but it's an income, the counselor said.

In Harry's view, his life had reached its nadir; he felt utter despair at having his employment opportunities limited to physical work. For the first time, Harry felt personally what it must have been like as a cadet washed out of flying: his future seemed hopelessly constricted. Harry forced himself to thank the counselor for the tip and left hurriedly to get on with his new life in the civilian world. Even if the opportunities available to him were as unpalatable as they sounded, there was no other choice.

Later that morning, Harry found Penn Station abuzz with passengers rushing to make their connections. He reported to the personnel office, saying he had been referred by the VA. An attendant ushered him to a freight elevator out of public view.

The elevator dropped slowly into the bowels of the station, down and down to an unimagined depth. It was eerie. Entering the equivalent of a warren of caves for the first time, Harry saw a subterranean enterprise of railcars busily pulling in and chugging their way back out after just enough downtime for offloading supplies to support topside industries and lifestyles. Groups of men not unlike chain gangs heaved to, lifting wrapped pallets of magazines onto electric carts to be transferred via the freight elevator to different levels for sorting.

Harry started his new job that day, but not without an incident of biting degradation. The company required its baggage handler prospects to submit to an onsite physical exam. Administered by a sadistic physician's assistant, it consisted of nothing more than the finger test for an inguinal hernia.

As he approached the exam area, Harry could hear shrieks of pain followed by a chorus of snickering laughter. Applicants got the finger pressed well beyond any diagnostic protocol, and when the inevitable high-pitched scream echoed through the dark and dank grotto, the old-timers on the lifting crew reacted with cruel chortling. This was a devilish sweatshop, a hellhole resembling a scene out of a novel like *Hard Times*.

Harry almost turned back towards the elevator, but he wouldn't let these ne'er-do-wells have the satisfaction of thinking they had scared him; he had faced greater challenges and been victorious. Besides, as much as Harry despised this horrid labyrinth, he needed a job. He forced himself to run the humiliating gauntlet and after emitting the unavoidable exclamation—more a groan—he went to work.

The lifting crew was made up mostly of African Americans, whom Harry promptly ascertained were illiterate and sadly resigned to their fate. Hoisting the loaded pallets was backbreaking and tedious grub-work. Every inhalation meant drawing in a cloud of suspended dust particles. By day's end Harry was exhausted and covered in soot, feeling like a cog in a begrimed underworld in which his labor was bereft of meaning or purpose.

The irony of working at the lowest rung in the railroad baggage handler system was not lost on Harry. He knew that A. Philip Randolph, the head of the Brotherhood of Sleeping Car Porters, had been one of the chief proponents of opening military flying to blacks. The theory was that having black Army pilots would advance the race by changing the employment dynamic, so that men of color could finally break out of society's second-class jobs.

Harry's plight started to eat at him. He felt now as his father had, laboring below decks in his ship's incinerator-like galley, sailing up and down coastal waters but going nowhere until he figured out where to walk the plank. Life was supposed to be what you made of it, not what others made of you. Just as his father had broken free from his place of torment, so too Harry plotted to escape from the clutches of his virtual prison, the forces holding him back, his purgatory.

During periods of introspection he realized that his ticket to a better life hinged on furthering his education. For all his worldly experience to that point, Harry had earned no formal academic credential. He spent his off-hours visiting local college campuses, comparing academic programs. Would any accept a combat veteran who had dropped out of high school?

New York University was willing to give him a chance despite his lack of preparatory schooling. The dean of the School of Engineering,

John R. Ragazzini, had worked on the Manhattan Project during the war and wanted to help the fellow New Yorker and veteran fighter pilot who had asked to meet with him to discuss the school's curriculum. But the special arrangement came with conditions: Harry would have to maintain at least a B average.

Harry's spirits were high, but from the start he found the course prerequisites in math and the natural sciences grueling. With his job filling the day, he had to attend classes at night. By the time he got back to the apartment, he was exhausted both physically and mentally, to the point where he could barely do homework.

There was really just enough time for him to doze off so that he could wake up early the next morning to go back to his job at Penn Station, all the while still coming to terms with his forced exit from the active-duty Air Force. Harry's life was clearly not panning out as he had hoped. Something would have to give.

Amid the constant frustration with work and school, Harry never stopped aching for his childhood dream of flying the big, beautifully decorated TWA and Pan Am passenger liners he had watched taking off from LaGuardia before he went to war. The dream burning in Harry's heart would simply not die. In the postwar years, the two airlines had become the country's indisputable flag carriers, with routes to the crossroads of the world.

It was a time of promise for the airlines as they expanded in the peacetime economy. Both Trans World Airlines and Pan American World Airways ran print advertisements seeking to hire pilots with as few as two hundred to four hundred flight hours. Harry had three to six times that much flight time, with instrument qualification. Harry doesn't remember where he saw the ads, only that they got him thinking again about his vision.

What he remembers is that one day while riding the train to his parents' home in Queens, he saw the familiar Pan Am logo displayed on the side of a building in Queens Plaza in Long Island City, as he had many times before. He got up from his seat a few stops before his destination, stepped off the train, and began walking towards the building with the sign at 28-19 Bridge Plaza North. On an impulse, Harry had decided to go into the Pan Am office, one of the airline's major administrative centers, to pop the question.

He had no fear or trepidation. He figured the worst they could do would be to say "no," and he could deal with that. Harry believed he had always done better when he went face-to-face with people, attempting to persuade them in person rather than going through a formal written process.

Of course, it was public knowledge in 1950 that airlines were off-limits to African Americans seeking flying jobs. But Harry put the thought of discrimination out of his mind and instead concentrated on the potential opportunity: someone would be the first black airline pilot and it might as well be me, he thought. How could he ever know if he might be the one unless he tried?

Up to this point, everyone who had offered an opinion on the possibility of an airline flying job was outside the industry—a teacher, a counselor, ordinary citizens in idle conversation—and their opinions were all based on long-standing assumptions stemming from practices that had been in place before the war, before black pilots had proved their flying prowess in combat. This would be the acid test, the airlines speaking for themselves.

The ads had given mailing addresses for submission of one's resume. Rather than risk a letter being ignored, Harry would initiate the process on the spot. After all, Pan Am was headquartered in the city and TWA, though based in Kansas City, had major operations in New York. If either was interested, Harry would be happy to forward his resume to the right department.

Harry swung the door open and went to the reception desk in the lobby. Calmly and deliberatively he asked the woman sitting behind the desk if he could submit his application to be a pilot. Though the lobby was quiet, with few people and little activity, tension immediately filled the air.

Flustered, the woman at first looked down and away but then, after gathering her thoughts, regained her composure and said in an even tone, suggestive of forced nonchalance, "We're not hiring at this time." The perfunctory rebuke was not a surprise to Harry, but nevertheless it was a dagger to the heart. Before the weight of the rejection could sink in, he retorted in his gentle voice, "An ad has run seeking pilots."

The woman, gaining confidence, reiterated her answer a little more firmly. Harry could see the futility of his venture. From the initial impulse on the train, Harry's idea had been a risky gambit, almost certain to fail.

He kept a stiff upper lip as he began to move away from the desk. Just then, a man in suit and tie who had overheard the brief exchange as he had been making his way across the lobby to the bank of elevators came over to Harry. Sizing up the circumstances, he took pity on Harry and introduced himself as a Pan Am personnel manager.

Seeking to assuage Harry's obvious distress, the man from the airline offered his regrets. He seemed genuinely discomfited that black pilots were summarily rejected. But he, like most people, was resigned to the status quo.

Escorting the deflated applicant back to the building door, the man put his arm around Harry, who tried to get a word in edgewise about his flying background. Clumsily, the man explained the airline's employment policy in the form of a rhetorical question, "Mr. Stewart, I'm sure you can understand our position. Just imagine what

passengers would think if during a flight they saw a Negro step out
of the cockpit and walk down the aisle in a pilot's uniform?"

Harry judged that he had no choice but to grin and bear it. While
the man was well-intentioned, his remarks were patronizing. As
Harry would learn, other honorably discharged Tuskegee Airmen had
also tried to find flying jobs in the airline industry, but they too had
run into the same brick wall. At the time, there simply were not any
major airlines offering in-cockpit opportunities for black pilots, no
matter how accomplished.

Harry took a deep breath out on the sidewalk. Despite the snub,
he was not ready to let go of his goal. While Pan Am was a no, who's
to say TWA would be the same? The other flag carrier was worth a
try. He wouldn't rest until he got the definitive word, and that would
require personally approaching the airline itself.

With the passage of so many years, Harry doesn't recall the TWA
office location where he made his stab at an application, but not surprisingly the result was substantively the same as in his encounter at
the Pan Am office. It had not been realistic for him to expect to break
the employment barrier, but he felt that he had to test the system to
remove any doubt in his mind before abandoning his preferred career
path and moving on to something else.

Harry had trouble reconciling the airline industry's discriminatory policy with the fact that the Air Force had integrated rapidly and
effectively the year before. It was not until around the mid-1960s that
the major airlines would begin to hire blacks as pilots, with only
incremental progress until then. Individual acts of courage by pilots
like Harry, who refused to be intimidated by long-held custom, were
instrumental in slowly chipping away at the obstructionism.

TWA took a big step in loosening its employment policy in
August 1957 when it hired James O. Plinton Jr., its first African
American in sales and promotion. Plinton, one of Harry's flight

instructors at Tuskegee, had tried repeatedly after the war to be hired as a pilot by major airlines but was turned down every time. He went south of the border where he helped organize Andesa, the national airline of Ecuador, and cofounded Quisqueya Ltd., a Caribbean airline that offered service from Haiti to the Turks and Caicos Islands.

And once on TWA's payroll, he helped develop the airline's operations in Africa. According to one of TWA's senior captains, Plinton "knew every government leader" on the continent. In 1971 the pioneering executive left TWA for Eastern Airlines, where he was promoted to vice president, then the highest position attained by a black person in the industry.

But those breakthroughs were in the future. For now, Harry was in desperate need of a change of fortune and, swallowing his pride, he approached his uncle Conrad for help. Having followed Harry's father from Virginia to Queens, Conrad had pursued an apprenticeship as an electrician and established a successful electrical contracting company, through which he had developed a range of contacts.

Harry's uncle, a smart man with a big heart, set up an appointment for Harry with a Harlem politician. In classic ward heeler fashion, the politician gave Harry a letter of introduction and told him to go down to city hall and show it to certain staffers in public works. The people Harry met with at city hall were standoffish until he presented them with the letter. Apparently the politician wielded a lot of power, because the clerks Harry was talking to suddenly became attentive.

Because of the courses Harry had taken at NYU, he was assigned to the city's engineering department at 125 Worth Street. It was patronage pure and simple, but Harry had the aptitude for the tasks at hand. In this case city taxpayers would be well served.

Harry adapted quickly. Some of the staff in the engineering department took a liking to him and mentored him. He watched the

draftsmen and the engineers at their tables with T-squares and com-
passes, learning from their example. In time he mastered drafting
techniques, working on such projects as the pipe mazes in the city's
sewerage treatment plants.

The feelings of inadequacy that had stemmed from his lack of
formal education gradually abated. As time passed, Harry got promotions to junior engineer and then assistant engineer. He admired his
engineer coworkers, and being around them boosted his self-confidence, especially with regard to revisiting college.

When Harry went to college this time it was different. Now he
was on more solid ground because of the support at work and because
his friend from military flying days, Roscoe Brown, gave valuable
counsel. Roscoe had pursued a postwar career in higher education,
and he guided Harry through the fine points of the process.

Rather than reenter NYU directly, Harry took community college
courses in Brooklyn. He did very well—all A's. Only after he had
earned an associate degree did he return to night classes at NYU,
where he hit his stride under the caring and watchful eye of E. A.
Salma, assistant dean of the College of Engineering. With financial
assistance from the G.I. Bill and with his mentors at his workplace as
his inspiration, Harry pursued a degree in mechanical engineering.

Of course, flying remained a passion. Some aviation experts
foresaw a future in which the helicopter and the seaplane would be
important factors in commercial air travel. Like other returning
military pilots who sought to take advantage of their skills and apply
them to the "next big thing" in aviation, Harry earned his rotorcraft
and seaplane ratings at civilian flight schools.

But the rosy predictions of large fleets of helicopters or seaplanes
shuttling commuters between Manhattan workplaces and suburban
residences or between the metroplex's major air terminuses didn't pan
out as hoped. Start-ups like helo operator New York Airways gave it

a try but struggled and ultimately failed. In any case, to supplement the household income Harry spent weekends giving instruction in light fixed-wing aircraft at Flushing Airport, near where his dream of flight had been born.

Sadly, after about a year it was becoming increasingly clear that his drafting job and college coursework did not leave enough time for his activities at the airport. When some of his college lab sessions were scheduled on Saturdays, he was left with no choice. Harry stopped flying; with a few aborted restarts, there would be a hiatus of five decades before a return to his first love.

In 1952, he and Delphine moved to an apartment in the old neighborhood in Corona. From 9:00 a.m. to 5:00 p.m. Harry was at his city job; then he attended the NYU night classes. Typically he didn't get home until 11:00 p.m. Delphine left milk and sandwiches in the refrigerator. He would sit down and study for a few hours, subsisting on no more than six hours of sleep.

Harry juggled work with his studies. It was a marathon in slow motion; at this pace, it would take at least two and a half times longer for him to graduate than for a regular day student. But after dogfighting with Luftwaffe pilots he was conditioned to pull out all the stops to reach his objective.

Saturday nights were set aside for a movie or a play with Delphine. Sunday nights were back to studying. During this time Delphine continued to supplement the household income with a new job at the New York Yankees' business office in the Bronx.

By 1956, Harry and Delphine were feeling more assured about their future, and they moved into the Dorie Miller housing development, also in Corona. The project, named after the Navy hero, was the first integrated co-op in New York. The couple lived on the same floor with Josephine Gordon, the mother of Joseph Gordon, Harry's childhood playmate and fellow trainee at Tuskegee. Being both widowed and without Joseph, who had been killed in combat, Mrs. Gordon treated Harry like a second son.

Harry's drawn-out academic grind finally bore fruit in 1963. Along the way he had been elected president of the student council and served as chairman of the campus chapter of the American Society of Mechanical Engineers. Now that he was armed with a degree, a new world opened to Harry. And the nascent civil rights movement was having a salutary effect on the hiring policies of corporate mainstays, which until that time had been, as a general rule, diffident at best about hiring minorities in anything but menial positions.

Harry's first choice was Grumman Aircraft in Bethpage on Long Island, but the manufacturer of naval fighters turned him down. Second choice was General Foods in Tarrytown, New York. An offer was made and Harry grabbed it.

At the cereal maker, Harry was insistent that he not be considered a token, but treated like anyone else—and that meant having equal responsibilities. Harry liked engineering the food processing equipment, but he sensed that his prospects for moving up within the company would be limited. After two years he made a switch.

For the next nine years he worked at Chemical Construction Company, known as Chemico. Headquartered at Fifty-Ninth Street and Fifth Avenue in Manhattan, the builder of ammonia-based fertilizer plants was in need of engineers because of a recent contract for a large plant in Manitoba. While on the job, Harry was able to log time flying to vendors in the client's Navion, a light plane for the civil market produced after the war by North American Aviation and later by the Ryan Aeronautical Company.

His big break came when Bechtel Corporation, the giant construction firm, offered him a position at its San Francisco headquarters. Harry's combination of soft-spoken team-playing, first-rate technical training, and diverse life experience made him a mover within the organization. He had offices at headquarters and also in Edmonton, Alberta, and Baton Rouge, Louisiana. Travel for the company involved regular trips to Europe, Japan, and Indonesia. His talents were recognized, and over time he became the manager of procurement for the Refinery and Chemicals Division. It was a big job, and the future held the promise of further promotions up the corporate ladder.

Despite the success he was enjoying, Harry knew that Delphine was homesick for her native New York. The couple decided they would be happier back East. Harry heard that one of Bechtel's utility customers in Detroit had an opening. The company in the "Motor Capital" was substantial, the position secure, and the pay good.

Detroit wasn't New York, but it would get them closer to their families and their roots. Moreover, a large number of Tuskegee Airmen had settled in the city after the war. Harry knew some of the veterans from days long gone. So in 1976 the couple moved, and Harry started working at the downtown headquarters of natural gas supplier ANR Pipeline Company. Harry stayed with ANR until his retirement about a decade later, by which time he had risen to the position of vice president of administrative services.

In August 1972, four years before Harry arrived in Detroit, Tuskegee Airmen from around the country gathered in the city for their first major postwar reunion. Some, like Air Force Major General Daniel "Chappie" James Jr., were still serving and others, like Michigan state senator Coleman A. Young, had long since entered civilian life. James, who would become the first African American to achieve the rank of four-star general in the U.S. military, said at the time that despite discrimination and arrests during the war, "at least we were in." Young, who would become Detroit's first African American mayor the following year, said, "We were fighting to prove our ability to fly, and we had another struggle, to preserve our dignity as men and officers."

The same year as the reunion, some of the Tuskegee Airmen resid-
ing in the city got together in the home of Alexander Jefferson, a
Tuskegee Airman who had become a teacher after the war. The local
veterans banded together with their colleagues elsewhere across the
country to form a nonprofit organization to preserve the history of
their wartime experiences and to assist deserving youth in pursuit of
aerospace careers. The organization was called Tuskegee Airmen Inc.
One of the better known veterans behind its formation was Mayor
Young, who had trained at Tuskegee during the war as a bombardier-
navigator for the 477th Bombardment Group, the all-black B-25
medium bomber unit.

In keeping with his early labor-organizing in the auto industry as
well as his later social activism, Young was among a group of 477th
personnel in April 1945 who protested the exclusion of blacks from
an officer's club at an Indiana air base, in an episode that came to be
known as the Freeman Field mutiny. Young was one of sixty-one black
officers arrested and confined to quarters over a two-day protest, an
experience that stayed with him; it wasn't until late in his life, during
his tenure as mayor of Detroit, that the Air Force expunged the insub-
ordination-related blemish from his service record.

Through the intervention of Young's administration in the 1980s,
a stately officer's home on the grounds of historic Fort Wayne was
turned over to the newly formed Tuskegee Airmen National Museum.
The small but dignified brick building near the banks of the Detroit
River was converted into a museum filled with scale airplane models,
uniforms, and other artifacts and memorabilia. Textual panels and
photo enlargements in the tastefully appointed interior told the story
of the pioneering black flyers and their support crews.

The Tuskegee Airmen saw their compact museum as a living
testament to their flying accomplishments. They believed that a natural adjunct would be a flight academy to inspire the area's young

people to follow in their footsteps—or, as some have put it, their contrails. Pursuing that vision in 2002, when word came that the Air Force Academy in Colorado Springs was going to divest itself of some of its Schweizer SGM2-37 motor-gliders (designated 7G-7A Terrazzo Falcons), phone calls were initiated that resulted in three of the aircraft being donated to the museum's fledgling program.

These used motor-gliders with Air Force pedigree were destined to restore Harry's wings.

Chapter Fourteen

AN EVERLASTING BEACON

*A simple ray of light can break into a world of
darkness and illuminate it.*
—Albert Einstein

By the early 1990s, Harry and Delphine had settled into a comfortable retirement in Bloomfield Hills, an affluent suburb north of Detroit. On a quiet autumn day in 1994, while they were relaxing at home, the telephone rang. When Harry answered he had no idea that the call would trigger a chain of events that would bring closure to a nagging issue left in the wake of the 1949 gunnery competition.

On the other end of the line was one of Harry's fellow Tuskegee Airmen, the highly regarded William Campbell, who had been the 332nd's operations group commander at the time of the competition. Campbell's call was prompted by an item that had appeared in the just-published annual almanac of the Air Force Association's *Air Force Magazine*. The almanac had listed the winners of the gunnery meets that had occurred in Nevada over the years.

Troublingly, the winners of the first postwar meet were recorded as "unknown." In hindsight, this was hard to understand because the magazine had run an article about the gunnery meet in its June

1949 edition, a mere month after the competition had occurred. In that article the 332nd's winning pilots were not only given full credit for their accomplishment but were pictured in a team photograph.

Campbell wanted to correct the magazine's recent glaring omission and asked Harry if he had any documentation to prove that he and his 332nd teammates had won the meet. Propitiously, Harry had saved a copy of the official scoring tabulation. He offered to send it to his friend to "put the record straight."

Shortly after Campbell's call, Harry received a call from another of the battle-hardened Tuskegee Airmen. Charles Dryden wanted to have his recollections of the historic gunnery meet refreshed for the memoir he was writing at the time. The next spring, in March 1995, Harry met with both Bill Campbell and Chuck Dryden.

Campbell mentioned that he was busy trying to get the Air Force Association to revise its records to reflect the Tuskegee Airmen's first-place finish in the propeller class at the gunnery meet. Meanwhile, Dryden sensed that hardly anyone outside a handful of people knew about the event and asked Harry to write an article describing it, for inclusion in the program booklet to be distributed at that year's Tuskegee Airmen convention in Atlanta. Harry gladly complied, penning a summary of the event that concluded on the note that the 332nd's two winning trophies had mysteriously disappeared long ago. Eventually, Harry's essay would set in motion a search for the missing treasures.

The breakthrough came nine years later when a private citizen entered the picture motivated by a desire to honor "forgotten" achievements of African Americans. Zellie Rainey Orr had led an effort in the early 2000s to honor the memory of Second Lieutenant Quitman Charles Walker, a Tuskegee Airman who had grown up in her hometown of Indianola, Mississippi. When Walker's fighter was downed by enemy groundfire over Lake Balaton in Hungary on November

15, 1944, he became the first African American pilot from the state to perish on a combat mission.

In large part because of Zellie Orr's research, in early March 2004 Lieutenant Walker's medals were presented to his family at Columbus Air Force Base in Mississippi. The base also dedicated a Tuskegee Airmen exhibit and hosted a panel discussion that featured several Tuskegee Airmen, including Alva Temple, who happened to be living in retirement right in town. This was Orr's first contact with one of the gunnery meet's team members, and she was moved by Temple's desire to see the trophies again.

Meanwhile, in August, Orr found her way to the American Battle Monuments Commission website and used it to locate the grave of Lieutenant Walker at the Ardennes American Cemetery at Neupré, Belgium. She passed the information on to Walker's relatives, bringing them closure. Having completed the project that had consumed her for years, she now turned her attention to locating the trophies, an undertaking she later chronicled in a self-published book titled *Heroes in War—Heroes at Home: First Top Guns*.

On August 23, Orr called Alva Temple at his residence to gather more background information, but she was informed that the ailing veteran had been hospitalized due to ongoing complications from cancer. Temple's grandson was able to supply limited information about the 1949 competition based on an old article. Orr immediately put out feelers to the Air Force Association; the service's archives at Maxwell Air Force Base in Montgomery, Alabama; and the National Museum of the U.S. Air Force at Wright-Patterson Air Force Base in Dayton, Ohio.

By the end of the week, on Friday, August 27, she had received an e-mail from Jeff Underwood, a museum historian, indicating that the large trophy was in "secure storage" at the museum. The small trophy has never been found. Apparently it was lost when the 332nd was inactivated shortly after the gunnery meet on July 1, 1949.

Exactly what path the large trophy had traveled to end up in storage at the main repository for the Air Force's historic artifacts remains unclear to this day. Records indicate that the National Museum of the U.S. Air Force put it into storage after receiving it from the National Air and Space Museum in 1979. It is ironic that for twenty-five years the trophy sat under wraps in Dayton, not far from the old Lockbourne Air Force Base in Columbus from which Harry and his teammates had set out to win the gunnery meet.

Encouraged by her progress in locating the large trophy's whereabouts in a week marked by a flurry of e-mails, Orr placed another call to the Temple residence on Sunday afternoon, August 29, this time to relay the good news. Sadly, she was told that Alva Temple had died the day before. It was a crushing blow, but Orr's efforts to unearth the trophy and bring it out into the open got a new boost the following weekend.

Harry attended the funeral of his old friend and team leader in the small town of Carrollton, Alabama. After final respects were paid, Orr approached Harry with the news that she had located the trophy. It was the first time they had met, and Harry was astounded that one of the trophies had been found.

As soon as Harry returned home, plans were initiated to feature the trophy at the Tuskegee Airmen National Museum's annual dinner in Detroit. It would be an opportunity for surviving team members to see the trophy again and for relatives and supporters to celebrate the team's accomplishment of fifty-five years earlier. Harry thanked Orr profusely, e-mailing her that "you are a dream come true."

Word of the discovery spread like wildfire throughout the circle of surviving Tuskegee Airmen, and emotions understandably ran high. The crated keepsake was pulled from its storage space and was found to no longer have the silvery figurine on top. In any case, the trophy underwent an extensive restoration involving an acetone bath, cleaning with a calcium carbonate and distilled water slurry, and gentle hand polishing. It was transported to the annual dinner under the watchful eye of the museum's senior curator at the time, Terry Aitken.

Harry headlined the gala affair on December 10, 2004, and also wrote an article about the 332nd team's gunnery meet experience for the dinner's program booklet. Unfortunately Harry's only surviving pilot teammate, James Harvey, was unable to attend. But additional guests of honor included retired Master Sergeant Buford Johnson, one of the team's ground support members; Lucille Temple, Alva's widow; and Hazel Alexander, Halbert's widow. A special place was reserved for Zellie Orr in consideration of her success in reuniting the trophy with those who had won it.

Rather than staging the dinner at a hotel ballroom, the decision was made to have it in the cavernous old brick hangar at the city's airport, not coincidentally named in memory of Coleman Young, Detroit's late mayor who had served with the all-black 477th Bombardment Group during World War II. It was a bit drafty, but none of the several hundred supporters in attendance seemed to mind. This was a portal to the sky, the kind of place where the dreams of the evening's headliner were born and where the dreams of coming generations might also take root—given the museum's plans, since realized, to collect a small fleet of flyable trainers including some that had been used at Tuskegee during the war.

For the occasion, one of the hangar's walls was draped in linen to soften the dais's backdrop. Table decorations included helium-filled balloons in the shape of stars that floated upwards to the high ceiling. Most of the Tuskegee Airmen in attendance came attired in the Detroit chapter's powder-blue blazers. The airport's ambiance brought out a levity not often seen at formal dinners.

The festivities highlighted the story of the gunnery meet and its triumphant participants. Harry delivered a heartfelt tribute to his teammates, emphasizing the role of the ground crews who made the first-place finish possible. When he completed his remarks, the tarp in front of the dais was unfurled amid great anticipation.

The elusive trophy, not seen in more than a half century, projected its silvery sheen under the hangar's floodlights. Harry, Delphine, and others who had been touched over the years by the trophy and its powerful symbolism gathered around it. The juxtaposition was uncanny, for the Stewarts exuded the very same vitality and cheer in the hangar that night as had been captured in the photograph snapped of them on the tarmac at Lockbourne on the day fifty-five years before, when Harry returned to his base as one of the Air Force's top guns.

When the after-dinner chitchat dissolved and the hangar's special adornments were removed, the trophy went back to the museum in Dayton. This time, though, it wasn't squirreled away in storage; instead it became an anchoring artifact in a permanent exhibit on the Tuskegee Airmen and the integration of the Air Force. The exhibit occupies space in a part of the gallery devoted to World War II, arguably the Air Force's finest hour.

The unearthing of the trophy after so many years in obscurity caused some people to wonder out loud why such a significant historical item was kept out of public view. In response, the National Museum of the U.S. Air Force issued a statement that dispelled any suggestion of sinister intent behind its decision-making. In answer to a June 2005 inquiry from Zellie Orr, one of the museum's public affairs representatives, Sarah Greiner, cleared the air with a comprehensive explanation: The museum's exhibit on the integration of the Air Force dates back to the late 1960s. As soon as the museum's website was established, information and photographs from the exhibit were posted online. An expansion in progress during 2005 allowed more display space, enabling the exhibit to include the trophy at that time. Also, Greiner pointed out, the roughly 4,500 historical items then displayed in the museum complex represented only about 7 percent of the artifacts in the museum's collection management facility.

On April 26, 2006, Harry and his sole surviving pilot teammate, James Harvey, along with retired Master Sergeant Johnson, presented a lecture about the gunnery meet at the museum's invitation. On hand to introduce them was the museum's director, retired Major General Charles Metcalf. The general's personal involvement in the evening program was no surprise to anyone who knew him.

General Metcalf recognized the importance of both amassing and disseminating the history of the Tuskegee Airmen. During his term as the museum's director, he emphasized the museum's role as "keeper of the stories," by which he meant that to know the Air Force you have to know the experience of its men and women through the years. Capturing the stories and then conveying them to the museum's one million visitors each year was his passion.

Also, he had a close relationship with Wardell Polk, the longtime head of the Tuskegee Airmen National Museum. This kept him plugged-in to the community of black aviation pioneers. When Zellie Orr submitted requests for information about the location of the trophy and later about display possibilities, the retired general made sure she got answers, sometimes responding himself.

In the summer of 2018, Harry returned to the National Museum of the U.S. Air Force for the first time since his joint presentation. He happened to be passing through Dayton on Interstate 75 during a drive back to Bloomfield Hills from a family matter in Atlanta. He was accompanied by his daughter Lori, who serves as his unofficial booster and dutiful caregiver in Delphine's absence. During their visit, they enjoyed taking advantage of their anonymity while wandering through the museum's vast collection of aircraft, spending most of their time in the galleries that cover the periods of Harry's youth and military service.

In the pre-World War II section of one of those galleries, the Martin B-10 stopped Harry cold. Restored in its authentic colors of Army blue and yellow, the relic brought back memories of seeing the ungainly bomber, when still new, pass over his home in Queens. It had represented the cutting edge of American aviation in the lead-up to the war, setting his youthful imagination afire.

Flashbacks of walking from his home in Corona to see the planes at LaGuardia flooded his head as he ambled slowly down the aisle between other transitory aircraft of the prewar era. The museum's exhibits tracked the steady progression of technology, and as Harry stepped to the next row with Lori by his side, the planes that had given him wings came into view. Before he knew it, his open-cockpit wood-and-fabric primary trainer was dangling overhead. Within sight, suspended from the ceiling further down the hall, was his basic trainer with its greenhouse canopy and big round engine.

It was inevitable that being with his old trainers again would bring recollections of hot afternoons cruising over the Alabama countryside. His recollections were further stirred as he made his way into the gallery's World War II section. Harry's combat plane, the P-51 Mustang, had been temporarily removed, but the bomber types he escorted and the model of the fighter he dueled against were on display, looking as pristine as he had ever seen them.

The B-17, B-24, and Fw 190 were the planes that had dominated Harry's attention on combat missions seventy-three years earlier. As Harry wandered through the gallery, wan mental images from that time were made fresh by the restorations around him. He had visions—alternately magnificent and terrible—of hundreds of bombers filling the sky at once, and of swarms of fast-moving interceptors spoiling for a fight.

No mere tourist, Harry had flown in the same sky with these old warplanes, contributing his share to the history of the titanic struggle for control of the air as projected by the gallery's narrative panels. With each step another mission, more planes, and familiar faces flashed in front of him. His emotions ran the gamut—grief for friends lost, feeling lucky for having survived, gratitude for comradeship forged in fire, pride in effectively performing assigned missions.

And yet there was something more. The exhibit that had opened around the time he last visited the museum as an invited speaker came into view. He approached it knowingly, respectfully.

This area of the gallery is unevenly illuminated, not by choice so much as by circumstance; the museum's buildings are voluminous hangar-like structures in the military style that favors utility over appearance. Because of a glare from the glass encasing the gunnery meet trophy, some visitors have to squint to make out Harry's name and the names of his teammates engraved in the plaque affixed to the trophy's base, but there the names are—in the open for the world to see. They share the trophy's base with the separately listed names of white fighter pilots from the 1949 and 1950 gunnery meets, a sign of the service's tortuous march to remake itself so that its anachronistic culture would be as up-to-date as its modern technology.

On a panel describing the postwar integration of the Air Force, Harry saw a blowup of the photo of himself and his teammates Alva Temple, James Harvey, and Halbert Alexander standing with the trophy they had won at the gunnery meet in 1949. He read the accompanying text about how the Tuskegee Airmen's winning performance over Frenchman Flat had been the last, symbolic straw that broke the back of the service's systemic segregation. He could hardly help but stare, absorbed in the events and personalities of that time.

Some visitors strolling through the gallery noticed the old man immersed in the exhibit. One sidled up to Lori, who was standing by her father's side. The stranger asked her if the man she was with had anything to do with those pilots featured in the exhibit.

Lori smiled and nodded affirmatively. "Oh yes," she whispered. "My dad is a Tuskegee Airman." The stranger extended his arm, and the next thing Harry knew he was being congratulated by an admirer asking for his autograph.

Other visitors observed the happenings and joined in, asking Harry a string of questions and forming an impromptu line to shake his hand and obtain his autograph. The unexpected encounter with well-wishers lasted for about an hour. Harry was moved.

Just before he and Lori left the museum that afternoon for the four-hour drive home, they gazed one last time at the trophy. Harry was at peace, confident that the trophy, long out of sight, would live on in public view. It would not be an artifact collecting dust but an inspiration for generations yet to come.

Indeed, the display case's overhead lamp casts its light in such a way that amplified beams ricochet almost blindingly in multiple directions off the trophy's shimmering, polished veneer. The refracted glow highlights the trophy as a sort of lantern in the darkness—an everlasting beacon that shines the brilliant rays originally sparked by outcasts who dreamed of soaring to glory on

In 2005, after a long period in storage, the 1949 gunnery meet trophy was put on permanent display at the National Museum of the U.S. Air Force in Dayton, Ohio. The rays of light that ricochet off the shimmering trophy make it a sort of lantern—an everlasting beacon to warm weary hearts and remind people of the resilience of the human spirit. *National Museum of the U.S. Air Force*

the noblest of wings. The flame that Harry and his fellow Tuskegee Airmen kindled in the skies of long ago warms today's weary hearts and serves as a reminder of the resilience of the human spirit.

Chapter Fifteen

A GRATEFUL
NATION

It may be we shall reach the Happy Isles . . .
—Alfred Tennyson, *Ulysses*

In the summer of 2002, more than half a century after the wartime exploits of the Tuskegee Airmen, the U.S. Congress began to mull over the idea of recognizing them with its highest civilian honor, the Congressional Gold Medal. The proposal was introduced by Michigan's Carl Levin in the Senate and New York's Charles Rangel in the House of Representatives. Gradually but ineluctably, like the historic flying program itself, the bill picked up momentum. In December 2005, Secretary of Defense Donald Rumsfeld, a onetime naval aviator, threw his considerable weight behind the legislation.

The next year the measure passed both chambers without a single vote in opposition. Most senators and representatives put their names on the bills as cosponsors in an admirable display of bipartisanship. Belatedly, through its elected officials, a grateful nation was paying homage to its heroic sons who had fought for the right to fight and then distinguished themselves in war-torn skies.

On the balmy Washington afternoon of March 29, 2007, nearly five years after the initiation of the legislative effort, the anticipatory

murmur reverberating against the gilded ceiling of the Capitol's
rotunda was hushed by an official voice announcing the entrance of
the surviving Tuskegee Airmen, about three hundred aged veterans—
pilots, mechanics, administrators, armorers, and so forth, from the
numerous specialized billets that made the hybrid flying program a
success. The country's top officeholders, including President George
W. Bush, were on the platform to greet the honorees, and the audience
was filled to overflowing with family, friends, and admirers.

The Tuskegee Airmen entered the rotunda from their assembly
point in Statuary Hall, where minutes before they had been joined
quietly and out of public view by the president and Speaker of the
House Nancy Pelosi. The two leaders of opposite parties, normally
fierce political opponents, posed together for formal pictures with the
honorees. From the White House photographer's elevated position,

The ultimate photo op! President George W. Bush and Speaker Nancy Pelosi, center right, surrounded by Tuskegee Airmen in their hallmark postwar blazers. In advance of the award of the
Congressional Gold Medal, the heroes assembled in the Capitol Building's Statuary Hall, March
29, 2007. *The White House*

the scene was simply magisterial, as close to regal as is possible for an American commemoration.

The Tuskegee Airmen came attired in their postwar organization's blazers, mostly crimson red and powder blue. Every single one of these vivid blazers represented a civil rights pioneer and a wartime patriot. Aggregated together they saturated the stately hall, turning it into a florid sea. Bush and Pelosi, standing next to one another and looking from a distance like the pepper-and-salt-tinted bride and groom figurines stuck into the top layer of a wedding cake, were visually conspicuous against the mix of intense hues.

With the honorees arrayed on either side and all around, the two political rivals were uncommonly exuberant. A cynic might suspect that the politicians' enthusiasm was put on for the fleeting moments it took to snap the official photograph. But their faces expressed a rapture that lasted beyond the instant of the shutter release. There seemed to be something different at work on this occasion, beyond the fake emotions often on display at politicians' photo ops.

Other than the photographer and a security detail, the president and the speaker were alone with the veteran flyers and their ground crews, men who had burnished their reputations through achievement of the Double V. In their old age these men brought with them the same seriousness of purpose and depth of character, the same pride and personal dignity that they had brought to Tuskegee as young recruits. These were the qualities that had gotten them through tests of will far away and long ago.

The gravitas of the Tuskegee Airmen and the pathos of their long and accomplished lives, now inevitably drawing toward an end, permeated the hall. It was hard to see how anyone present at this gathering of heroes could be left untouched, unmoved. Later Bush would say, "I was impressed by the fact that I wasn't amongst heroes who were statues. I was impressed that I was amongst heroes who still live."

As the hour for the presentation approached, the honorees were ushered into the rotunda. It would be the last time so many Tuskegee Airmen would ever appear together. They did not march with a spring in their step as they had as young men with something to prove on the parade grounds at Tuskegee, for advanced age now trapped their boundless spirits in frail bodies. Many of the honorees were supported by canes, used walkers, or had to be pushed along in wheelchairs.

The muted reception that greeted the honorees as they began to enter was a fleeting reflex spurred by awe. The lull quickly turned to a thunderous ovation that seemed like it could last forever. For the whole time it took the Tuskegee Airmen to slowly file one by one to their seats in a reserved section directly in front of the podium, everyone who had come to pay their respects stood and cheered. Mixed in anonymously among the admirers and clapping along with them was former Secretary of Defense Donald Rumsfeld. Pressured to resign from the Bush cabinet in the wake of the 2006 midterm elections, he had come as a private citizen.

The audience's applause echoed off the rotunda's high walls, which are crowned by a recessed frieze depicting the nation's history. Wrapping the dome's entire three-hundred-foot circumference, the painted panorama starts with a scene that shows Christopher Columbus landing on the shore of America and ends with a panel that celebrates the birth of flight at Kitty Hawk, North Carolina. It was as if the three principal artists, Constantino Brumidi, Filippo Costaggini, and Allyn Cox, were saying that America's beginning depended on a courageous act of discovery and that its future hinged on an equally great leap into the unknown—as symbolized by the Wright brothers lofting into the sky.

The ceremony unfolding on the floor below was a validation of this optimism about the irrepressible arc of the country's technological and spiritual progress. After all, here were the remnants of the first military squadrons of African Americans being hailed as they entered the centerpiece of the Capitol, a national landmark that, beginning in the late eighteenth century and continuing through the early years of the Civil War, had been erected largely by slaves. Even the Statue of Freedom that straddles the top of the building's dome was, ironically, fabricated in part by Philip Reid, an African American laborer owned by the sculptor Clark Mills.

Notably, one of the honorees' most ardent devotees among the dignitaries on the platform was a contemporary of theirs, braced by canes in both hands. West Virginia's eighty-nine-year-old Robert C. Byrd, the Senate's president pro tempore, clumsily but enthusiastically brought his hands together in a clapping motion to show his veneration of the Tuskegee Airmen. The senator, ill and unable to control the tremors that caused his limbs to quiver intermittently, did not have to stand; under the circumstances no one would have faulted him for sitting through the grand entrance of the Tuskegee Airmen.

But fighting through obvious physical pain that caused periodic wincing, he did stand. Washingtonians in attendance did not lose sight of the irony of the ailing Senate leader's conspicuous outpouring of support for the Tuskegee Airmen. At an earlier time in his life, Byrd's political ambitions had almost been undone by the revelation that he had been a member of the Ku Klux Klan. Even after downplaying his affiliation with the white supremacist organization, the lawmaker fiercely opposed the historic civil rights legislation of 1964.

More than four decades later, Byrd's adulation for the honorees entering the rotunda was another piece of evidence of how far the Tuskegee Airmen and other freedom fighters had moved the country. In Byrd's eyes you could see an importuning, a beseeching of the

veterans passing before him to accept his own agonizing metamor-
phosis on race as the last sitting senator known to have belonged to
the Klan. For the senator, as for the country writ large, the occasion
was cathartic, a form of redemption, an expression of contrition for
past sins.

Because the event had been in the planning stages for a long time,
Harry knew the program's agenda in advance. Nevertheless, the event
was overwhelming for him. After all, he had entered the Army Air
Forces as a starry-eyed eighteen-year-old so fearful of the reaction he
might provoke in the company of Tuskegee's white townspeople that
he dared not venture off the campus or the airfields during the entirety
of his training in Alabama. Never in a million years did he imagine
that he and his fellow Tuskegee Airmen would be feted like this.

A panoply of leading elected officials was on the agenda. Each
dignitary was allotted a few minutes to deliver a tribute. Most of the
speechmaking was predictable and not particularly memorable. One
representative played up his personal friendships with a couple of the
Tuskegee Airmen. Another wasn't able to resist pandering by repeat-
ing the old myth that the Tuskegee Airmen had never lost a bomber
to enemy interceptors. Still another had trouble properly pronouncing
"Tuskegee," making it rhyme with "squeegee," to audible groans from
the audience.

In an entirely different class of speaker was Colin Powell, the first
African American secretary of state and chairman of the Joint Chiefs
of Staff. When he came to the podium he did not pull out folded
papers to read, as had most of the speakers. Looking not at printed
pages or a teleprompter screen, but into the eyes of the Tuskegee Airmen, he began: "My Tuskegee Airmen brothers, I stand so proudly
before you today … but I know from the depth of my heart that the
only reason I'm able to stand proudly before you today is that you
stood proudly for America sixty years ago."

Acknowledging that his rise through the ranks was made possible by the accomplishments of the Tuskegee Airmen, Powell noted the rich history of African Americans in uniform and enumerated examples of other black military units that had paved the way for those who would come later. He specifically mentioned the black troops who served under George Washington, the three hundred thousand black Union soldiers in the Civil War, and the black troopers who charged up San Juan Hill with Teddy Roosevelt. In a rising cadence, he ticked off black units whose service overlapped with that of the Tuskegee Airmen, including the 555th Parachute Infantry Battalion—the so-called "Triple Nickle"—the 92nd and 93rd Infantry Divisions, and the 761st Tank Battalion.

Powell singled out the Navy's first black officers, known as the Golden Thirteen, and the first black Marines, known as the Montford Point Marines. Coupling these pioneering black servicemen of World War II with the Tuskegee Airmen, he proclaimed that they all "did splendidly." It was clear from his opening words that Powell was talking not as an outside observer or an impartial commentator but as someone who had worn his country's uniform most of his adult life and who spoke with the passion that comes from life-altering experience at the frontlines.

His words struck a tone befitting the nation's historical march to freedom, as related in the rotunda's magnificent works of art. The backdrop included John Trumbull's *Surrender of Lord Cornwallis*, a huge canvas that depicts George Washington accepting the British surrender at Yorktown on October 19, 1781. That victory, in the Revolutionary War's last major campaign, signified the consummation of America's independence. Also behind the platform was Vinnie Ream's marble statue of a solemn Abraham Lincoln. Clad in his familiar double-breasted frock coat, the Civil War president stares down contemplatively at his right hand, which holds the Emancipation Proclamation.

Powell's talk was mostly the private soliloquy of a seasoned and erudite officer confiding in his attentive and respectful soldiers convened nearby. The rest of the room was privileged to listen in. The retired statesman and Army general knew well the struggles of the brave veterans arrayed before him, for he too—during his arduous climb to the pinnacle of national security, starting as an infantryman in the late 1950s—had experienced the ugliness of prejudice. Believing that all achievers stand on the shoulders of giants, he was letting the Tuskegee Airmen know that they were giants.

As both a beneficiary of giants and a latter-day giant himself, Powell asked: Why would a class of citizens serve a country that would not serve them? The question hung in the still air of the rotunda. You could hear a pin drop as the audience awaited the explanation.

Powell hazarded a two-part answer. It was, he opined, because the Tuskegee Airmen and the other aforementioned black servicemen had dared to dream that America would waken one day to the promise of its underlying principles. The second reason that these ostracized minority members chose to serve, he ventured, was that the military afforded them a way to prove love of country and to demonstrate the ability to deliver performance.

Doubling down on the latter idea, Powell told the honorees that despite all the hurdles they had encountered they never lost sight of the goal: to perform. Success and the acceptance into the larger society that it enabled was all about the performance, he stressed. And he extolled the Tuskegee Airmen for having made a conscious effort to pass on their legacy of performance to the next generation.

As he was nearing the conclusion of his speech, Powell surveyed the black veterans, gazing admiringly at them and taking in their faces slowly. He thanked them for what they had done for the African American community. But more important, he said, was what they had done for America.

Swallowing hard but not losing his rhythm—it was not Powell's practice to fall victim to his emotions—he said fervidly, "You caused America to look into the mirror of its soul—you showed America that there is nothing a black person couldn't do, there's nothing a human being with a sense of purpose cannot do if given the opportunity, if given the training, the skills...." Then, ending on the same personal note on which he had begun, he said, "As somebody who benefited from your service, I thank you as you receive this most worthy symbol of your courage and sacrifice, the Congressional Gold Medal."

It was a tour de force. Harry felt goosebumps, and he was not alone. As Powell walked back to his seat, the rotunda erupted into deafening applause.

As the saying goes, it would be a hard act to follow. Expectations for President Bush were not high. His oratorical skills were less than impressive: in the five and a half years since his most eloquent declamatory flourish, on the site of the 9/11 terrorist attack in Lower Manhattan, his pronouncements on everything from natural disasters to a slackening economy had failed to galvanize an increasingly skeptical and polarized public. Nevertheless, all eyes were on the president as he took his turn at the podium as the final speaker before the medal's presentation.

At this atypically amicable Washington event, where the bitterest of partisans sat together in unified purpose, it seemed that the tender harmony lightened the chief executive's bearing and added a lilt to his voice. Wisely, Bush eschewed hollow platitudes. Instead, like Colin Powell, he personalized his message.

"I have a strong interest in World War II airmen. I was raised by one." Referring to George H. W. Bush, who had piloted a Grumman Avenger off the deck of the *San Jacinto* aircraft carrier in the war's Pacific theater, he said, "He flew with a group of brave young men who endured difficult times in the defense of our country."

Bush then highlighted the obvious differences in wartime experiences between those naval aviators and the Tuskegee Airmen. His father and the other flyers aboard the carrier were "very fortunate because they never had the burden of having their every mission, their every success, their every failure viewed through the color of their skin.... Nobody expected them to bear the daily humiliations while wearing the uniform of their country."

Bush described a young African American who had been so anxious to join the Army Air Corps when flying positions opened to blacks that he left his car parked with a thousand dollars' worth of photography equipment at the train station, never to be seen again. He also described how Noel Parrish, the white commander at Tuskegee Army Airfield, responded to the naïve if not insolent question, "How do African Americans fly?" Parrish's answer: "'Oh, they fly just like everybody else flies—stick and rudder.'" The quip drew bursts of laughter.

Bush emphasized the effect the honorees had had on the current generation of service personnel. He pointed out that "one of our young soldiers today took pictures of you for a scrapbook for his children." In his praise for the legacy of the Tuskegee Airmen, he quoted another currently serving soldier: "It is not often that you get a chance to meet the guys who have paved the path for you."

Amid the growing problems Bush faced as the head of state, he somehow managed to put the heavy weight of his office aside—and to overcome his usually tortured syntax to connect with the audience as someone who had been moved by the deeds of the Tuskegee Airmen. Maybe it was the influence of his aviator father, to whom he had alluded, or perhaps it was the fact that, as a young man during the Vietnam years, he had briefly flown Air Force fighters, albeit far from war. Or perhaps it was the renown of the heroes being honored that inspired the embattled president to rise to the occasion.

His surprising wit was balanced by a cool seriousness, telegraphed by pursed lips and crinkled nose. The president said, "I thank you for the honor you have brought to our country." He reminded the audience that the Tuskegee Airmen "were fighting two wars: One was in Europe and the other took place in the hearts and minds of our citizens … And little by little every victory at war was translated to a victory here in the United States."

In helping to win the war, Bush said, the Tuskegee Airmen had also helped to change the nation for the better. In conferring the Congressional Gold Medal, he declared, the government's leaders were ensuring that the story of the first black veterans of the air "will be told and honored for generations to come." Placing his hand over his heart, he called it "the story of the human spirit, and it ends like all great stories do—with wisdom and lessons and hope for tomorrow."

What more could the president say to the gallant gentlemen he had come to honor? "And I would like to offer a gesture to help atone for all the unreturned salutes and unforgivable indignities." Harry, sitting in the front row, pondered for a split second what the gesture might be—the naming of a monument, the opening of a new training base?

Before Harry could speculate further, Bush continued, "And so, on behalf of the office I hold and a country that honors you, I salute you for the service to the United States of America." As he spoke those final words, the president raised his right hand crisply to his brow.

It was a salute—literally, a salute—from the commander in chief of the United States to the Tuskegee Airmen. Bush held the salute as he panned his head from right to left and back again to encompass all of the honorees. And the most remarkable thing happened.

Spontaneously, the honored veterans hastened to their feet in a ripple from front to back, Harry in the lead. The veterans fought the effects of age and illness as they straightened themselves into the posture of attention they had learned at Tuskegee. They snapped back purposeful salutes of their own, as if to say one last time, "Ready for duty, sir!"

The Tuskegee Airmen's instinctive reaction revealed much about them and their enduring values, their tradition of honor, and their undying bond with fellow flyers. Those values had remained robust against the tide of insults and provocations. The scene could hardly help but bring to mind the old warriors celebrated in the stirring verses of Lord Tennyson's *Ulysses*:

> Tho' much is taken, much abides; and tho'
> We are not now that strength which in old days
> Moved earth and heaven, that which we are, we are;
> One equal temper of heroic hearts,
> Made weak by time and fate, but strong in will
> To strive, to seek, to find, and not to yield.

A half-dozen preselected Tuskegee Airmen ascended the platform to receive the Congressional Gold Medal on behalf of the approximately fifteen thousand trailblazers who had been part of the historic military flying program. This contingent was not chosen at random. Each was a standout, an exemplar among heroes. To no one's surprise, Harry was one of them.

As he mounted the platform with his comrades in arms, Harry glanced to the side, where he made eye contact with Delphine. Confined to a wheelchair because of compound medical issues, Delphine clasped her hands together and beamed with pride. Harry winked. They had come a long way together since Harry's flight suit days, and he knew that his latest climb up the riser's steps to be hailed along with his wartime buddies by the country's leaders—like so many other upward strivings in his life—would have been doubtful without Delphine as the wind under his wings.

First in the procession was Roscoe Brown, Harry's fellow NYU alum and postwar mentor. Next was Alexander Jefferson, who had survived a German prison camp and after the war become a science teacher in Detroit. He was followed by Lee Archer, another NYU alum who, depending on how kill scores were tallied, was arguably an ace. Charles McGee, who had flown hundreds of missions spread across three wars and had the distinction of being the highest-ranking officer among the surviving members of the group, was next. Right behind him was Harry, followed by retired Technical Sergeant George Watson, a mechanic whose inclusion reflected the pilots' recognition that their success depended on the myriad subspecialties of those, especially among the enlisted ranks, who had worked behind the scenes and out of the spotlight.

Six representatives from among the Tuskegee Airmen were selected to receive the Congressional Gold Medal on behalf of the estimated fifteen thousand participants in the segregated flying program. In the rotunda of the Capitol Building, left to right: George Watson, Harry, President George W. Bush, Speaker Nancy Pelosi, Charles E. McGee, Lee A. Archer, and Alexander Jefferson. Out of the frame to the right is Roscoe C. Brown. *The White House*

Meanwhile, President Bush had walked over to Senator Byrd to help him stand. Clutching Byrd's hand, Bush steadied the Senate leader as he inched his way to the center of the platform, where Speaker Pelosi joined them. All three would stand through the medal's presentation and the Tuskegee Airmen's remarks. A velvet case was handed to Bush, and with no additional fanfare he cracked it open, bringing the resplendent medallion's golden sheen into view.

Roscoe Brown, being the first in line, was welcomed by the president, who patted him on the back with his right hand. With his left hand, Bush placed the Congressional Gold Medal's opened case into the Tuskegee Airman's cupped hands. The moment had arrived; with Brown's acceptance, the sparkling symbol of a grateful nation had been conveyed to its intended recipients, the Tuskegee Airmen.

Brown's jubilant expression was electric. The other representative Tuskegee Airmen stood line abreast across the platform, looking towards their glowing colleague who had taken receipt of the Congressional Gold Medal. After the ceremony it would be transferred to the Smithsonian Institution, where it would reside in the permanent collection, as mandated by the enabling legislation. Bronze replicas were to be provided to each of the honorees immediately following the program.

■   ■   ■

It had taken months for the medal honoring the Tuskegee Airmen to be produced because each medal, dating back to the first one presented to George Washington in 1776, is a unique award with a distinct design. The U.S. Mint's sculptor-engravers Phebe Hemphill and Don Everhart had the daunting task of capturing the essence of the Tuskegee Airmen's story on the two sides of the medal. Their designs proved how a couple of carefully planned and well executed renderings can encapsulate an entire saga.

On the topside, or obverse, of the medal, three Tuskegee Airmen are depicted in profile— first is a pilot in leather helmet with goggles, and backing him up are a mechanic in billed cap and an administrative officer in service cap. This makes the point that the flying succeeded because of a team effort; the aviators were the most visible, the ones garnering headlines, but, as they knew so well, their success hinged on the unsung support personnel. Block letters arched above the three figures spell out "TUSKEGEE AIRMEN" and to the right and left are the dates—"1941" and "1949"—when the segregated program was in operation. The three figures are cradled on the outstretched wings of an eagle, which according to the U.S. Mint's description, symbolizes "flight, nobility, and the highest ideals of the nation."

The reverse side of the medal shows some of the aircraft in which the Tuskegee Airmen burnished their reputation. The warplanes appear stacked in formation, as in the logo of Tuskegee Airmen Inc., after which the image was patterned. At the top is the P-40 Warhawk, the first fighter that the 99th Fighter Squadron rode into combat; in the middle is the P-51 Mustang, the 332nd Fighter Group's last fighter to see combat during the war; and, below is the B-25 Mitchell, the medium bomber operated by the all-black 477th Bombardment Group, which did not prepare in time to be deployed abroad. The bottom of the medal contains the succinct inscription: "OUTSTANDING COMBAT RECORD INSPIRED REVOLUTIONAY REFORM IN THE ARMED FORCES."

■ ■ ■

The medal was left in its case as Roscoe Brown, on cue, strode towards the podium to make responsive remarks. Robert Byrd, the longtime senator who had had to live down his past association with the KKK, intercepted Brown, reaching out and gripping his hand hard, pulling it towards himself and holding it close to his chest. As he squeezed the Airman's hand, Byrd uttered a few words—too far from the microphones to be audible, but it was obvious from his smile that the words were warm and congratulatory. In the instant that the two men of diametrically opposite backgrounds shook hands with mutually approving nods, time stood still, like in a freeze-frame of a videotaped history lesson. A spell that had long cast its glum and melancholy pall over America had been broken.

Roscoe Brown, still aglow, introduced his colleagues on the platform by rank and name, looking at each of them proudly, like a brother, as he did so. Then he turned to the audience and, referencing the Double V, stated that the Tuskegee Airmen were "very, very pleased to have been at the forefront of the struggle for freedom and justice." After Brown had set the bar, some of his fellow flyers stepped to the podium.

Alexander Jefferson spoke on behalf of the thirty-two Tuskegee Airmen who had been taken prisoner by the Germans during the war. Lee Archer waxed nostalgic about the compliments he had received over the years for his service but suggested that the current ceremony was unique because the country's leaders were asserting that the country owed a debt of gratitude to the Tuskegee Airmen. To that he said, "Paid in full!"

Harry was the last to speak, symbolically pulling up the rear of the formation, much as he had as a new addition to the 332nd in 1945, flying Tail End Charlie on escort missions. Always the quiet one, more an engineer than a public speaker, he read a two-line statement on behalf of the Tuskegee Airmen "expressing our gratitude for all those responsible for this poignant and memorable occasion." It was vintage Harry—unruffled, respectful, gracious: the quintessential Tuskegee Airman.

In a way it didn't matter what the men receiving the medal said. As would be expected, the audience responded politely, at times enthusiastically. What really mattered was the Tuskegee Airmen's combined feats, the fullness of their record, the purity of their motives, their triumph over impossible odds, and their imperturbable humility.

The dissonance for which Washington is notorious did not disappear, but it receded for the duration of the ceremony in the rotunda. Like flights that soar to new heights, the success of the Tuskegee Airmen was a reminder of how high people can rise when faithful to a noble ideal, an audacious quest, a distinguished enterprise, something glorious. Indeed, for the time the rotunda was dominated by the presence of the Tuskegee Airmen, it harbored no partisans, only Americans.

Chapter Sixteen

KEEPING THE DREAM ALIVE

I'll fly away, O Glory,
I'll fly away.
—Albert E. Brumley, "I'll Fly Away"

From its founding in 1987, the Tuskegee Airmen National Museum in Detroit was envisioned as a living testament to the flying accomplishments of the country's first African American military pilots. This meant having a flight academy to inspire the city's young people. As previously mentioned, when word came in 2002 that the Air Force Academy in Colorado Springs was going to divest itself of some of its Schweizer motor-gliders, the museum requested and received three of the aircraft.

Harry's flying had languished; work and family commitments had taken precedence, crowding out one of the things he loved to do. In 2004 that would change. He was asked if he wanted to go for a ride in a restored P-51, the type he had flown in combat during World War II.

It had been fifty-nine years since his last flight in a Mustang, and the experience of being in the cockpit again, soaring like the fighter pilots of old, reignited the wonder he had known. A short time later, he described his experience: "When I got in the plane and flew, I was bitten by the flying bug again." In March 2005, he linked up with an instructor and refreshed his dormant skills, earning a glider rating at the same time.

Operating out of the city's Coleman A. Young Municipal Airport, Harry started giving rides to youngsters in the museum's motor-gliders. He hoped to kindle in his young passengers the same passion that he had had for flight when growing up near New York's LaGuardia Airport. The museum's leaders, for their part, were thrilled to have an original Tuskegee Airman flying the motor-gliders; they had Harry's name emblazoned on one of them.

By the fall of 2007, Harry was eighty-three years old, and he reluctantly decided the time had come to ground himself. In the two years that he had participated in the museum's aviation program, he

After a ride in a restored P-51, Harry had found his first love again. In former Air Force Academy motor-gliders operated by the Tuskegee Airmen National Museum at Coleman A. Young Municipal Airport in Detroit, Harry introduced young people to their first plane rides, hoping to instill in them a sense of the magic of flight that he had experienced as a youngster watching planes at LaGuardia and as a cadet learning stick-and-rudder technique at Tuskegee. *Harry Stewart Jr.*

had personally introduced scores of children to the joys of flight. He gave many their first plane rides.

After taking off, he often steered north to sparsely used airspace underlain by virgin pastures and verdant farmlands, which presented a stark contrast to the daily sight-picture taken in by the program's inner-city youth. At cruise altitude, while enveloped by the fresh breezes wafting in from over the blue waters of Lake Huron, Harry liked to pull the long wing of the motor-glider through graceful maneuvers that he had learned a generation ago in the skies above Tuskegee, sharing the liberating force—the magic—of the flyer's world with his onboard companions.

■　■　■

Museum officials, led by president Brian R. Smith, had often ruminated about the museum one day having each of the aircraft types flown by the Tuskegee Airmen during World War II, starting with the Stearman biplane trainer all the way through the red-tailed fighters. In 2008, they made contact with the owner of one of only two flyable advanced trainers known to have been stationed at Tuskegee Army Airfield during the war. Negotiations ensued, and by the next year a deal was struck to store the plane at the museum's hangar in Detroit. In September 2010, the museum consummated the purchase.

North American Aviation AT-6C, serial number 42-48884, had rolled off the assembly line in Dallas and been handed over to the Army Air Forces on March 27, 1943. It was promptly pressed into service as an advanced trainer at Tuskegee, where it remained for the duration of the war except for a deployment in June–July 1945 to Eglin Army Airfield in Florida. Harry checked his records, and while it's not certain from the weathered logbook's notations, indications are that he almost certainly flew this ship back when he was a cadet.

After the war, the plane hopscotched around the country, with postings at bases in Kansas, Tennessee, and New Hampshire. At one point it even wound up back in Alabama, assigned to the Air University at Maxwell Army Airfield. In January 1951 the trainer went to the North American Aviation plant at Downey, California, where it was remanufactured to the standard of a later model. On May 7, 1951, it was handed back to the Air Force as a T-6G with serial number 49-3292.

The rebuilt plane was then used by flight instruction contractors under Air Training Command's aegis in Georgia and Missouri. In mid-1955 it was flown to the sprawling desert storage area at Davis-Monthan Air Force Base in Arizona. Piston-powered taildraggers had little relevance to the Air Force a decade after the war, so in January 1956 the well-worn trainer was sold off as surplus property. For more than a half-century it plied the skies in private hands, until finally

In the spring of 2009, the Tuskegee Airmen National Museum in Detroit took delivery of one of only two still flyable AT-6 advanced trainers that had been used at Tuskegee Army Airfield during World War II. Harry rode along on the last leg of the delivery flight, helping to guide his old trainer to its new home. Sitting behind ferry pilot Bill Shepard, Harry flashes the victory sign, a poignant reference to the campaign to achieve the Double V—victory against totalitarianism abroad and racism at home. In subsequent years, while in the company of the plane on the air show circuit, Harry has delighted in explaining that he was "one of the luckiest people in the world to be able to fly this great airplane." *Tuskegee Airmen National Museum*

returning to the hands of some of those who had stamped it with its unique historical character.

In connection with the plane's museum delivery flight from Oshkosh, Wisconsin, to Detroit in spring 2009, arrangements were made for Harry to fly with the ferry pilot, Bill Shepard, on the final leg from Jackson, Michigan. On this ship's wings Harry had been baptized in the ocean of air more than six decades before. As he wrapped his fingers around the control stick, memories of old glories came to mind. For much of the flight and for a time afterwards, Harry beamed like he was one of the youngsters he had taken on a motor-glider ride.

The "old girl," as he referred to the antique, hadn't changed fundamentally in all the intervening years. She remained an honest lady who, if handled respectfully, would reciprocate the favor. And in the half-hour or so that Harry guided his long-separated mistress to her new home, his flight retraced a familiar trajectory—the course that allows for the dream that anything is possible.

Starting with the 2011 flying season, the rare aircraft has been displayed at a succession of air shows and fly-ins, frequently showcased in the premier exhibit space in deference to its historical significance. When time and health permit, Harry accompanies it, standing proudly alongside his ship. When bystanders approach with questions about his flights in it long ago, a smile invariably lights his face. He has been heard explaining, with a twinkle in his eyes, that he was "one of the luckiest people in the world to be able to fly this great airplane."

■ ■ ■

But even before Tuskegee there was LaGuardia. As a fifteen-year-old in love with aviation and growing up in the Corona section of

Queens, Harry was at the airport on the occasion of its renaming in honor of New York's mayor in 1939. He stood on the ramp in front of a shiny all-metal airliner decked out in the markings of Transcontinental & Western Air, the precursor of Trans World Airlines, or TWA. The next spring, he watched from LaGuardia's fence as large flying boats, the exquisite Pan Am Clippers, launched from the Marine Air Terminal to destinations across the Atlantic.

The TWA and Pan Am transports were tantalizing examples of a new age in commercial air transportation. For an impressionable adolescent they were the impetus for dreams of worlds awash in adventure. With tears in her eyes, Harry's junior high school history teacher and guidance counselor had warned him not to get his hopes up. And indeed, when he tried to apply—as a decorated air combat veteran—to the airlines whose silver ships had lit his passion for flight, they turned him down on the spot.

But the story did not end there. The offensive employment practices at the airlines eventually changed with the times, spurred on by civil rights organizations promoting legal and legislative protections against discrimination. Also, private citizens stepped forward. Trailblazers included Perry H. Young Jr., who was hired in 1956 as the first black pilot for New York Airways, the commuter helicopter airline. Two years later, Ruth Carol Taylor was hired as Mohawk Airlines' first black flight attendant. A major breakthrough occurred in 1965 when Marlon D. Green, a black pilot, won a protracted lawsuit against Continental Airlines to become one of the company's pilots.

As things unfolded, Pan Am went bankrupt in 1991. Its vaunted transatlantic routes, the ones pioneered by the famous Clippers that had fueled Harry's dreams of being a globe-trotting airline pilot, were taken over by Delta Air Lines in that year. And five years earlier, Delta had purchased Western Airlines, which could trace its origins to a

1930s offshoot of TWA. TWA itself went bankrupt in 2001 and was absorbed by American Airlines.

Both Delta and American are proud of their heritage airlines, Pan Am and TWA. American even maintains one of its aircraft in TWA heritage livery. The history is important, in part because many airline employees believe what they do is more than just a job.

More than seventy years after Harry's dream of flight was born at LaGuardia's fence, friends of his asked the two successor airlines if honorary captain's wings could be awarded to him, given his distinguished military flying career and the unfortunate refusal of the legacy carriers to accept his application to fly for them. Delta was the first to agree.

On February 19, 2015, Harry was flown to Delta's headquarters in Atlanta for the presentation. The honorary captain's wings were accompanied by a typed tribute and a plaque reading, "In Recognition of Achievement in Aviation/Presented to: Honorary Delta Captain Harry Stewart."

The accompanying tribute was on Delta letterhead. It recited Harry's career highlights and included his military decorations. It concluded:

> Your courage, hard work and perseverance are traits we look for when training Delta pilots and promoting them to the position of Captain. Be it known to all those present that Lt Col Harry Stewart, USAF, Ret. is hereby conferred the title of Honorary Delta Captain.
>
> On behalf of Delta's 12,000 pilots, we are honored and humbled to call you one of our own.

The tribute was signed by Captain Jim Graham, Delta's vice president of flying operations and chief pilot. In August 2018,

American Airlines followed Delta's lead and announced that it would award honorary captain's status not only to Harry but to all the surviving Tuskegee Airmen, in recognition of their selfless service to the country under exceptionally burdensome circumstances. During Black History Month, February 2019, the airline sent individualized certificates designating Harry and each of his surviving colleagues as an "Honorary American Airlines Captain."

Harry held the document in its leather diploma-style cover, peering at it with a gleam in his eyes. The certificate referred to his "having served with distinction as one of the original Tuskegee Airmen" and noted that it was awarded as evidence of his "attaining a special place of high honor and as a sign of appreciation from the more than 130,000 American Airlines team members around the world." It was signed by Kimball Stone, American Airlines' senior vice president of flight operations and the Integrated Operations Center.

The magnitude of American Airlines' transformation from its offhand acceptance of the industry's prevailing attitudes of the mid-twentieth century can be seen in the top management's quick and unequivocal reaction in recent times to isolated incidents involving passengers of color. On October 25, 2017, CEO Doug Parker sent a letter to his company's employees stating: "We do not and will not tolerate discrimination of any kind."

Today many African Americans, members of other minority groups, and women are acutely aware that their opportunity to fly for the airlines was forged through individual acts of courage by trailblazers like Harry. By refusing to be intimidated and by being unafraid to stare the evil of prejudice in the face, Harry was one of the steadfast souls who opened up the staircase to the skies for people of all colors and creeds and walks of life.

Harry and his fellow Tuskegee Airmen never stopped dreaming, never stopped believing that one day America would waken to the promise of equal opportunity for all citizens. More than three-quarters of a century since the little boy from Queens went to the local airport with the improbable dream of captaining the exquisite and alluring TWA and Pan Am airliners, those airlines, in their modern form, had blessed his dream. He is now Captain Stewart!

In reaching for the heavens and defying gravity, Harry advanced the cause of freedom. The successes that stemmed from his gallantry and quiet dignity are reminders that no one needs to accede any longer to the encumbrances that he

Soaring to glory! Aviation artist Stan Stokes captured Harry on the wing of a postwar F-47N, gazing skyward. Above is his red-tailed P-51D *Little Coquette* and the P-47, in which he had the bulk of his fighter lead-in training. To the left are the patches of the 332nd Fighter Group and the 301st Fighter Squadron. *Palm Springs Air Museum*

encountered throughout his flying life. Instead, as the astute commentator Walter Lippmann wrote in praise of Amelia Earhart and her ilk, who had pushed the proverbial envelope ever farther in flight's golden age, in the dust of which we are made "there is also fire, lighted now and then by great winds from the sky."

Harry helped to kindle that fire, which has illuminated the way for all who fly!

Epilogue

AFFIRMING THE LEGACY

I will not falter,
And I will not fail.

—United States Air Force, "The Airman's Creed"

Cognizant of the value to morale in preserving the heritage of outstanding historic units, the Air Force reconstituted the 332nd Fighter Group as the 332nd Air Expeditionary Group in 1998, forty-nine years after the historic all-black flying outfit had been inactivated. The modern 332nd was stationed at Ahmad al-Jaber Air Base in Kuwait, where it supported Joint Task Force–Southwest Asia in the enforcement of no-fly zones throughout Operation Southern Watch. The group heeded modern operational doctrine by rotating modular forces in and out of expeditionary deployments.

It dawned on someone in the chain of command that inviting representative members of the original unit from its glory days in the 1940s would likely be a shot in the arm to the men and women serving at the desert base. The two Tuskegee Airmen invited were Harry Stewart and Lucius Theus, a retired major general who had trained in part at Tuskegee and who as a non-pilot had a distinguished Air Force career in administration. Gratified, they did not hesitate to leave the comfort of home to visit with the heirs of their legacy.

The two pioneers arrived at the base in mid-February 2001 and were treated grandly for the several days of their visit. The personnel of the reconstituted 332nd were in awe of the visiting veterans. Harry and Lu drew on their wartime experience to urge the young service members to stick to their principles in the face of adversity, remain loyal to their comrades-in-arms, and give their all for the country. The veterans' example and their pep talks provided sustenance for the challenges to come.

On February 16, 2001, one of the group's F-15E Strike Eagles flew a mission against Iraqi command and control centers in Baghdad. The pilot and his weapon systems officer had carried an American flag with them. Upon their return to base they presented the flag to Harry as a token of their respect.

The certificate accompanying the presentation was emblazoned with the modern group's emblem, which was in major part a replica of the emblem originally adopted by the first 332nd during World War II, with an image of a panther spitting fire. The latest airmen to operate with it as their badge of honor were upholding the tenacious ferocity that it symbolizes.

The next year, as part of the lead-up to the second Gulf War, the air expeditionary group expanded into the 332nd Air Expeditionary Wing. The new incarnation of the Tuskegee Airmen's storied group was the largest wing in the Air Force. At its peak, more than eight thousand men and women from all walks of life, representing the breadth of America's rich diversity, operated a variety of fighter, attack, reconnaissance, tanker, and search-and-rescue aircraft under the fire-spitting panther emblem and the Red Tail sobriquet.

Charged with providing air power for the combatant commander during Operation Iraqi Freedom, the wing moved to Tallil Air Base near Nasiriyah in 2003 and then to Joint Base Balad, about sixty miles north of Baghdad, in 2004. The leadership of the wing made it a priority to communicate the unit's renowned heritage to all who were serving in its ranks. Newsletters, e-blasts, and commander's bulletins told of courage under fire and of standing fast to underlying principles. Because of the seminal contributions of the precursor unit, the modern wing adopted "The Legend Continues" as its official battle cry. The wing's airmen proudly referred to each other as "Tuskegee Airmen."

When the conflict turned into an unconventional war complicated by ancient sectarian rivalries and characterized by a series of seemingly endless suicide bombings, revenge killings, and roadside explosions, a chorus of officeholders, self-anointed experts, and media commentators chimed in to question the worth of America's commitment. Some of the U.S. government's highest-profile officials even went so far as to declare in their gravest tone that staying the course was hopeless. The war, they said, was lost.

Yet amid the naysaying, the 332nd Wing's airmen hunkered down, and the Air Force called in its prized resource again: additional visits by Tuskegee Airmen from 2005 onward bolstered spirits. The visiting veterans included Harry's fellow pilots from the original 332nd—friends like Lee Archer, Alexander Jefferson, and Charles McGee. They spread cheer and encouragement, both by their chipper personalities and their stories of winning air battles while overcoming endemic racism. Whether white or black, the service members at Balad cherished the face time with old heroes who in their prime had also heard the refrain that their cause was futile.

During their whirlwind tours, the Tuskegee Airmen told how they had withstood the withering challenges of World War II out of a love for their country. It is hard to quantify the impact that the venerated aviators had on operations. But the men and women they met with during their trips to Balad spread the word as they pressed on in performance of their duties, clearly inspired by the one-on-one encouragement from the original Red Tails.

By mid-2008, a dramatic turnaround began to take hold in Iraq. The stalemate that once appeared intractable even to some supporters of America's intervention had been snapped. Of course, there were many factors at work, including a troop surge and an indigenous "awakening" in segments of Iraq's population, and it would be presumptuous to attribute the improvement to morale-building trips. It would be plausible, though, to infer that the visits by Harry and the other old-timers had an impact that added at least a nudge in tipping the balance.

Ironically, the hard-won stability in Iraq was squandered. Political promises of an arbitrarily set end-date of the American troop presence took precedence over military necessities. The relative calm that prevailed gave a false confidence that renewed violence would not fill the vacuum left by the departing U.S. combat forces. Against the advice of senior military commanders, the withdrawal occurred in late 2011 under the aerial escort of the 332nd.

Ground troops in armed convoys moved safely from Iraq to neighboring Kuwait. The escort missions were mostly perfunctory, which spoke volumes about the work the 332nd had done during its long deployment to Iraq. The men and women of the 332nd, old and new, could hold their heads high.

The Iraq War was now left in the hands of the Iraqis, and the mistaken decision to withdraw prematurely was compounded by a failure to recognize the continued need for the expeditionary wing in the theater of operations. In May 2012 the 332nd was inactivated for the second time in its history. But three years later, in May 2015, the wing had to be stood back up to deal with the resurgence of terrorist activity that had been foreseen by perceptive commanders and analysts as a possible consequence of the ill-advised withdrawal.

In Operation Inherent Resolve, the 332nd has had to refight some of the battles it had already won with U.S. troops and their partners. Under demanding circumstances, including the requirement to avoid civilian casualties, it has provided essential air power to friendly ground forces. Extremists of the Islamic State in Iraq and Syria have lost virtually all the territory they once held. Within the wing, the influence of the Tuskegee Airmen continues to resonate.

■ ■ ■

The mystique of the Tuskegee Airmen also persists elsewhere in the Air Force. The four World War II fighter squadrons made famous by the black flyers live on. Notably, the last squadron in which Harry served on active duty, the 100th, has had its ties to Alabama solidified. Mere months after the Congressional Gold Medal was awarded to the Tuskegee Airmen in 2007, the Alabama Air National Guard became the host to a reactivated 100th Fighter Squadron. In 2009 the squadron was attached to the 332nd Air Expeditionary Wing at Balad, which represented the first time since the 1940s that the squadron was united with the wing.

These days the squadron flies its F-16 Fighting Falcons from Montgomery Regional Airport, also known as Dannelly Field, which is located only about forty miles from Tuskegee, where the squadron was born in 1942. To mark the bond with the first 100th, the fin of one of the modern squadron's otherwise dull-gray fighter jets is symbolically emblazoned in bright red paint. It is expected that the Red Tail tradition will continue in 2023, when the squadron is scheduled to take delivery of its next fighter jets, the highly advanced F-35 Lightning IIs.

More than seven decades after the first Red Tails followed their dreams and soared above the Alabama countryside, their latter-day brethren regularly climb through nearly the same piece of the sky. As they prepare for their next challenge, the modern Red Tails are strengthened by the example of their forebears who established the standard so very high and who remained ever faithful to "The Airman's Creed": "I will not falter, And I will not fail." Each time the squadron's fighter jets launch on a mission, led by the plane that wears the identifier of the Tuskegee Airmen, their pilots are never really alone in their single-seat cockpits. Wherever they fly, the spirit of Harry Stewart and the other original Tuskegee Airmen rides with them.

ACKNOWLEDGMENTS

Deep appreciation goes to the central subject of this book, retired Air Force Lieutenant Colonel Harry T. Stewart Jr. Fighter pilots sometimes get a bad rap for being overbearing and egotistical, as if the personality of those at the tip of the spear in armed conflict must project omniscience and invincibility. Fortunately, Harry is far removed from this caricatured stereotype.

He is quite the opposite—exceedingly modest, incurably soft-spoken, and unfailingly humble. He personifies the values Americans should want in their heroes. And he is not alone among his special group of veterans who are invariably identified by the name of the location in rural Alabama where they earned their wings.

The Tuskegee Airmen have the best possible excuse to lash out in fits of rage. Even when they were putting their lives on the line for their country, some of their countrymen went out of their way to belittle and berate them, for no good reason at all. But as the targets of this shameful treatment, they usually didn't take the bait. With rare exceptions, the black veterans who soared to new heights during World War II resisted the temptation to become like their tormentors and exhaust themselves in spite.

In some ways, the Tuskegee Airmen's rejection of the ugly side of human nature is their greatest accomplishment. These gallant men of the air returned to an unwelcoming environment and yet overcame obstacles at home that foreclosed opportunities that would naturally have extended their military aviation careers into flying for the airlines. When this pathway forward was cut off for them, they succeeded at second careers as teachers, lawyers, doctors, engineers, government officials, and so forth, becoming leading citizens of their communities. They refused to be distracted from what was decent and noble, perhaps by keeping their sights on the possibilities looming on the horizon ahead as opposed to delving into the evils of the past.

It has been an honor to call Harry a friend for many years and a real treat to have had him as a flying companion in my World War II-era Stearman and to have been a passenger of his in one of the Schweizer motor-gliders of the Tuskegee Airmen National Museum. How lucky I have been to share the controls in flight with this lion of the air! And how lucky I have been to have known as friends so many of Harry's comrades-in-arms, most of whom have sadly gone West in the inexorable march of time.

Today, of the Tuskegee Airmen, only twelve fighter pilots who deployed and saw combat in World War II are still alive. One of these is Harry Stewart, which makes recording his story all the more imperative. Like the other Red Tails, Harry fought for liberty abroad while being denied its fruits at home. In the gamut of his experiences, ranging from tragic to triumphant, are lessons to be heeded and inspiration to be found.

At first, Harry wasn't sure about recounting the ups and downs of his flying life. But with the gentle urging of Dr. Brian Smith, president of the Tuskegee Airmen National Museum and a leading light of the Detroit Chapter of Tuskegee Airmen Inc., Harry was persuaded to do it. A big source of encouragement at every step of the way has been Harry's ever cheerful daughter Lori.

Various museums and libraries, whose officials and volunteers work diligently to retain a particular slice of aviation history, have contributed to this book in different ways. At the Tuskegee Airmen National Museum, the aforementioned Brian Smith has been helpful in providing seemingly arcane tidbits of history while juggling many responsibilities pertaining to the museum's youth flight academy, exhibit content, and mundane operational matters, among the multiple other jobs of a museum leader. He and his late wife Tammy were early to recognize Harry's important place in aviation history, and they helped unlock the door for me.

At the TWA Museum, thanks go to Pamela R. Blaschum, Karen Holden Young, and John Mays. At the Pan Am Historical Foundation, a shout-out to Doug Miller, who promptly steered me onto certain paths in search of long-lost materials. At the Otto G. Richter Library at the University of Miami, which oversees an extensive Pan American World Airways collection, I give high marks to Jay Sylvestre, Nicola Hellmann-McFarland, and Adrian Legaspi for giving their best to find truly rare items.

The Palm Springs Air Museum has evolved into a major repository of aviation history with an outstanding collection of old warplanes that continues to attract a growing number of visitors. Among the prized possessions is *Bunny*, the P-51 Mustang expertly restored in the markings of Robert Friend, Harry's brother-in-law. The museum also commissioned well-known aviation artist Stan Stokes to create portraits of both Bob and Harry as permanent parts of the collection. It's a testament to the museum's commitment to preserve the Tuskegee Airmen story for years to come. My thanks go to the museum's vice chairman, Fred Bell, and the museum's education-program coordinator, Greg Kenny.

The nonprofit Commemorative Air Force keeps the old warbirds going, bringing them to life at air shows around the country to give the public an idea of what it was like to see the sky teeming with piston-powered planes whose pilots strove to preserve freedom. In Minnesota, the CAF Red Tail Squadron maintains an immaculately restored P-51 in red tail markings to honor the legacy of the Tuskegee Airmen. My thanks go to the squadron's marketing director LaVone Kay for photo assistance.

Navy veteran and independent historian Craig Huntly has become a well-known source of information about the Tuskegee Airmen. He has a wealth of materials about the historic flying program and was kind enough to share some documents with me. His cooperation is greatly appreciated.

Old friend and sometime collaborator Walter Boyne, the former director of the Smithsonian Institution's National Air and Space Museum, has been a constant source of encouragement. Walt has long supported the effort to bring the Tuskegee Airmen story out of the shadows and into full public view. While heading the museum, he authorized the first major national museum exhibit on African American flight. Titled *Black Wings*, the exhibit opened at the museum on September 23, 1982, accompanied by a groundbreaking booklet of the same title.

In the booklet's foreword, Walt made the point that "Those in search of models for the youth of today could scarcely find a better set than the black men and women who fought for the right to fly." That statement is as true today as it was then, and hopefully both young and old will embrace Harry Stewart as exactly such a role model after reading *Soaring to Glory*. My thanks go to Walt for his suggestions throughout the writing of this book.

Scholars, historians, and writers have contributed to the vast and expanding literature on blacks in aviation, especially the Tuskegee

Airmen, with outstanding books and articles. There isn't space here to highlight every example, but it is hoped that the sources listed in this book's bibliography will be considered a recommended reading list for those who want more information.

Alex Novak and Margaret Vander Woude of Regnery History are to be congratulated for publishing this story about a young man's quest to fly and his aviation achievements. Their specialty imprint has become a significant conveyor of military and aviation history. I am grateful to Alex and Maggie, along with their teammates Elizabeth Kantor, Kathleen Curran, Nicole Yeatman, and Kylie Frey, for making this book a reality.

Before you can get to publication, you need a committed advocate, and mine has been the insightful and persevering Grace Freedson. She recognized early on that this book was more than a flying story. At its core, it is the story of the resilience of the human spirit, which is the kind of story that cuts across genres and appeals to everyone who has ever dared to dream that humanity can rise to ennobling heights. For her advocacy I remain deeply appreciative.

It goes almost without saying, but I must say it: Mary is the one deserving of the highest praise. There is no way that this book, like others before it, could ever get done without such a patient and loving spouse.

The sparkle in Mary's face that showed itself when she went for her first plane ride with me decades ago continues to radiate now, lighting up my life. I know how lucky I am because the light that she represents is a constant, like the North Star. No matter where I am, whether in the air or on the ground, that light, the ray of perpetual sunshine—which gives off feelings of friendship, caring, respect, and hope—is with me, sustaining me.

When I depart on a flight, I know that upon my return Mary will be there, making it dawn regardless of the hour of the day. And it's the same with the writing of a book, which is just another kind of journey. When it ends, you are back home, in the same place—wherever that might be in the geographical sense—with the love of your life, in the glow of the flame that makes your life special.

To Mary, my undying love along with, once again, my thanks for your understanding on this latest sky-high adventure!

BIBLIOGRAPHY

BOOKS

Amick, Jeremy Paul. *Together as One: Legacy of James Shipley, World War II Tuskegee Airman*. Harrisonville, Missouri: Burnt District Press, 2017.

Bird, Kai. *The Chairman: John J. McCloy, the Making of the American Establishment*. New York: Simon & Schuster, 1992.

Black Americans in Defense of our Nation. Washington, D.C.: Office of the Deputy Assistant Secretary of Defense for Equal Opportunity and Safety Policy, 1985.

Bracey, Earnest N. *Daniel "Chappie" James: The First African American Four Star General*. Jefferson, North Carolina: McFarland & Company, 2003.

Bragg, Janet Harmon and Marjorie M. Kriz. *Soaring Above Setbacks: The Autobiography of Janet Harmon Bragg, African American Aviator*. Washington, D.C.: Smithsonian Institution Press, 1996.

Broadnax, Samuel L. *Blue Skies, Black Wings: African American Pioneers of Aviation.* Westport, Connecticut: Praeger Publishers, 2007.

Brown, Harold H. and Marsha S. Bordner. *Keep Your Airspeed Up: The Story of a Tuskegee Airman.* Tuscaloosa, Alabama: The University of Alabama Press, 2017.

Bucholtz, Chris. *332nd Fighter Group—Tuskegee Airmen.* Oxford, England: Osprey Publishing Limited, 2007.

Carisella, P. J. and James W. Ryan. *The Black Swallow of Death: The Incredible Story of Eugene Jacques Bullard, the World's First Black Combat Aviator.* Boston: Marlborough House, 1972.

Caro, Robert A. *The Power Broker: Robert Moses and the Fall of New York.* New York: Alfred A. Knopf, 1974.

Caver, Joseph, Jerome Ennels, and Daniel Haulman. *The Tuskegee Airmen: An Illustrated History, 1939–1949.* Montgomery, Alabama: New South Books, 2011.

Cooper, Charlie and Ann. *Tuskegee's Heroes: Featuring the Aviation Art of Roy LaGrone.* Osceola, Wisconsin: Motorbooks International, 1996.

Dabbs, Henry E. *Black Brass: Black Generals and Admirals in the Armed Forces of the United States.* Charlottesville, Virginia: Howell Press, 1997.

Davis, Jr., Benjamin O. *Benjamin O. Davis, Jr., American: An Autobiography.* Washington, D.C.: Smithsonian Institution Press, 1991.

Davis, Richard G. *Carl A. Spaatz and the Air War in Europe.* Washington, D.C.: Smithsonian Institution Press, 1992.

De Seversky, Alexander P. *Victory Through Air Power.* New York: Simon and Schuster, 1942.

Diner, Hasia R. *Julius Rosenwald: Repairing the World.* New Haven, Connecticut: Yale University Press, 2017.

Donald, David, ed. *Warplanes of the Luftwaffe.* London: Aerospace Publishing Ltd., 1994.

Dryden, Charles W. *A-Train: Memoirs of a Tuskegee Airman.* Tuscaloosa, Alabama: The University of Alabama Press, 1997.

Fleischman, John. *Black and White Airmen: Their True History.* Boston: Houghton Mifflin Company, 2007.

Francis, Charles E. *The Tuskegee Airmen: The Men Who Changed a Nation.* Boston: Branden Publishing Company, 1988.

Gardner, Michael R. *Harry Truman and Civil Rights: Moral Courage and Political Risks.* Carbondale and Edwardsville, Illinois: Southern Illinois University Press, 2002.

Graff, Cory. *P-51 Mustang: Seventy-five Years of America's Most Famous Warbird.* Minneapolis, Minnesota: Zenith Press, 2015.

Greenly, Larry W. *Eugene Bullard: World's First Black Fighter Pilot.* Montgomery, Alabama: New South Books, 2013.

Grinsell, Robert. *Focke-Wulf Fw 190.* New York: Crown Publishers, 1980.

Gropman, Alan L. "Benjamin O. Davis, Jr.: History on Two Fronts" in *Makers of the United States Air Force.* Edited by John L. Frisbee. Washington, D.C.: Office of Air Force History, 1987.

_____. *The Air Force Integrates, 1949-1964.* Washington, D.C.: Office of Air Force History, 1985.

Gruenhagen, Robert W. *Mustang: The Story of the P-51 Fighter, World War II's Most Famous Fighter.* New York: Arco Publishing Company, 1976.

Gubert, Betty Kaplan. *Invisible Wings: An Annotated Bibliography on Blacks in Aviation, 1916–1993.* Westport, Connecticut: Greenwood Press, 1994.

Gubert, Betty Kaplan, Miriam Sawyer, and Caroline M. Fannin. *Distinguished African Americans in Aviation and Space.* Westport, Connecticut: Oryx Press, 2002.

Hardesty, Von. *Black Wings: Courageous Stories of African Americans in Aviation and Space History.* New York: Collins (in association with the Smithsonian National Air and Space Museum), 2008.

_____. *Great Aviators and Epic Flights.* Fairfield, Connecticut: Hugh Lauter Levin Associates, 2002.

Hardesty, Von and Dominick Pisano. *Black Wings: The American Black in Aviation*. Washington, D.C.: National Air and Space Museum/ Smithsonian Institution, 1983.

Haulman, Daniel L. *The Tuskegee Airmen Chronology: A Detailed Timeline of the Red Tails and Other Black Pilots of World War II*. Montgomery, Alabama: New South Books, 2017.

Holway, John B. *Red Tails, Black Wings: The Men of America's Black Air Force*. Las Cruces, New Mexico: Yucca Tree Press, 1997.

Homan, Lynn M. and Thomas Reilly. *Black Knights: The Story of the Tuskegee Airmen*. Gretna, Louisiana: Pelican Publishing Company, 2001.

Jakeman, Robert J. *The Divided Skies: Establishing Segregated Flight Training at Tuskegee, Alabama, 1934-1942*. Tuscaloosa, Alabama: The University of Alabama Press, 1992.

James Jr., Rawn. *The Double V: How Wars, Protest, and Harry Truman Desegregated America's Military*. New York: Bloomsbury Press, 2013.

Jefferson, Alexander and Lewis H. Carlson. *Red Tail Captured, Red Tail Free: The Memoirs of a Tuskegee Airman and POW*. New York: Fordham University Press, 2005.

Juptner, Joseph P. *U.S. Civil Aircraft Series, Volume 3*. Blue Ridge Summit, Pennsylvania: Tab Aero, 1993.

Laslie, Brian D. *Architect of Air Power: General Laurence S. Kuter and the Birth of the U.S. Air Force*. Lexington, Kentucky: The University Press of Kentucky, 2017.

Lee, Ulysses. *The Employment of Negro Troops*. Washington, D.C.: Center of Military History, United States Army, 1966.

Libbey, James K. *Alexander P. de Seversky and the Quest for Air Power*. Washington, D.C.: Potomac Books, 2013.

Lloyd, Craig. *Eugene Bullard: Black Expatriate in Jazz-Age Paris*. Athens, Georgia: University of Georgia Press, 2006.

McCullough, David. *Truman*. New York: Simon & Schuster, 1992.

McGovern, James R. *Black Eagle: General Daniel "Chappie" James, Jr*. University, Alabama: The University of Alabama Press, 1985..

Moore, Christopher Paul. *Fighting for America: Black Soldiers—the Unsung Heroes of World War II*. New York: One World/Ballantine Books, 2005.

Morgan, Len. *The AT-6 Harvard*. New York: Arco Publishing Co., 1965.

Moye, J. Todd. *Freedom Flyers: The Tuskegee Airmen of World War II*. New York: Oxford University Press, 2010.

Nalty, Bernard C. *Strength for the Fight: A History of Black Americans in the Military*. New York: The Free Press, 1986.

Nugent, John Peer. *The Black Eagle*. New York: Stein and Day, 1971.

Orr, Zellie Rainey. *Heroes in War—Heroes at Home: First Top Guns*. Marietta, Georgia: Communication Unlimited, 2008.

Osur, Alan M. *Blacks in the Army Air Forces During World War II*. Washington, D.C.: Office of Air Force History, 1977.

Phelps, J. Alfred. *Chappie: America's First Black Four Star General, The Life and Times of Daniel James, Jr.* Novato, California: Presidio Press, 1991.

Powell, William J. *Black Aviator: The Story of William J. Powell* (new edition of *Black Wings*, 1934), Washington, D.C.: Smithsonian Institution Press, 1994.

Rich, Doris L. *Queen Bess: Daredevil Aviator*. Washington, D.C.: Smithsonian Institution Press, 1993.

Rose, Robert A. *Lonely Eagles: The Story of America's Black Air Force in World War II*. Los Angeles: Tuskegee Airmen Inc., Los Angeles Chapter, 1982.

Sandler, Stanley. *Segregated Skies: All-Black Combat Squadrons of World War II*. Washington, D.C.: Smithsonian Institution Press, 1992.

Scott, Lawrence P. and William M. Womack Sr. *Double V: The Civil Rights Struggle of the Tuskegee Airmen*. East Lansing, Michigan: Michigan State University Press, 1994.

Scutts, Jerry. *Mustang Aces of the Ninth & Fifteenth Air Forces & the RAF*. Oxford, England: Osprey Aerospace, 1999.

Shacklady, Edward. "The North American P-51D Mustang" in *Aircraft in Profile, Profile Nos. 1–24*. Edited by Martin C. Windrow. Garden City, New York: Doubleday and Company, 1965.

Simmons, Thomas E. *The Brown Condor: The True Adventures of John C. Robinson*. Silver Spring, Maryland: Bartleby Press, 1988.

Smith, Charlene E. McGee. *Tuskegee Airman: The Biography of Charles E. McGee, Air Force Fighter Combat Record Holder*. Boston: Branden Publishing Company, 2000.

Smith, J. Richard. "The Focke-Wulf Fw 190D/Ta 152 Series" in *Aircraft in Profile, Profile Nos. 73–96*. Edited by Martin C. Windrow. Garden City, New York: Doubleday and Company, 1968.

Smith, Tammy L. and Susan G. Robinson (Illustrations). *The Tuskegee Airmen: The Verdict in Vegas*. Self-Published, 2013.

Spencer, Chauncey E. *Who Is Chauncey Spencer?* Detroit: Broadside Press, 1975.

Stentiford, Barry M. *Tuskegee Airmen*. Santa Barbara, California: Greenwood/ABC-CLIO, 2012.

Stimson, Henry L. and McGeorge Bundy. *On Active Service in War and Peace*. New York: Harper & Brothers, 1948.

Stroup II, Robert M. *Crossroads of Liberty: A Pictorial Tribute to Lockbourne/Rickenbacker AFB*. Missoula, Montana: Pictorial Histories Publishing, 2008.

Tillman, Barrett. *Forgotten Fifteenth: The Daring Airmen Who Crippled Hitler's War Machine*. Washington, D.C.: Regnery History, 2014.

Tucker, Phillip Thomas. *Father of the Tuskegee Airmen, John C. Robinson*. Washington, D.C.: Potomac Books, 2012.

Wagner, Ray. *Mustang Designer: Edgar Schmued and the Development of the P-51*. New York: Orion Books, 1990.

Wagner, Wolfgang. *The History of German Aviation: Kurt Tank – Focke-Wulf's Designer and Test Pilot*. Atglen, Pennsylvania: Schiffer Military/Aviation History, 1998.

Warren, James C. *The Freeman Field Mutiny: A Tuskegee Airman's Story.* San Rafael, California: Donna Ewald, 1995.

Westbrook, Shelby. *Tuskegee Airmen, 1941 – 1945.* Chicago: Tuskegee Airmen Inc., Chicago Chapter, 2003.

Windrow, M. C. "The Focke-Wulf Fw 190A" in *Aircraft in Profile, Profile Nos. 1 – 24.* Edited by Martin C. Windrow. Garden City, New York: Doubleday and Company,1965.

Wright, Kai. *Solders of Freedom: An illustrated History of African Americans in the Armed Forces.* New York: Black Dog & Leventhal Publishers, 2002.

ARTICLES

Bernstein, Mark. "How Perry Young Broke the Color Barrier: A Black Pilot and a Small Helicopter Airline Moved Faster Than the Speed of Law," *Air & Space/Smithsonian*, February/March 2019.

Blevins, Danny K. "The Military Plane Crash of 1948 Revealed: The Facts Behind the Crash of a P-47 in Butcher Hollow in 1948 and More. . ." *The Bankmule*, The Official Publication of the Van Lear, Kentucky Historical Society, March 2005.

Borja, Elizabeth. "African American Pioneer Dale White and the 1939 Goodwill Flight," Smithsonian National Air and Space Museum, www.airandspace.si.edu, February 28, 2017.

Brown, Deneen L. "How Harry S. Truman Desegregated the Military 70 Years Ago," *Washington Post*, July 26, 2018.

Correll, John T. "The Feeder Force: Graduates of the Civilian Pilot Training Program Had a Head Start Toward Flying for the AAF in World War II," *Air Force Magazine*, January 2014.

Douglas, Helen Gahagan. "The Negro Soldier," *Appendix to the Congressional Record*, February 1, 1946.

DeMarco, Carolyn. "Revving His Jets: Former Tuskegee Airman Achieves Sky-High Goals," *Birmingham-Bloomfield Eccentric*, March 23, 1989.

"Fighters Up—Again: Don't Kid Yourself—The Day of the 'Little Friend' Isn't Over by a Long Shot," *Air Force Magazine*, June 1949.

Flint, Jerry M. "Black Ex-Pilots Recall Bias in World War II," *New York Times*, August 14, 1972.

Goldstein, Richard. "Gen. Benjamin O. Davis, Jr., 89, Dies: Dispelled Racial Myths as Leader of Pilots' Unit," *New York Times*, July 7, 2002.

Hamby, Alonzo L. "1948 Democratic Convention: The South Secedes Again," *Smithsonian Magazine*, August 2008.

Handleman, Philip. "The Tuskegee Airmen," *Private Pilot*, June 1990.

_____. "The Heroic Odyssey of Chief Anderson," *Friend's Journal* (Air Force Museum Foundation), Spring 1997.

_____. "With Wings as Eagles: A Tribute to Late Tuskegee Airman Lt. Col. Walter Moore Downs," *Warbirds*, July 2002.

_____. "The Liberating Sky: Pioneering Black Pilots Broke Barriers and Climbed to New Heights—Part 1," *Vintage Airplane*, January 2012.

_____. "The Liberating Sky: Pioneering Black Pilots Broke Barriers and Climbed to New Heights – Part 2," *Vintage Airplane*, February 2012

_____. "Tuskegee Triple: Harry Stewart Earned a Distinguished Flying Cross in his First Dogfight as a Tuskegee Airman," *Aviation History*, September 2013.

_____. "Best of the Best: Tuskegee Airman Harry Stewart and the Air Force's First Top Guns – Part 1," *Warbirds*, October 2013.

_____. "Best of the Best: Tuskegee Airman Harry Stewart and the Air Force's First Top Guns—Part 2," *Warbirds*, December 2013.

Hanser, Kathleen. "Black Wings: The Life of African American Aviation Pioneer William Powell," http://blog.nasm.si.edu.

Haulman, Daniel L. "The Tuskegee Airfields: The Famous Airmen Were Actually Trained at Five Airfields, Surrounding Tuskegee Institute," *Air Force Magazine*, June 2014.

_____. "The Tuskegee Airmen and the 'Never Lost a Bomber' Myth," *The Alabama Review*, January 2011.

Hopkins, Carol. "Remembering Victory: World War II Pilot Recalls the Day 60 Years Ago When Victory in Europe Was Declared," *Oakland Press*, May 8, 2005.

Kellogg, Alex P. "Still on the Wing," *Detroit Free Press*, November 10, 2005.

Lambertson, Giles. "The Other Harlem: At a Small Airfield in 1930s Chicago, Blacks Found the First Schools that would Teach Them to Fly," *Air & Space/Smithsonian*, February/March 2010.

Laris, Michael. "Freedom Flight: Chauncey Spencer and Dale White Risked Life and Limb to Fly a Rickety, Rented Biplane from Chicago to Washington but Their Real Destination Was the Future," *Washington Post*, February 16, 2003.

Law, John. "Tuskegee Squadron Battled on Two Fronts," *The Review* (Niagara Falls, Ontario), October 29, 1998.

Libby, Justin H. "More Than a Pilot: The Life and Career of a True Aviation Pioneer, Robert N. Buck," *American Aviation Historical Society Journal*, Summer 2018.

Maksel, Rebecca. "The Unrecognized First: Emory Malick, the First African American Pilot, Wasn't Known to Historians Until Recently," *Air & Space/Smithsonian*, March 2011.

Newell, Mike. "Honors, Finally, for a Tuskegee Airman from Philly, Lynched by the Nazis," www.philly.com, April 23, 2018.

Patterson, Brandon. "Tuskegee Airman Honored After He's Shot Down, Lynched in World War II," *Sunday Free Press*, May 27, 2018.

Salpukas, Agis. "James Plinton, Jr., 81; Broke Color Barriers at U.S. Airlines," *New York Times*, August 14, 1996.

Schulz, Dana. "Before LaGuardia, There Was Glenn H. Curtiss Airport," www.6sqft.com, August 27, 2015.

Scott, Phil. "The 'Blackbirds': The Story of the First All-Black Aerobatic Team," *AOPA Pilot*, July 2009.

Stewart, Jr., Harry T. "The Last Hurrah," *Tuskegee Airmen: The First Top Guns*, December 10, 2004.

Tackett, Loretta. "Tuskegee Airman Visits Van Lear," *Paintsville Herald*, August 10, 2005.

"30 Years Post Delta Merger: A Look Back at Western Airlines," www.airwaysmag.com, April 3, 2017.

Wilkinson, Stephan. "Tuskegee Top Guns," *Aviation History*, March 2012.

Wood, Michael. "Battle for the Heart of a Park ... and the Soul of a Borough, The NYC World's Fair: 1939–1940 in Flushing Queens," www.queensbuzz.com, 2007–2018.

"World War II Hero Visits Johnson County Alternative School," *Eagle Express*, The Official Publication of the Johnson County Schools, August 2005.

TRAINING MANUALS

German Aircraft and Armament: Informational Intelligence Summary No. 44-32. Washington, D.C.: Office of the Assistant Chief of Staff, Intelligence, U.S. Army Air Forces, October 1944.

Pilot's Flight Operating Instructions for Army Models RP-47B & C and P-47D & G Airplanes, British Model Thunderbolt. Patterson Field, Fairfield, Ohio: Commanding General, Fairfield Air Service Command, Army Air Forces, November 20, 1943.

Pilot's Flight Operating Instructions P-51B and P-51C Airplanes. Inglewood, California: North American Aviation, Inc., February 1, 1944.

Pilot's Handbook for Army Model AT-6C, Navy Model SNJ-4, British Model Harvard IIA Airplanes. Washington, D.C.: Commanding General, Army Air Forces, undated.

PILOT LOGS

Air Force Form 5, Individual Flight Record, Pilot, Harry T. Stewart, December 1943–January 14, 1950.

Pilot Logbook, Harry T. Stewart Jr., September 19, 1943–April 5, 1946.

Pilot Logbook, Harry T. Stewart Jr., January 12, 1952–July 1, 1980.

MONOGRAPHS

A Brief History of the 332nd "Red Tail" Fighter Group, authorized by Major George S. Roberts, Commanding, undated.

Haulman, Daniel L. *A Short History of the Tuskegee Airmen.* Maxwell Air Force Base, Alabama: Air Force Historical Research Agency, January 8, 2015.

_____. *Misconceptions About the Tuskegee Airmen.* Maxwell Air Force Base, Alabama: Air Force Historical Research Agency, July 23, 2013.

Unit History. (320th Army Air Forces College Training Detachment [Aircrew]) Tuskegee, Alabama: Tuskegee Institute, December 4, 1943.

WEBSITES

"Air Travel and Segregation," www.airandspace.si.edu, undated.

"Family Tree," www.deltamuseum.org, undated.

"History of the 485th Bomb Group," www.485thbg.org, undated.

GOVERNMENT DOCUMENTS

"Harry T. Stewart, Jr. Appreciation Day," *Proclamation.* R. T. Daniel, Johnson County Judge/Executive, August 3, 2005.

Defense Attache Office, Embassy of the United States of America, Vienna, Austria, Letter of Colonel David M. Knych, U.S. Army, (and attachments), April 6, 2018.

VIDEOS

Congressional Gold Medal Ceremony. C-SPAN, March 29, 2007.

New Year's at Ramitelli: A Safe Haven for Change. Tarnaby Production, 2011.

Ramitelli Reunion. Lucasfilm Ltd., 2012.

INTERVIEWS

Harry T. Stewart Jr. with the author, 2017–2019.

INDEX